Full Legal Disclaimer

This book was prepared by the Author. The Author makes no warranty, express or implied, or assumes any legal liability or responsibility for the accuracy, completeness, or any third party's use or the results of such use of any information, apparatus, product, or process disclosed, or represents that its use would not infringe privately owned rights. Reference herein to any specific commercial product, process, standard or service by trade name, trademark, manufacturer, or otherwise, does not necessarily constitute or imply its endorsement, recommendation, or favoring by the Author.

Trademark Disclaimer

Reference herein to any specific commercial product, process, standard or service by trade name, trademark, manufacturer, or otherwise, does not necessarily constitute or imply its endorsement, recommendation, or favoring by the Author, any Company or any agency thereof or its contractors or subcontractors.

Any reproduction or re-transmission in whole or in part of this work is expressly prohibited without the prior consent of the Author.

Copyright Notice

© Copyright 2024 Matt Coutu

Note: This book assumes the reader has some proficiency in Number Systems, some Automation and some Networking exposure as well. If the reader has no or little Networking exposure or education we recommend The Technicians Guide to Industrial Networking. The book is not an all encompassing guide to Precision Time Protocol rather it is intended to get the reader using and understanding Precision Time Protocol on the Factory Floor or On-Site as quickly as possible

Introduction

This book covers the intricacies of Precision Time Protocol(PTP) otherwise known as IEEE 1588. The 2019 version of the protocol is the main focus and how it can be made to function in an Industrial Network.

Synchronization: The internal clocks of Network Devices will always drift in time from each other unless regularly updated. For the purpose of this book Synchronization is the aim of coordinating the time, phase and/or frequency of these otherwise Independent Real World Clocks. Unless otherwise stated the term Synchronization is limited to Time Synchronization

Note: Terms, concepts, definitions and acronyms are defined as they are needed

Why do we even need Time Synchronization between Devices? There are many applications and systems that simply require Synchronization between Devices for them to even operate or to operate optimally. As Network and data transmission speeds have increased the various forms of Synchronization(time, frequency and phase) have been utilized to allow these technologies and protocols to function.

When it comes to Electrical, Telecom and Network Systems events occur extremely quickly and knowing exactly when they occurred is very important. Being able to determine which order events occurred is also important when trouble shooting problems. All electronic Devices will drift with their time if they are not Synchronized with a Master Clock. If the Devices are off even by a few milliseconds you may not be able to establish which event occurred first and thus you cannot accurately discover the root problem or event.

Within the Electrical Utilities Industry Phasor Measurement Units(PMUs) are utilized to oversee the phase angle of Voltage or Current of the electrical grid to allow for its proper operation. If the electrical grids loads and supply are not matched stress on the grid and poor power distribution will occur. Sampled Values, Synchrophasors, control of Switching activities and Travelling Wave Fault are other instances of where Electrical Utilities require better than microsecond Synchronization accuracy.

Industrial Plant Automation under normal circumstances would not require high levels of accurate Synchronization but is another area that under special conditions can be necessary. This can include the control of Drive Systems with Multiple Axes as well as the accurate Timestamping of historical process data.

Synchronization allows many Network Services to function including the transmission of data and voice. As well employing Synchronization can increase the bandwidth of a Network Link.

Time, phase and frequency are all important components of Synchronization. Within specific sectors and applications they are all relevant in some way. The Financial Industry, Academia and Research, Defense Industry, Transmission, Distribution, Government, Mining and Manufacturers all utilize Synchronization in some manner.

Providing high precision Synchronization to End Devices using the same Ethernet Network infrastructure as how all other data is transported has been a want for many years.

A Master Clock as well as generating a correct Time Signal must also have the proper infrastructure to transport that Time Signal correctly to the Slave Clocks. This can be a time consuming, costly and tiresome engineering problem. Ethernet based Networks are under normal circumstances inherently resistant to the needs of Time Synchronization due to the fact that Ethernet is separated by multiple Layers(OSI Model, etc). The best Ethernet based Time Synchronization protocols require access to the Physical Layer since it necessitates a Physical Signal. Access to and handling of the Physical Layer hardware is key for the most accurate Synchronization protocols as will be shown throughout this book. In short this is due to the fact that a protocol using a Time Signal can have the data sitting at any OSI Layer and it can take an indeterminate amount of time to pass the Time Signal Packet up the Protocol Stack. Inconsistent Network Traffic also increases variability in how fast or slow a Packet is processed.

Because of this Ethernet based Time Synchronization protocols have suffered from lack of reliability, availability and determinism and were up until PTP considered incapable of providing the most accurate Time Signals.
Determinism: Determinism simply means something is predictable. When the Packet is transmitted, it should be received in an expected and predictable period of time
Master Clock: Master Clocks transmit Time Signals to Slave Clocks

Slave Clock: Slave Clocks receive Time Signals from Master Clocks

Network Time Protocol(NTP) and its various versions is widespread and extremely common among IT professionals and the IT Networks they typically manage. NTP as a Time Synchronization protocol owes its widespread adoption to Network Professionals who gave it a huge advantage over other Time Protocols when it comes to Ethernet based Networks. If a PC is connected to the internet it is a practical certainty that it is Synchronized using NTP.

The most common practice to Synchronize Slave Clocks is by passing a Time Signal over the Internet from a NTP Server. NTP uses a Client-Server model for messaging between Devices. The NTP Servers job is to provide precise time to the respective clients who will intermittently request the NTP Server for the time information. The Client requests sent to the NTP Server are typically about 15minutes apart from each other.

With hundreds of NTP Servers spread across the world the majority of them even being Synchronized to the atomic Clocks of their respective National Time Services.

On IT or OT Networks there can be multiple NTP Master Clocks however the more common practice is to have either a standalone NTP Server or to have the NTP Server operating internally on a Router or Ethernet Switch.

With NTPs popularity it comes standard on nearly every Network enabled consumer or business Device. NTP is the choice of Time Protocol when it comes to Stock Market Transactions, Banking Transactions, Database Coordination, Air Traffic Control and many more.

NTP can only Synchronize Devices to within tens of milliseconds under optimum conditions. PTP can Synchronize those same Devices to be under hundreds of nanoseconds. As well NTP when exposed to Network Congestion or a large Network infrastructure can decrease performance even worse where Synchronization can be greater than hundreds of milliseconds.

Simple Network Time Protocol(SNTP) is a slimmed down version of NTP that is only employed by Client Devices. SNTP Devices are unable to transfer a Time Signal to other Devices. They are only able to obtain a Time Signal from a NTP Server.

What about Inter-Range Instrumentation Group Timecodes(IRIG) Signals? Historically IRIG Signals were a very common method of transferring timing information between Devices and still is depending on the application. The IRIG Timecode Standards was originally developed in the late 1950's by the US Army and the first version was introduced in 1960. To say that this method of Synchronization is old is saying something. Many of us will not have family members this old! The Telecommunications and Timing Group(TTG) has revised it several times over the years. The most recent version being put out in 2004.

The IRIG standard in reality specifies a range of Serial Time Codes based on different Bit Rates delivered over a co-ax cable. With the most common type and industry standard IRIG-B having a resolution down to 1ms which for many applications is more than adequate. IRIG co-ax Time Signals are Deterministic meaning once the 1kHz carrier frequency signal is transmitted from the Master Clock the system knows how long it will take to reach the Slave Clock.

IRIG-B defines a format of encoding time including the Day of Year, Second, Minute and Hour.

With the use of Converters IRIG Co-Ax Signals can be converted to Fiber Optic and thus can be extended over considerable distances. However the long distances will introduce Latency issues.

A standard IRIG signal is common to many GPS(Global Positioning System) receiver outputs with IRIG-B being the standard in many industries including: The Defense Industry, Generating Plants, Transmission Utilities, Distribution Utilities, Government, Mining and some Manufacturing.

However, there are drawbacks when using an IRIG-B Signal. For one Devices using IRIG-B Signals require their own dedicated system or dedicated infrastructure including co-ax or serial cables to carry the Time Signals and special IRIG-B Clocks to generate them. The additional cost and time of setting up an IRIG-B Network and infrastructure is an important consideration with the selection of any Time Synchronization protocol. Another consideration is as mentioned IRIG-B can only Synchronize down to 1ms while PTP can realize Synchronization down to better than hundreds of nanoseconds. A third drawback is that Path Delays need to be set manually. IRIG-B Signals are not as commonly accepted as they once were. With many vendors only offering a few or even no products to be used with this aging but still vaunted Time Signal. A small consideration as well is the further calibration of the signal Propagation Time between the Master Clock and the Slave Clocks over the co-ax cables.

With the advent of cheap GPS receivers becoming ubiquitous among consumer and commercial Devices using Satellites UTC Synchronized Time Signals can be transmitted to Devices located at the far reaches of our planet. GPS enabled Devices can be accurately Synchronized to within tens of nanoseconds.

All Devices that need to be Synchronized in a Network must be able to directly access GPS Signals as well as have the necessary GPS receiver. Each End Device having their own outdoor antenna is not practical or cost effective. GPS is used in a wide variety of applications including Synchronizing NTP Time Servers to UTC, Professional and Amateur Astronomy, Cellular Telephony and providing a reference Time Signal for PTP GrandMaster Clocks.

Summary of Time Synchronization protocols:

Synchronization Protocols:	PTP:	NTP:	IRIG-B:	GPS Only:
Hierarchy:	Master Slave	Client Server	Master Slave	Master Slave
Medium:	Ethernet	Ethernet	Typically Co-Ax Cable	Satellite Receiver
Accuracy(dec):	~100ns	1-100ms	~1ms	30-40ns
Cost:	Medium	Low	High	Very High
Devices Needed:	All Devices Including: Master, Slave, Boundary And Transparent Clocks(For Best Results)	Master Clock Only	Master and Slave Clocks	All Devices
Transit Time Compensation:	Yes	Yes	Yes	Yes
Interval Between Synchronization Signals(dec):	~1s	Minutes	1s	~3s

When the best Time Accuracy is required, at a moderate cost and the least cumbersome the coupling of PTP with a GPS Time Signal is the superior timing solution for modern day local Ethernet Networks requiring precision Time Synchronization.

PTP Development

Precision Time Protocol(PTP) outlined in the IEEE Standards Associations standard IEEE 1588-2019 is what this document focuses on. For the original standard there were multiple purposes first being it must be easily configured. Meaning a Device having PTP functionality must be almost entirely plug and play. This was seen as a huge advantage and would make PTP a much more desirable time protocol. The second being PTP must be able to work with multiple Devices of varying Clock accuracies. The third is PTP was only intended to function on smaller local Ethernet Networks. The fourth is it must work with the least amount possible of CPU usage, memory and Network bandwidth. The fifth is it must support Multicast Ethernet Frames. And lastly it must allow for the under microseconds Synchronization of multiple Network Devices on a local Ethernet Network.

Note: PTP can theoretically work with other Network types but this book will only focus on using it on Ethernet Networks. For more information on the basics of Ethernet based Networks we recommend The Technicians Guide to Industrial Networking

IEEE 1588 that defines PTP is a living document and is updated regularly at least every 5 years. New conditions, options, features, profiles, parameters and expected Synchronization accuracies are being revised in this protocols current state as of this writing. IEEE 1588-2002(Version1) of PTP was released in 2002 with the updated IEEE 1588-2008(Version2) being released in 2008. Version1 and Version2 are not compatible with one another and a Network containing Devices with both will not work when it comes to PTP. This book as mentioned will focus almost entirely on IEEE 1588-2019 which as of this writing has seen widespread use across multiple industries and companies.

Generally speaking IEEE 1588-2019 is compatible with IEEE 1588-2008 but only if the optional features, services, etc typical of both versions that are to be used are setup almost exactly the same. As well these different versions are also compatible if no options of either are used. It is highly recommended to not mix versions of PTP so as to reduce compatibility issues between devices that are very likely to occur. If the two versions are to be used together in single Network consult the IEEE 1588-2019 standard for more information on how to perform this feat.

PTP Basics

PTP is widely used and due to the fact it can ensure Synchronization of frequency and time better than 100s of nanoseconds in accuracy for Packet-based Ethernet Networks. As well PTPs limited bandwidth and processing needs for PTP Packets is a huge advantage as well.

Local Slave Clocks are Synchronized with a local Network GrandMaster Clock or Master Clock. GrandMaster and Master Clocks transmit distinct PTP Messages containing Timestamps that allow the Synchronization of PTP Slave Clocks to occur. With the most basic of settings the PTP protocol requires nearly no user management or involvement. The precise Timestamps of these PTP Messages sent between Master and Slave Clocks is what makes all this possible.
Within a normal Ethernet Network Ethernet Switches transmit Packets using Full-Duplex Network links between Network Devices. Within these Packets contains the Destination Address of the Device the Packet is intended for. Ethernet Switches will at times have a multitude of Packets they must transmit all at once and the Switch would become overwhelmed. At this time Packets are passed to the Ethernet Switches' Input and Output Buffers so they are not misplaced/accidently deleted. When the Ethernet Switch continues being overwhelmed and the Buffers become full they will even stop transmitting Packets momentarily. When an Ethernet Switch goes through this Slave Clocks can becomes Desynchronized from their associated Master or GrandMaster Clock.

There are also inconsistent Delays when a Packet is received and while the CRC Field is being checked. The Packet is placed into the Ethernet Switches local memory while it combs the MAC Address Table to do the CRC Check. The CRC Check operation will cause differences in the time the Packets are forwarded. The inconsistent Delays for Packets associated with this operation will cause Asymmetrical Delay Errors.

Asymmetrical Delay Error: When the Transit Time for a given Packet is not the same transmitting to Device2 from Device1 as transmitting to Device1 from Device2

PTP is designed to remedy and mitigate these inconsistent delays associated with Ethernet Switching. When Ethernet Switches are PTP capable PTP Packets are updated with corrections as they traverse the Ethernet Network. Ethernet Switches are divided into two separate groups: PTP capable Ethernet Switches are called Transparent Clocks and regular Ethernet Switches are called NonTransparent Clocks.

PTP is intended to act as a distributed protocol. Where every Device on a Network runs the identical Synchronization protocol program. It exclusively runs with the data contained in the Ethernet based PTP Messages transmitted between Devices. As mentioned earlier an attractive feature of PTP is it is designed to be plug and play with the individual Device default settings. This is only true as long as all other connected Devices are also using the default settings as well.

PTP is designed to set system boundaries of which Devices are to be Synchronized, to allow for the configuration of the system and each Clock individually, allow for the controlled initial operation and settings of a modified Network or System. As well PTP will divide said Synchronized End Devices between two groups: Master Clocks and Slave Clocks. And lastly will supply the data for Slave Clocks to Synchronize to Master Clocks.

The excellent Synchronization time accuracy is only realized when the PTP standard is properly followed and understood. Network Topology Layout, Network Asymmetry and how PTP Messages transit the Network(and their associated delays) will all affect how accurate PTP is.

TAI And UTC The Real World Timescales

There are two different real world timescales the reader should be aware of UTC and TAI.

TAI: Is French and stands for International Atomic Time and is a time standard determined by hundreds of atomic clocks located in national laboratories across the world

UTC: Stands for Universal Coordinated Time and is the main standard the world measures time in

UTC and TAI are off from each other by over 40 seconds these days. Since TAI does not consider leap seconds the gap will continue to grow.

To calculate UTC the following formula is used:

UTC = TAI – DLS

Note: The DLS value is maintained in the CurrentUTCOffset data set member of the TimeProperties Data Set

PTP And ARB Epochs

When was the beginning of time? It's a good question. According to the IEEE 1588-2019 standard there are two origins of time(called epochs) and which one you end up using will depend on your selected IEEE 1588-2019 selected timescale: PTP or ARB

PTP Epoch: The PTP Epoch is January 1st 1970 00:00:00 TAI

ARB Epoch: The ARB Epoch is specific to that particular PTP Domain and not traceable to an international standard clock. The time may not be traceable but the frequency can be

PTP And ARB Timescales

PTP Timescale: For the PTP Timescale time is defined as the time passed since the PTP Epoch

ARB Timescale: For the ARB Timescale time is defined as the time passed since the epoch was created and the time is only relevant to that PTP capable Network or Domain. DLS would in this case not be used or even able to calculate UTC

The TimeProperties data set member PTPTimescale is what governs which timescale is to be used. If PTPTimescale is true then PTP Timescale is enabled. If PTPTimescale is false then the ARB Timescale is running.

The PTP Timescale is the preferred timescale for Implementing PTP as it is traceable to an atomic clock and an internationally agreed upon timescale.

Universal Coordinated Time

DLS is a 16bit signed integer, is in seconds and is preserved in the TimeProperties data set member CurrentUTCOffset. DLS is transmitted by the GrandMaster Clock to each Slave Clock. DLS is not used to compute UTC from TAI if the TimeProperties data set member CurrentUTCOffsetValid is not true.

If the TimeProperties data set member PTPTimescale is false the timescale is ARB and the epoch is only relevant to that PTP capable Network or Domain. DLS would in this case not be used to calculate UTC.

PTP Clock Types

Before we begin our in-depth discussion of how PTP operates we first need to define the types of Clocks and other Devices that make up a PTP capable Network. In PTP almost all Devices on an Ethernet Network are considered a Clock. There are many different Clock types and Clock groups a Device could be categorized as.

Master Clock

Master Clocks create the PTP Time Messages and transmit them to the Slave Clocks. Slave Clocks will Synchronize their time to a Master Clock. Master Clocks are typically End Devices and are considered Ordinary Clocks.

Slave Clock

Slave Clocks will receive PTP Time Messages and Synchronize their time to a Master or GrandMaster Clock. Slave Clocks are End Devices and are considered Ordinary Clocks.

SlaveOnly Clock

SlaveOnly Clocks can only receive PTP Time Messages and Synchronize their time to a Master or GrandMaster Clock. They will never become a Master Clock. Most Slave Clocks are SlaveOnly Clocks but will rarely be called as such. Many Clocks can be configured as SlaveOnly Clocks. SlaveOnly Clocks are End Devices and are considered Ordinary Clocks.

GrandMaster Clock/Preferred GrandMaster Clock

A GrandMaster Clock is a device which only acts as a Master Clock and will never act as a Slave Clock. All Clocks on a PTP capable Network(including Masters and Slaves) will ultimately derive their time from the GrandMaster Clock or Preferred GrandMaster Clock. The GrandMaster Clock usually has a very accurate Time Source such as an atomic clock or GPS Time Signal.

If the Network does not need an outside Time Signal and only needs to be Synchronized locally the GrandMaster can free run. Of course a free running Clock will drift further and further from UTC as time goes on. GrandMaster Clocks are considered Ordinary Clocks.

Alternate GrandMaster Clock/Alternate Master Clock

When the Alternate GrandMaster Clock optional feature is enabled this kind of PTP Clock may exist on a PTP capable Network. An Alternate GrandMaster Clock is a PTP Clock which is basically an active Backup GrandMaster Clock. During the Best Master Clock Algorithm selection process that particular Master Clock would not have been selected as the GrandMaster Clock it will instead designate itself an Alternate GrandMaster Clock. It will transmit Announce Messages with the AlternateMasterFlag on. An Alternate GrandMaster Clock will even transmit Sync(and if required the associated Follow_Up) Messages however once again with the AlternateMasterFlag on. Slave Clocks will typically ignore Alternate GrandMaster Clock Messages unless the GrandMaster Clock goes offline or fails. Alternate GrandMaster Clocks will only act as a Master Clock and will never act as a Slave Clock. Alternate GrandMaster Clocks are considered Ordinary Clocks.

Ordinary Clock

An Ordinary Clock is an End Device on a Network meaning it is not an Ethernet Switch, Bridge, Hub or Router. They are the most commonplace Clock type in a PTP capable Network. An Ordinary Clock can only transmit a Time Signal or receive the Time Signal and Synchronize to it. Ordinary Clocks include: SlaveOnly Clocks, GrandMaster Clocks, Preferred GrandMaster Clocks, Master Clocks, Slave Clocks, etc.

Note: Ordinary Clocks will usually only have one PTP capable Physical Port unless they are connected PRP/HSR and in that case they will have two

Boundary Clock

A Boundary Clock has at least one Slave Port and one Master Port. The PTP Sync Packet will be received on a Port designated as a Slave Port and the Boundary Clock will adjust for the delay and then create a new PTP Sync Packet to transmit out on a Master Port usually belonging to another PTP Domain. A Boundary Clock is used when there are too many Slave Clocks on a Network for a single Master Clock, the Network needs to be scaled up, there are long distances involved in the Network, if you need to convert a signal from PTP to IRIG-B for legacy Devices, if you are bridging between two different Network Transport Protocols or PTP Profiles.

There are many reasons to make use of a Boundary Clock. In this way it acts as an intermediary between the GrandMaster Clock and Slave Clocks. Boundary Clocks reduce the amount of Network hops and resulting delays that occur in a PTP enabled Network.

A major advantage to Boundary Clocks is they reduce the need for GPS GrandMaster Clocks on each PTP Domain or Network segment. This in turn could decreases the cost of implementing a PTP capable Network. A Boundary Clock can be assigned to be a GrandMaster Clock by the Best Master Clock Algorithm(BMCA) for a particular PTP Domain.

A Boundary Clock is similar to a Transparent Clock but it operates differently and is used in different circumstances. Boundary Clocks like Transparent Clocks can supplant standard Ethernet Switches as they will stop and process all PTP Messages separately. All other Network Traffic will be allowed to pass unhindered.

Slave Clocks that are downstream of the GrandMaster Clock or are in a different PTP Domain will instead Synchronize to the Boundary Clock's Master Port which is closer or is simply what is available. Boundary Clocks often have many PTP capable Ports and each one can be connected to a separate PTP Domain or can allow for multiple PTP communication paths between PTP Domains.

Boundary Clocks can be connected to more than one PTP Domain but can only Synchronize to one Master or GrandMaster Clock on one PTP Domain as per the BMCA. A Boundary Clock must have more than one PTP capable Port.

All Multicast PTP Message(excluding Announce Messages) will be stopped and not retransmitted once received at a Boundary Clock Port. Boundary Clocks are never considered Ordinary Clocks.

Transparent Clock

A Transparent Clock like a Boundary Clock is an Ethernet Switch that can handle PTP Messages separate from normal Network Traffic. Transparent Clocks do have the advantage over Boundary Clocks of generating less delay jitters and errors. How Transparent Clocks operate come down to two different types of Transparent Clocks that use different Path Delay Mechanisms. Both kinds of Transparent Clocks are defined in the next sections and are further explained in greater detail in later sections.
The two kinds of Transparent Clocks are completely incompatible with each other. If a PTP capable Network or single PTP Domain will use both types of Transparent Clocks a Boundary Clock must be used to separate them. A Boundary Clock must be used to separate two different Path Delay Mechanisms.

Transparent Clocks replace normal Ethernet Switches which are at best generally inaccurate and can cause further inaccuracy when the Network gets congested. Transparent Clocks are never considered Ordinary Clocks.

All Transparent Clocks will calculate the ResidenceTime of the PTP Event Message by the following formula:

ResidenceTime: ResidenceTime is the total time it takes for a PTP Event Message to be processed by a Transparent Clock or NonTransparent Clock. It is measured from the time the Message is received on an ingress Port to when it is then retransmitted out an egress Port. Only Transparent Clocks will measure the Residence Time of PTP Event Messages

ResidenceTime = Transmitted Timestamp - Received Timestamp

Transparent Clocks Ports operate differently from Boundary Clocks or Ordinary Clocks in that they do NOT maintain a Master, Slave or Passive PortState. Boundary Clocks are never considered Ordinary Clocks.

End-to-End Transparent Clock

An End-to-End Transparent Clock supports the Delay Request-Response Path Mechanism(used to measure the End-to-End Path Delay) and will not support the Peer Delay Path Mechanism. This type of Transparent Clock will update the Sync(or associated Follow_Up) PTP Message's CorrectionField with the total time the Sync Message spent being processed(called the ResidenceTime) by that End-to-End Transparent Clock.

Note: The terms End-to-End and Delay Request-Response can be used interchangeably

Measuring the Residence Time helps reduce any differences in PTP Message Delays or Asymmetry Delays brought on by that specific Transparent Clock. Each End-to-End Transparent Clock will add their own ResidenceTime for that particular PTP Event Message to the CorrectionField. End-to-End Transparent Clocks will not add corrections based on link delays or path delays.

End-to-End Transparent Clocks are superior to Peer-to-Peer Transparent Clocks only if the Network they are embedded into has any NonTransparent Clocks(Non-PTP capable Ethernet Switches).

Note: PTP Ports that only support or are configured for Delay Request-Response Path Mechanism will only work with other Delay Request-Response Path Mechanism Ports

Peer-to-Peer Transparent Clock

A Peer-to-Peer Transparent Clock supports the Peer Delay Path Mechanism(used to measure the Peer-to-Peer Delay) and will not support the Delay Request-Response Path Mechanism. This type of Transparent Clock will determine the Link Delay Time of every one of its Ports. It will then update the Sync(or optional associated Follow_Up) PTP Message's CorrectionField with the Link Delay Time and the ResidenceTime.

Note: The terms Peer-to-Peer and Peer Delay can be used interchangeably

Each Peer-to-Peer Transparent Clock will add their own ResidenceTime for that particular PTP Event Message to the CorrectionField. Just like the End-to-End Transparent Clock this helps reduce any differences in PTP Message Delays or

Asymmetry Delays brought on by that specific Transparent Clock.

An extra advantage with Peer-to-Peer Transparent Clocks is that the Slave Clock does not need to determine the Path Delay between itself and the GrandMaster Clock. Each Link Delay is determined in advance and added to the relevant PTP Message's CorrectionField by each Peer-to-Peer Transparent Clock as the Sync(or optional associated Follow_Up) Message transits the Network. Peer-to-Peer Transparent Clock will only forward Sync, Follow_Up and Announce PTP Messages that are received. All other PTP Messages are terminated upon being received. Peer-to-Peer Transparent Clocks will for every Link calculate the Link Delay.

Peer Delay Path Mechanism also reduces Network Traffic as less PTP Messages are required to transit the entire Network. As well any Master Clock and GrandMaster Clock would receive less PTP Messages(Delay_Req) and have to respond with less PTP Messages(Delay_Resp) to every Slave Clock that is receiving time from them. In fact, Peer-to-Peer Transparent Clocks will delete all received Delay_Req and Delay_Resp Messages as they are not used in the Peer Delay Path Mechanism.

PTP Ports that only support or are configured for Peer Delay Path Mechanism will only work with other Peer Delay Path Mechanism Ports. As well it is not just Peer-to-Peer Transparent Clock Ports that can employ this Path Mechanism, any Clock PTP Port may be able to support it-consult the Clock's documentation for more information.

A Boundary Clock that supports both Path Delay Mechanisms may be used to connect between Network Segments(or PTP Domains) that use the different Path Delay Mechanisms.

Note: Peer-to-Peer Transparent Clocks are especially advantageous for Networks with multiple paths between the Slave Clock and the GrandMaster Clock. No matter which path the Sync Message travels the actual Total Network Delay the Message experienced will be contained within(or the associated optional Follow_Up Message).

Under the Peer Delay Path Mechanism Sync Messages(or their associated Follow_Up Messages) are updated with the Link Delay Time and ResidenceTimes as they transit the Network any changes to the Path they take through the Network will be automatically accounted for. In this way Peer Delay Path Mechanism is superior to the Delay Request-Response Path Mechanism.

NonTransparent Clock:

A NonTransparent Clock is an Ethernet Switch that does not support PTP and treats PTP Messages like any other Network Traffic. It will not account for the ResidenceTime the PTP Message spends being processed by itself or the Link Delay Time. A NonTransparent Clock will not update the CorrectionField of Sync(or optional associated Follow_Up) Messages. NonTransparent Switches are never considered Clocks.

Note: Peer-to-Peer Transparent Clocks cannot be on the same PTP Domain as End-to-End Transparent Clocks or NonTransparent Clocks. This is because Peer-to-Peer Transparent Clocks use special Peer Delay PTP Messages that the other types of Ethernet Switches do not know how to properly handle. Peer-to-Peer Transparent Clocks can share the same PTP Domain as Boundary Clocks configured for the Peer-to-Peer mechanism though. In short only one Path Delay Mechanism can be on the same PTP Domain: Request-Response Mechanism or Peer Delay Mechanism

PTP Management Node

A Management Node is an End Device that allows the Network Professional to make changes and monitor PTP Clocks with PTP Management Messages. A PTP Management Node may use software that can manage PTP Clocks without PTP Management Messages. Management Nodes are never considered Clocks.

PTP Node

A PTP Node is otherwise known as a Clock or a PTP capable Network Device. The terms Clock and PTP Node may be used interchangeably in PTP documentation.

PTP Instances

The term PTP Instance can be confusing when reading PTP related documentation, lets see if we can clarify the term. A PTP Clock can have one or multiple PTP Instances. Consulting the Clocks documentation can indicate how many PTP Instances it has(If the manual even cares to mention this detail).

A PTP Instance will only work in one PTP Domain and will ignore PTP Messages that belong to a different PTP Domain. The PTP Protocol is used to Synchronize the Clocks of all PTP Instances in a specific PTP Domain. The IEEE 1588-2019 standard allows for more than one PTP Domain to exist on a PTP capable Network but this is not advised.

A Boundary Clock will have multiple instances as it will be usually required to operate in one or more PTP Domain.

In most cases the term PTP Instance is just another term for PTP capable Device or just PTP Clock. This document will where possible simply use the term PTP Clock or just Clock for simplicities sake.

PTP Instances are broken down into four different types:
1. Boundary Clocks
2. Ordinary Clocks
3. Peer-to-Peer Transparent Clocks
4. End-to-End Transparent Clocks

All PTP Instances have the following:
1. ClockIdentity
2. PortNumber

Boundary Clocks and Ordinary Clocks have the following data set members that describe them:
1. Priority1
2. Priority2
3. ClockClass
4. ClockAccuracy
5. TimeSource
6. OffsetScaledLogVariance
7. NumberPorts

PTP Port

The term PTP Port can be a confusing one and is not helped by the broad definition in the IEEE 1588 standard. Since the PTP standard specifies a protocol that is meant to be transported by a wide selection of Network Transport Protocols it is very broadly defined.

A PTP Port as defined by the standard connects a PTP Clock to a PTP capable Network. Each PTP Clock needs to have at least one PTP Port to operate. Some Clocks such as Boundary Clocks will have multiple PTP Ports.

A PTP Port is able to separate PTP Event Messages and PTP General Messages. PTP General Messages are handled by the General Interface and PTP Event Messages are handled by the Event Interface.

A PTP Port must operate using only one version of the PTP protocol and must use only one Network Transport Protocol. A single Physical Port connected to a PTP capable Network may be used by multiple PTP Ports.

How a PTP Port is depicted in the standard is outlined below.

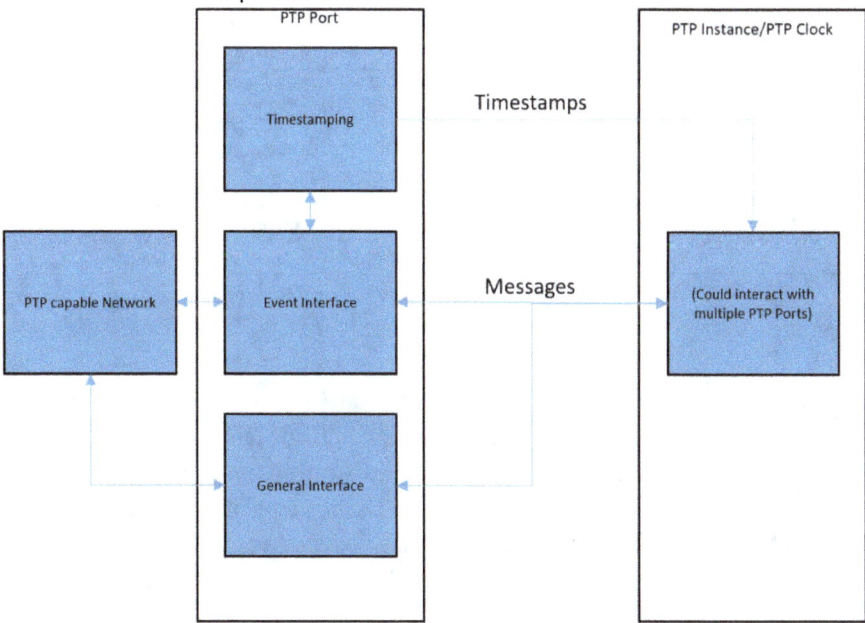

So how does this convention work with Ethernet?

There are Logical PTP Ports or Sockets that will always belong to a particular PTP capable Physical Port and there are PTP capable Physical Ports as well that will always have at least one operational Logical PTP Port. Since both are very similar to each other the shorthand is to refer to both combined as a PTP Port. If a section of this document needs to refer to a specific one it will directly refer to it otherwise assume PTP Port refers to a combination of both at the same time.

PTP Messages

PTP Messages are what PTP uses to communicate and exchange information between PTP Clocks. PTP Messages allow for the Synchronization and Management of PTP capable Network Devices.

PTP Message Types

PTP has many Packet based Message Types used in different ways by different types of Clocks:

PTP Message Types:	Used by:	Message Class:
Sync	Ordinary and Boundary Clocks	Event Message
Follow_Up		General Message
Delay_Req		Event Message
Delay_Resp		General Message
Pdelay_Req	Transparent Clocks	Event Message
Pdelay_Resp		Event Message
Pdelay_Resp_Follow_Up		General Message
Announce	Master Clocks	General Message
Management	Master and Slave Clocks	General Message
Signaling	Master and Slave Clocks	General Message

Sync Message

The Sync Message is transmitted at regular intervals(usually every 1s). If the Sync Message is an One-Step(1S) Sync Message it will contain the Timestamp(OriginTimestamp) of when it was transmitted by a Master Clock(or a PTP Master Port). During the One-Step Sync Messages transit over the Network between the Master Clock and the Slave Clock the Sync Message may have its CorrectionField updated to account for the Link Delays and the Residence Times of Transparent Clocks.

However if the Sync Message is a Two-Step(2S) Sync Message the Transmitted Timestamp(OriginTimestamp) contained in the Sync Message will be set to zero. The Follow_Up Message will instead contain the Timestamp(PreciseOriginTimestamp) of when the Sync Message was originally transmitted from the Master Clock. The Follow_Up Message is transmitted after the Sync Message. As well for a Two-Step Sync Message during Network transit between Master Clock and Slave Clock the Follow_Up Message's CorrectionField would be updated with any Link Delay Times(if the Peer Delay Mechanism is used) and the ResidenceTimes of any Transparent Clocks.

The Sync Message is used in the Synchronization process between Master and Slave Clocks.

Note: Sync Messages are allowed to use a Unicast Transmission Model as determined by their selected PTP Profile but must maintain the function of the Multicast Transmission Model

Follow_Up Message

The Follow_Up Message is as described earlier deliberately transmitted by the Master Clock and contains the Two-Step Sync Message's Timestamp(PreciseOriginTimestamp) of when the Sync Message was originally transmitted by the Master Clock or more accurately the Master Port. The Follow_Up Message would not be used for a One-Step Master Clock. The Follow_Up Message is used in the Synchronization process between Master and Slave Clocks.

Note: Follow_Up Messages must use the same Transmission Model(Unicast or Multicast) as their associated Sync Message

Delay_Req Message

The Delay_Req Message is transmitted by a Slave Clock to a Master Clock to ask the Master Clock to respond with a Delay_Resp Message. The Delay_Resp Message would contain a Timestamp(ReceiveTimestamp) of when the Delay_Req Message was received by the Master Clock. The Delay_Req Message is used in the Synchronization process between Master and Slave Clocks.

Note: Delay_Req Messages are allowed to use a Unicast Transmission Model as determined by their selected PTP Profile but must maintain the function of a Multicast Transmission Model

Delay_Resp Message

The Delay_Resp Message is transmitted by the Master Clock and contains the Master Clocks Timestamp(ReceiveTimestamp) of when the Delay_Req Message was received. The Delay_Resp Message is used in the Synchronization process between Master and Slave Clocks.

Note: Delay_Resp Messages are to use the same Transmission Model(Unicast or Multicast) as the received Delay_Req Message

Pdelay_Req Message

The Pdelay_Req Message is transmitted by the Delay Requestor Port to the Delay Responder Port and will have the Delay Requestor Ports Timestamp(OriginTimestamp) of when the Pdelay_Req Message was transmitted. The Pdelay_Req Message is used to start the process to calculate the Link Delay between two Peer Delay Ports.

Pdelay_Resp Message

The Pdelay_Resp Message is transmitted by the Delay Responder Port to the Delay Requestor Port and will have the Delay Responders Ports Timestamp(RequestReceiptTimestamp) of when the Pdelay_Req Message was received. The Pdelay_Resp Message is used as part of the process to calculate the Link Delay between two Peer Delay Ports.

However if the Delay Responder Port belongs to a Two-Step Clock the Timestamp(RequestReceiptTimestamp) contained in the Pdelay_Resp Message will be a zero.
The Pdelay_Resp_Follow_Up Message will instead contain the Timestamp(ResponseOriginTimestamp) of when the Pdelay_Resp Message was transmitted and is sent afterwards.

Note: Be aware, instead of a Timestamp of when the Pdelay_Resp Message was transmitted the time difference between when the Pdelay_Req Message was received and when the Pdelay_Resp Message was transmitted may also be used

Pdelay_Resp_Follow_Up Message

The Pdelay_Resp_Follow_Up Message is as described in the previous section deliberately transmitted by the Delay Responder Port belonging to a Two-Step Clock and contains the Pdelay_Resp Messages Timestamp of when it was transmitted(ResponseOriginTimestamp). The Pdelay_Resp_Follow_Up Message would not be used by a Delay Responder Port belonging to a One-Step Clock. The Pdelay_Resp_Follow_Up Message is used as part of the process to calculate the Link Delay between two Peer Delay Ports.

Announce Message

The Announce Message is only transmitted by PTP Ports in the Master PortState in order to create a Synchronization Master-Slave Hierarchy and details out the specifications(Class, Priorities, Qualities, etc) of the Transmitting Clock to the other Clocks in the same PTP Domain. The specifications of the Clock is contained in its data sets and is what the Announce Message contains. The specifications of the Clock and therefore the data sets of the Clock are not static and are subject to change. For example the degradation of the Clocks internal Oscillator may occur and will affect the Clocks specifications(ClockClass). Announce Messages are transmitted at regular intervals as Multicast Messages.

Note: Announce Messages are allowed to use a Unicast Transmission Model determined by their selected PTP Profile but must maintain the function of a Multicast Transmission Model

Management Message

Management Messages are used by a PTP Management Node to pull PTP Clock information from Clocks and to configure the data sets of Clocks(PTP Instances) in the Network. It is used to monitor, configure and maintain a PTP capable Network.

Signaling Message

Signaling Messages are employed for regular non time sensitive communication between Clocks. Some Clocks are not equipped to support Signaling Messages and will delete them when received without being further processed.

PTP Message Classes

All PTP Messages are assigned as ether an Event Message or a General Message Class:

PTP Message Types:	Message Class:
Sync	Event Message
Follow_Up	General Message
Delay_Req	Event Message
Delay_Resp	General Message
Pdelay_Req	Event Message
Pdelay_Resp	Event Message
Pdelay_Resp_Follow_Up	General Message
Announce	General Message
Management	General Message
Signaling	General Message

Event Message

An Event Message is a PTP Message that is time sensitive. This means the PTP Message will need its transmitted time and received time recorded(Timestamped). Transmission Timestamps, Received Timestamps, Residence Times, Link Delays are all important to Event Messages and will affect the accuracy of the Synchronization of Slave Clocks. Event Messages will be treated differently from normal Network Traffic by Transparent Clocks.

General Message

PTP General Messages are not time sensitive meaning they will not need to take into account the transmitted time or received time. However some General Messages may contain the Original Transmitted Timestamp, ResidenceTimes or Link Delays for their associated Event Message partner.

Note: The term Message can be used interchangeably with the term Packet when it comes to PTP over Ethernet

Transporting PTP Messages

PTP Messages can be contained and transmitted within a wide selection of Network Transport Protocols. PTP can be transported with:

Ethernet(IEEE 802.3)
UDP IPv4
UDP IPv6
DeviceNET
ControlNET

In this book we will only focus on transporting PTP over Ethernet(IEEE 802.3).

Transporting A PTP Message with Ethernet

The PTP Message is enclosed in the payload of the Ethernet Frame as defined by the standard IEEE 802.3. The Ethernet Frame is specified as containing a PTP Message by setting the Ethernet Type Field found in the Ethernet Header as 88F7(hex).

Ethernet Frame:		
Ethernet Header	Payload(PTP Message)	Ethernet FCS

Note: Hexadecimal numbers are expressed as 0123(hex)

Note: Decimal numbers are expressed as 123 or 123(dec)

PTP allows for the use of Unicast or Multicast Messages. The PTP IEEE standard was written with Multicast Messages in mind. Specific PTP Profiles may restrict Messages to one or the other though.

Note: If the reader has no or little Networking exposure we recommend The Technicians Guide to Industrial Networking

Traffic Class

If using the IPv6 Header or any other Ethernet Transport Mechanism that uses Traffic Classes PTP Event Messages will need to have the highest priority set. This will allow any PTP Event Messages to be processed faster or with a higher priority compared to other Network Traffic thus improving the Synchronization accuracy.

PTP Message Parts

Every PTP Message subsists of three parts: Header, Body and Suffix.

PTP Message:		
Header	Body	Suffix
34bytes	Variable	Not Always Required

Note: Reserved Fields will only contain a value of zero

Note: A byte(or octet) is assumed to be 8bits in length for the purpose of this document

IEEE 1588-2019 Common PTP Message Header

All PTP Messages have a PTP Header. The IEEE 1588-2019 PTP Header is 34bytes in length and contains the following:

Byte1		Byte2	
MajorSdoID	MessageType	MinorVersionPTP	VersionPTP
MessageLength			
DomainNumber		MinorSdoID	
FlagField			
CorrectionField			
CorrectionField(cont)			
CorrectionField(cont)			
CorrectionField(cont)			
MessageTypeSpecific			
MessageTypeSpecific(cont)			
SourcePortIdentity			
SourcePortIdentity(cont)			
SourcePortIdentity(cont)			
SourcePortIdentity(cont)			
SourcePortIdentity(cont)			
SequenceID			
ControlField		LogMessageInterval	

MajorSdoID: The MajorSdoID Field's value unless otherwise specified by the selected PTP Profile or is a PTP Management Message is to be the four most significant bits of the Transmitting Clock's SdoID. The possible values of SdoID and what the values are intended to be used for are defined in the next table. If the Network Device understands the MajorSdoID Field value the Network Device receiving the Message will process the Message as a PTP Message. Otherwise if the Network Device does not understand it will process the PTP Message as it would any other received Message. The MajorSdoID Field contains an unsigned integer and is 4bits in length

SdoID Value Range(hex):		DomainNumber values when PTP uses Ethernet as per IEEE 802(dec):	Description:
Major SdoID:	Minor SdoID:		
From: 0	00	*0-127 are allowed *128-255 are reserved	*If using IEEE 1588-2008 or the PTP specifies as such
To: 0	00		
From: 0	01		*For use only with the IEEE 1588-2008 version, for backwards compatibility
To: 0	FF		
From: 1	00	*0-239 are allowed *240-255 are reserved	*If using IEEE 802.1 PTP Profiles
To: 1	00		
From: 1	01		*For use only with the IEEE 1588-2008 version, for backwards compatibility
To: 1	FF		
From: 2	00	*240-255 are reserved	*Used by IEEE 1588 Common MeanLinkDelay
To: 2	00		
From: 2	01	*reserved	*Used by IEEE 1588 Working Group
To: 2	FF		
From: 3	00	*0-239 are allowed *240-255 are reserved	*If using QSDOs PTP Profiles
To: F	FC		
From: F	FD	*0-239 are allowed *240-255 are reserved	*For temporary or testing
To: F	FE		
From: F	FF	*reserved	*Used by IEEE 1588 Working Group
To: F	FF		

Note: The term reserved simply indicates that it is to be retained for future use or for a specific groups use usually for testing or research

MessageType: The MessageType Field specifies which PTP Message is enclosed in the body of the PTP Message. This field specifies whether the PTP Message is a Sync, Follow_Up, Delay_Req, Delay_Resp, Pdelay_Req, Pdelay_Resp, Pdelay_Resp_Follow_Up, Announce, Management or a Signaling Message. The MessageType Field contains an unsigned integer and is 4bits in length

MessageType:	Value(hex):
Sync	0
Delay_Req	1
Pdelay_Req	2
Pdelay_Resp	3
Reserved	4-7
Follow_Up	8
Delay_Resp	9
Pdelay_Resp_Follow_Up	A
Announce	B
Signaling	C
Management	D
Reserved	E-F

MinorVersionPTP: The MinorVersionPTP Field is used to specify the minor version of PTP the PTP Message and transmitting PTP Clock are using. The Port Data Set contains the MinorVersionNumber data set member from the original transmitting Clock. VersionPTP and MinorVersionPTP together specify the version of the PTP standard the Clock that first transmitted the Message is using. For the IEEE 1588-2019 version the MinorVersionPTP value is 1(dec). The MinorVersionPTP Field contains an unsigned integer and is 4bits in length

VersionPTP: The VersionPTP Field is used to specify the version of PTP the PTP Message and transmitting PTP Clock are using. The Port Data Set contains the data set member VersionPTP in the original transmitting PTP Clock. VersionPTP and MinorVersionPTP together specify the version of the PTP standard the Clock that first transmitted the Message is using. For the IEEE 1588-2019 version the VersionPTP value is 2(dec). The VersionPTP Field contains an unsigned integer and is 4bits in length

MessageLength: The MessageLength Field value is used to define the complete length in octets of the PTP Message. Including all octets of the Header, the Body and the Suffix. The MessageLength does not include any Padding. If there are TLV's attached to the PTP Message they will not be counted as part of the MessageLength. For these two reasons this makes the MessageLength of limited use. The MessageLength Field contains an unsigned integer and is 2bytes in length

DomainNumber: The DomainNumber Field defines which PTP Domain the PTP Message and Transmitting Clock belongs to. For PTP Messages transmitted from Peer-to-Peer Transparent Clocks and for PTP Management Messages the DomainNumber value are specified differently. PTP Domains and Subdomains are discussed further in a later section. The DomainNumber must be between 0-255 and which values that can be used are defined by the SdoID value. The DomainNumber Field contains an unsigned integer and is 1byte in length

MinorSdoID: The MinorSdoID Field unless otherwise specified by the selected PTP Profile or is a PTP Management Message is to be the 8 least significant bits of the Transmitting Clock's SdoID. The possible values of SdoID and what the values are intended to be used for are defined in the next table. The MinorSdoID Field is 8bits in length

SdoID Value Range(hex):		DomainNumber values when PTP uses Ethernet as per IEEE 802(dec):	Description:
Major SdoID:	Minor SdoID:		
From:		*0-127 are allowed	*If using IEEE 1588-2008 or
0	00	*128-255 are reserved	the PTP specifies as such
To:			
0	00		
From:			*For use only with the IEEE
0	01		1588-2008 version, for
To:			backwards compatibility
0	FF		
From:		*0-239 are allowed	*If using IEEE 802.1 PTP
1	00	*240-255 are reserved	Profiles
To:			
1	00		

From:			*For use only with the IEEE 1588-2008 version, for backwards compatibility
1	01		
To:			
1	FF		
From:		*240-255 are reserved	*Used by IEEE 1588 Common MeanLinkDelay
2	00		
To:			
2	00		
From:		*reserved	*Used by IEEE 1588 Working Group
2	01		
To:			
2	FF		
From:		*0-239 are allowed *240-255 are reserved	*If using QSDOs PTP Profiles
3	00		
To:			
F	FC		
From:		*0-239 are allowed *240-255 are reserved	*For temporary or testing
F	FD		
To:			
F	FE		
From:		*reserved	*Used by IEEE 1588 Working Group
F	FF		
To:			
F	FF		

FlagField: The FlagField contains individual flags that specify a particular PTP status. Of them the Flag that indicates One-Step or Two-Step is used most commonly. If the PTP Message Type does not indicate the Flag bit status the Flag bit status is assumed to be zero. The FlagField is 2bytes in length. The PTP Flags from most significant(left) to least significant(right):

Bit0: Bit0 is called the AlternateMasterFlag and if true means the transmitting PTP Port is an Alternate Master Port. The AlternateMasterFlag is used by Sync, Follow_Up, Delay_Resp and Announce Messages

Bit1: Bit1 is called the TwoStepFlag and if a Sync Message has this flag set as true the Sync Message is a Two-Step Sync Message and an associated Follow_Up Message will be following it. If a Pdelay_Resp Message has this flag set as true then it will be followed by a Pdelay_Resp_Follow_Up Message. The TwoStepFlag is used by Sync and Pdelay_Resp Messages

Bit2: Bit2 is called the UnicastFlag and if a PTP Message has this flag set as true the Message was transmitted unicast. If the UnicastFlag is set as false the Message was transmitted multicast. The UnicastFlag is used by PTP Messages

Bit3: Bit3 is reserved

Bit4: Bit4 is reserved

Bit5: Bit5 is called the PTP Profile Specific 1 Flag and is dependent on the selected PTP Profile. If not used is to be set as false. The PTP Profile Specific 1 Flag is used by PTP Messages

Bit6: Bit6 is called the PTP Profile Specific 2 Flag and is dependent on the selected PTP Profile. If not used is to be set as false. The PTP Profile Specific 2 Flag is used by PTP Messages

Bit7: Bit7 is reserved

Bit8: Bit8 is called the Leap61 Flag and is used to indicate the status of the data set member Leap61 of the TimeProperties Data Set. The Leap61 Flag is used by Announce Messages

Bit9: Bit9 is called the Leap59 Flag and is used to indicate the status of the data set member Leap59 of the TimeProperties Data Set. The Leap59 Flag is used by Announce Messages

Bit10: Bit10 is called the CurrentUTCOffsetValid Flag and is used to indicate the status of the data set member CurrentUTCOffsetValid of the TimeProperties Data Set. The CurrentUTCOffsetValid Flag is used by Announce Messages

Bit11: Bit11 is called the PTPTimescale Flag and is used to indicate the status of the data set member PTPTimescale of the TimeProperties Data Set. The PTPTimescale Flag is used by Announce Messages

Bit12: Bit12 is called the TimeTraceable Flag and is used to indicate the status of the data set member TimeTraceable of the TimeProperties Data Set. The TimeTraceable Flag is used by Announce Messages

Bit13: Bit13 is called the FrequencyTraceable Flag and is used to indicate the status of the data set member FrequencyTraceable of the TimeProperties Data Set. The FrequencyTraceable Flag is used by Announce Messages

Bit14: Bit14 is called the SynchronizationUncertain Flag and is used to indicate the status of the data set member SynchronizationUncertain of the Current Data Set. The SynchronizationUncertain Flag is used by Announce Messages

Bit15: Bit15 is reserved

CorrectionField: The CorrectionField can contain the values for ResidenceTimes, DelayAsymmetrys, MeanPathDelays or MeanLinkDelays. The CorrectionField of a PTP Message is updated by Transparent Clocks as the Message transits the Network between two PTP Clocks. How the CorrectionField is updated by Transparent Clocks depends on the specific implementation of PTP. The CorrectionField is measured in nanoseconds multiplied by 65,536. For Example 10.5ns would be 688,128. If the CorrectionField(represented in bit format) is all ones except for the most significant bit being a zero than the correction value is too large to fit into the CorrectionField. The CorrectionField is used by Sync, Follow_Up, Delay_Req, Delay_Resp, Pdelay_Req, Pdelay_Resp, and Pdelay_Resp_Follow_Up Messages. The CorrectionField is a signed integer and is 8bytes in length

MessageTypeSpecific: The MessageTypeSpecific Field can be used by Sync, Delay_Req, Pdelay_Req and Pdelay_Resp Messages for all other PTP Messages it is to be assigned as reserved and not used. When it is used it is only to be done so by a Clock's specific internal hardware. If the PTP Clock has several internal hardware systems that are not Synchronized together it can be used to transmit a Timestamp between those internal systems. There are other uses for the MessageTypeSpecific that are not covered here. For the Network Professional this field has little meaning and is not well defined or explained in the IEEE 1588-2019 standard. The MessageTypeSpecific Field contains an unsigned integer and is 4bytes in length

SourcePortIdentity: The SourcePortIdentity Field is the PTP Port Number of a particular PTP Port of a particular Clock that originally transmitted the PTP Message. The Transmitting Ports Port Data Set contains the data set member PortIdentity-its value will be that of the SourcePortIdentity Field. PortIdentity has two fields: ClockIdentity and PortNumber. The SourcePortIdentity Field contains the PortIdentity special data type and is 10bytes in length

SequenceID: The SequenceID Field is a record of what sequence number the PTP Message is. Certain PTP Message are given an original SequenceID number but others copy another associated PTP Messages SequenceID number. Either way each PTP Message is assigned their SequenceID when they are originally transmitted. The SequenceID Field contain an unsigned integer and is 2bytes in length

ControlField: The ControlField is only used when UDP with IPv4 is employed otherwise it is not used. The ControlField is beyond the scope of this document. If not used for UDP IPv4 all bits of this field are to be set to zero. The ControlField Field contains an unsigned integer and is 2bytes in length

LogMessageInterval: The LogMessageInterval Field's value is different depending on the PTP MessageType as per the next table. LogMessageInterval is used to determine the mean time between different PTP Messages. The LogMessageInterval Field is 1byte in length

PTP Message Type:	Value(dec):
Sync	*For Unicast PTP Messages the value 127 is to be used *For Multicast PTP Messages the Transmitting Ports LogSyncInterval value is to be used
Follow_Up	*For Unicast PTP Messages the value 127 is to be used *For Multicast PTP Messages the Transmitting Ports LogSyncInterval value is to be used
Delay_Req	127
Delay_Resp	*For Multicast PTP Messages the Transmitting Ports LogMinDelayReqInterval *For Unicast PTP Messages the value 127 is to be used *For Unicast PTP Messages used In the optional Multicast/Unicast Operation see the IEEE standard
Pdelay_Req	127 or PTP Profile Specific

Pdelay_Resp	127
Pdelay_Resp_Follow_Up	127
Announce	*For Unicast PTP Messages the value 127 should be used *For Multicast PTP Messages the Transmitting Ports LogAnnounceInterval value should be used. Either value could be used
PTP Management	127
Signaling	127

IEEE 1588-2019 Common PTP Message Suffix

After the PTP Message Body, at the end of the PTP Message is the PTP Message Suffix containing one or more TLVs. The Suffix can have a length of zero and contain no TLVs. Transmitting Clocks will not add TLV's to a PTP Message unless they are required to by the TLV semantics or the optional Message Length Extension is being used.

Multiple TLVs can be attached to a PTP Message. The order position of a TLV in a PTP Message will not affect how it is understood. This is unless the specified PTP Profile indicates differently. If including a particular TLV to a PTP Message would cause that Message to exceed its maximum frame size than the TLV will not be added.

Asymmetry Delays are likely to happen if TLV laden PTP Messages are used in a Network that includes NonTransparent Clocks. Synchronization accuracy will be degraded slightly by the use of TLVs unless the optional Message Length Extension is turned on.

Message Length Extension

When this option is turned on by the selected PTP Profile the PTP Event Messages will all have the same length. If there are NonTransparent Clocks included in a Network utilizing PTP the Path Delay values of PTP Event Messages will vary based the length of the Message. This errors belongs in the category of asymmetry errors and can be mitigated by the use of the optional Message Length Extension.

Each MessageLength for each PTP Message mentioned in the PTP Profile will be indicated in the PTP Profile. If the specific MessageLengths are not indicated in the PTP Profile but that the Message Length Extension is consult the IEEE 1588 standard for the default value calculations.

Announce Message Body

All PTP Messages have a PTP Body. This is the Body of the Announce Message:

Byte1	Byte2
OriginTimestamp	
OriginTimestamp(cont)	
OriginTimestamp(cont)	
OriginTimestamp(cont)	
OriginTimestamp(cont)	
CurrentUTCOffset	
Reserved	GrandmasterPriority1
GrandmasterClockQuality	
GrandmasterClockQuality(cont)	
GrandmasterPriority2	GrandmasterIdentity
GrandmasterIdentity(cont)	
GrandmasterIdentity(cont)	
GrandmasterIdentity(cont)	
GrandmasterIdentity(cont)	StepsRemoved
StepsRemoved(cont)	TimeSource

OriginTimestamp: The OriginTimestamp Field can contain a Timestamp of when the PTP Message was originally transmitted by the Transmitting Clock. Otherwise the value is set to zero. The OriginTimestamp Field contains the Timestamp special data type and is 10bytes in length

CurrentUTCOffset: The CurrentUTCOffset Field will contain the value of the TimeProperties data set member CurrentUTCOffset received from the Grandmaster Clock. The CurrentUTCOffset is the offset value between the TAI Timescale and the UTC Timescale. The CurrentUTCOffset Field contains an integer and is 2bytes in length

Reserved: This Reserved Field is 1byte in length

GrandmasterPriority1: The GrandmasterPriority1 Field will contain the value of the data set member GrandmasterPriority1 of the Parent Data Set. In other words it will contain the Grandmaster Clock's Priority1 value. The GrandmasterPriority1 Field contains an unsigned integer and is 1byte in length

Note: Each Ordinary Clock and Boundary Clock has a Priority1 value that is configurable by the Network Professional and helps determine which Clock is to be the GrandMaster Clock or Master Clock

GrandmasterClockQuality: The GrandmasterClockQuality Field will contain the value of the data set member GrandmasterClockQuality of the Parent Data Set. In other words it will contain the Grandmaster Clock's ClockQuality value. The GrandmasterClockQuality Field contains the ClockQuality special data type and is 4bytes in length

GrandmasterPriority2: The GrandmasterPriority2 Field will contain the value of the data set member GrandmasterPriority2 of the Parent Data Set. In other words it will contain the Grandmaster Clock's Priority2 value. The GrandmasterPriority2 Field contains an unsigned integer 1byte in length

Note: Each Ordinary Clock and Boundary Clock has a Priority2 value that is used by the BMCA. It is configurable by the Network Professional and helps with the finer detail of ordering between comparable Clocks that have the same or similar quality

GrandmasterIdentity: The GrandmasterIdentity Field will contain the value of the data set member GrandmasterIdentity of the Parent Data Set. In other words it will contain the Grandmaster Clock's ClockIdentity value. The GrandmasterIdentity Field contains the ClockIdentity special data type and is a 8octet array and is 8bytes in length

StepsRemoved: The StepsRemoved Field will contain the value of the original Transmitting Clocks data set member StepsRemoved of the Current Data Set. A Clocks StepsRemoved is the number of Boundary Clocks that exist between the transmitting Master Clock and the original GrandMaster Clock. The StepsRemoved Field is also important in eliminating Rogue(Looping) Announce Messages by comparing its value to either 255 or the Default Data Sets MaxStepsRemoved data set member.

If the StepsRemoved Field value is equal to or greater than the MaxStepsRemoved or 255 the Announce Message it is embedded into is deleted. The StepsRemoved Field contains an unsigned integer 2bytes in length

TimeSource: The TimeSource Field will contain the value of the data set member TimeSource of the TimeProperties Data Set specifying the origin of the Time Signal used by the GrandMaster Clock as per the table below. The TimeSource Field contains an unsigned integer 1byte in length

Value(hex):	TimeSource:
10	ATOMIC_CLOCK
20	GNSS
30	TERRESTRIAL_RADIO
39	SERIAL_TIME_CODE
40	PTP
50	NTP
60	HAND_SET
90	OTHER
A0	INTERNAL OSCILLATOR
F0-FE	PTP Profile Dependent
FF	Reserved

Sync Message Body

All PTP Messages have a PTP Body. This is the Body of the Sync Message:

Byte1	Byte2
OriginTimestamp	
OriginTimestamp(cont)	
OriginTimestamp(cont)	
OriginTimestamp(cont)	
OriginTimestamp(cont)	

OriginTimestamp: The OriginTimestamp Field will contain a Timestamp of when the One-Step Sync Message was originally transmitted by the Master Clock or GrandMaster Clock. Otherwise if the Sync Message was Two-Step the OriginTimestamp Field value will be set to zero. The OriginTimestamp Field contains the Timestamp special data type and is 10bytes in length

Follow_Up Message Body

All PTP Messages have a PTP Body. This is the Body of the Follow_Up Message:

Byte1	Byte2
PreciseOriginTimestamp	
PreciseOriginTimestamp(cont)	
PreciseOriginTimestamp(cont)	
PreciseOriginTimestamp(cont)	
PreciseOriginTimestamp(cont)	

PreciseOriginTimestamp: The PreciseOriginTimestamp Field will contain a Timestamp of when the associated Two-Step Sync Message was originally transmitted by the Master Clock. Follow_Up Messages are only used when the associated Sync Message is a Two-Step Sync Message. The PreciseOriginTimestamp Field contains the Timestamp special data type and is 10bytes in length

Delay_Req Message Body

All PTP Messages have a PTP Body. This is the Body of the Delay_Req Message:

Byte1	Byte2
OriginTimestamp	
OriginTimestamp(cont)	
OriginTimestamp(cont)	
OriginTimestamp(cont)	
OriginTimestamp(cont)	

OriginTimestamp: The OriginTimestamp Field can contain a Timestamp of when the Delay_Req Message was transmitted by the Slave Clock otherwise the value is set to zero. The OriginTimestamp Field contains the Timestamp special data type and is 10bytes in length

Delay_Resp Message Body

All PTP Messages have a PTP Body. This is the Body of the Delay_Resp Message:

Byte1	Byte2
ReceiveTimestamp	
ReceiveTimestamp(cont)	
ReceiveTimestamp(cont)	
ReceiveTimestamp(cont)	
ReceiveTimestamp(cont)	
RequestingPortIdentity	
RequestingPortIdentity(cont)	
RequestingPortIdentity(cont)	
RequestingPortIdentity(cont)	
RequestingPortIdentity(cont)	

ReceiveTimestamp: The ReceiveTimestamp Field will contain a Timestamp of when the Delay_Req Message was received by the Master Clock. The ReceiveTimestamp Field contains the Timestamp special data type and is 10bytes in length

RequestingPortIdentity: The RequestingPortIdentity Field of the Delay_Resp Message will contain the same value as the associated Delay_Req Message's Header SourcePortIdentity Field value. The RequestingPortIdentity Field contains the PortIdentity special data type and is 10bytes in length

Pdelay_Req Message Body

All PTP Messages have a PTP Body. This is the Body of the Pdelay_Req Message:

Byte1	Byte2
OriginTimestamp	
OriginTimestamp(cont)	
OriginTimestamp(cont)	
OriginTimestamp(cont)	
OriginTimestamp(cont)	
Reserved	
Reserved(cont)	
Reserved(cont)	
Reserved(cont)	
Reserved(cont)	

OriginTimestamp: The OriginTimestamp Field will contain a Timestamp of when the Pdelay_Req Messages was transmitted by the Delay Requester Port. The OriginTimestamp Field contains the Timestamp special data type and is 10bytes in length

Reserved: The Reserved Field for the Pdelay_Req Message is used simply to make the Pdelay_Req Message the same length as the corresponding Pdelay_Resp Message. This is done to reduce the risk of Asymmetry Delay Errors as some networks are configured to have separate transmission times for various Message lengths. The Reserved Field is 10bytes in length

Pdelay_Resp Message Body

All PTP Messages have a PTP Body. This is the Body of the Pdelay_Resp Message:

Byte1	Byte2
RequestReceiptTimestamp	
RequestReceiptTimestamp(cont)	
RequestReceiptTimestamp(cont)	
RequestReceiptTimestamp(cont)	
RequestReceiptTimestamp(cont)	
RequestingPortIdentity	
RequestingPortIdentity(cont)	
RequestingPortIdentity(cont)	
RequestingPortIdentity(cont)	
RequestingPortIdentity(cont)	

RequestReceiptTimestamp: The RequestReceiptTimestamp Field will contain a zero or a Timestamp of when the associated Pdelay_Req Message was received by the Delay Responder Port. The RequestReceiptTimestamp Field contains the Timestamp special data type and is 10bytes in length

Note: Be aware, instead of a Timestamp of when the Pdelay_Resp Message was transmitted the time difference between when the Pdelay_Req Message was received and when the Pdelay_Resp Message was transmitted may also be used

RequestingPortIdentity: The RequestingPortIdentity Field of the Pdelay_Resp Message will contain the same value as the associated Pdelay_Req Message's Header SourcePortIdentity Field value. The RequestingPortIdentity Field contains the PortIdentity special data type and is 10bytes in length

Pdelay_Resp_Follow_Up Message Body

All PTP Messages have a PTP Body. This is the Body of the Pdelay_Resp_Follow_Up Message:

Byte1	Byte2
ResponseOriginTimestamp	
ResponseOriginTimestamp(cont)	
ResponseOriginTimestamp(cont)	
ResponseOriginTimestamp(cont)	
ResponseOriginTimestamp(cont)	
RequestingPortIdentity	
RequestingPortIdentity(cont)	
RequestingPortIdentity(cont)	
RequestingPortIdentity(cont)	
RequestingPortIdentity(cont)	

ResponseOriginTimestamp: The ResponseOriginTimestamp Field will contain a zero or Timestamp of when the associated Pdelay_Resp Message was transmitted by the Two-Step Delay Responder Port or the time elapsed between receiving the Pdelay_Req Message and the transmission of the Pdelay_Resp Message. The ResponseOriginTimestamp Field contains the Timestamp special data type and is 10bytes in length

RequestingPortIdentity: The RequestingPortIdentity Field of the Pdelay_Resp_Follow_Up Message will contain the same value as the associated Pdelay_Req Message's Header SourcePortIdentity Field value. The RequestingPortIdentity Field contains the PortIdentity special data type and is 10bytes in length

Signaling PTP Message Body

All PTP Messages have a PTP Body. This is the Body of the Signaling PTP Message:

Byte1	Byte2
TargetPortIdentity	
TargetPortIdentity(cont)	
TargetPortIdentity(cont)	
TargetPortIdentity(cont)	
TargetPortIdentity(cont)	
TLVs	
TLVs(cont)	

TargetPortIdentity: The TargetPortIdentity Field of the Signaling Message will contain the value for the intended PTP Port and PTP Clock. The TargetPortIdentity Field contains the PortIdentity special data type and is 10bytes in length

TLV: The TLV Field is filled with one or more discretionary or PTP Profile dependent TLVs. Select TLVs are covered by this document but is by no means extensive. Consult the newest IEEE 1588 standard for more information

Management PTP Message Body

All PTP Messages have a PTP Body. This is the Body of the Management PTP Message:

Byte1	Byte2
TargetPortIdentity	
TargetPortIdentity(cont)	
TargetPortIdentity(cont)	
TargetPortIdentity(cont)	
TargetPortIdentity(cont)	
StartingBoundaryHops	BoundaryHops
Reserved / ActionField	Reserved
ManagementTLV	
ManagementTLV(cont)	

TargetPortIdentity: The TargetPortIdentity Field of the Management Message will contain the value for the intended PTP Port and PTP Clock to receive the Message. The intended receiving PTP Port will be the Port the Management Message is intending to act upon. If the value contained in the TargetPortIdentity Field is all ones the Management Message acts on all PTP Ports of that PTP Clock. The TargetPortIdentity Field contains the PortIdentity special data type and is 10bytes in length

StartingBoundaryHops: The StartingBoundaryHops Field value of a Management Message is either dependent on the selected PTP Profile or the StartingBoundaryHops Field value is populated in response to another received Management Message. In response to another Management Message the value of the StartingBoundaryHops Field is determined by taking the other Management Message's StartingBoundaryHops and BoundaryHops and subtracting them from each other(StartingBoundaryHops minus BoundaryHops). The StartingBoundaryHops Field value is the times this Management Message can be retransmitted from a Boundary Clock. The StartingBoundaryHops Field contains an unsigned integer and is 1byte in length

BoundaryHops: The BoundaryHops Field value indicates the number of Boundary Clocks the Management Message can still be retransmitted from. The BoundaryHops Field and the StartingBoundaryHops Field of the Management Message will start with the same value when first transmitted by the originating PTP Clock. The BoundaryHops Field value is decreased by one each time a Boundary Clock retransmits the Management Message. The BoundaryHops Field contains an unsigned integer and is 1byte in length

Note: The value of the difference between a Management Message's StartingBoundaryHops Field value and the same Management Message's BoundaryHops Field value specifies the total amount of Boundary Clocks the Management Message passed through

Reserved: This Reserved Field for the Management Message is 4bits in length

ActionField: The ActionField value signifies what kind of Management Message it is and what needs to be done when the Message is received as per the table directly below. The ActionField contains an unsigned integer 4bits in length

Value (dec):	ActionField Name:	Description of the Management Message:
0	GET	A sole MANAGEMENT TLV will be carried by the GET Management Message. The MANAGEMENT TLV's ManagementID Field will specify what data will be pulled. The correct responding PTP Clock or PTP Port will answer with another Management Message except with the ActionField assigned as RESPONSE. The TLV in the responding Management Message will be a MANAGEMENT_ERROR_STATUS TLV if an error happens. When operating correctly the TLV in the responding Management Message will have the enclosed data requested by the original Management Message's ManagementID.

1	SET	A sole MANAGEMENT TLV will be carried by the SET Management Message. The MANAGEMENT TLV's ManagementID Field will specify what data needs to be assigned. If there is more than one data field specified by the ManagementID and if any one field is not updated the item is designated an error. Nonconfigurable fields that were attempted to be written over will be answered with a MANAGEMENT_ERROR_STATUS TLV.The responding PTP Clock or PTP Port will answer with another Management Message except with the ActionField assigned as RESPONSE. When operating correctly the TLV in the responding Management Message will have the enclosed data requested by the original Management Message's ManagementID. The TLV in the responding Management Message will be a MANAGEMENT_ERROR_STATUS TLV if an error happens.
2	RESPONSE	A RESPONSE Management Message will have one MANAGEMENT TLV or a MANAGEMENT_ERROR_STATUS TLV attached. The RESPONSE Management Message ManagementID Field will be the same value as the Requesting Management Message. When operating correctly the TLV in the RESPONSE Management Message will be a MANAGEMENT TLV and will have the information requested by the original Management Message's ManagementID Field. The TLV in the responding Management Message will be a MANAGEMENT_ERROR_STATUS TLV if an error happens. The RESPONSE Management Message is for responding to GET or SET Management Messages.
3	COMMAND	A COMMAND Management Message will have one MANAGEMENT TLV. When the COMMAND Management Message is received the event specified by the COMMAND Message will be carried out by the specified PTP Port or PTP Clock. Once the event is finished the responding Clock will transmit an ACKNOWLEDGE Management Message back to the requesting Clock or Management Node.

4	ACKNOWLEDGE	The ACKNOWLEDGE Management Message will have attached one MANAGEMENT TLV or a MANAGEMENT_ERROR_STATUS TLV. When everything operated correctly the Acknowledge Management Message will have the same MANAGEMENT TLV Field as the associated Command Management Message. By extension, the ManagementID and DataField values will be the same as the associated Command Management Message it is acknowledging. The TLV in the responding Management Message will be MANAGEMENT_ERROR_STATUS TLV if an error happens.
5-F	Reserved	

Reserved: This Reserved Field for the Management Message is 8bits in length

ManagementTLV: The ManagementTLV Field is filled with either one MANAGEMENT TLV or one MANAGEMENT_ERROR_STATUS TLV. MANAGEMENT TLVs can either modify/manage PTP Clock or PTP Port Data Sets or they can start events. MANAGEMENT_ERROR_STATUS TLVs are used to respond to Management Messages where the responding PTP Port or PTP Clock has encountered an error or problem. The ManagementTLV Field is variable in length

Note: TLV stands for Type, Length and Value. It is a generic data type and way of organizing data. TLV's are attached to PTP Messages usually Management Messages

MANAGEMENT TLV Format

Some Management PTP Messages will have a MANAGEMENT TLV attached. This is the format of the MANAGEMENT TLV:

Byte1	Byte2
TLVType	
LengthField	
ManagementID	
DataField	

TLVType: The TLVType Field value indicates the type of TLV. For MANAGEMENT TLVs the value is 0001(hex). All TLVType values are defined by the below table. The TLVType Field contains an unsigned integer 16bits in length

Value (hex):	TLVType Name:	Propagated by Boundary Clock?
0000	Reserved	No
0001	MANAGEMENT	No
0002	MANAGEMENT_ERROR_STATUS	No
0003	ORGANIZATION_EXTENSION	No
0004	REQUEST_UNICAST_TRANSMISSION	No
0005	GRANT_UNICAST_TRANSMISSION	No
0006	CANCEL_UNICAST_TRANSMISSION	No
0007	ACKNOWLEDGE_CANCEL_UNICAST_TRANSMISSION	No
0008	PATH_TRACE	Yes
0009	ALTERNATE_TIME_OFFSET_INDICATOR	Yes
000A - 1FFF	Reserved	No
2000 - 2003	Reserved	No
2004 - 202F	Reserved	No
2030 - 3FFF	Reserved	No
4000	ORGANIZATION_EXTENSION_PROPAGATE	Yes
4001	ENHANCED_ACCURACY_METRICS	Yes
4002 - 7EFF	Reserved	Yes
7F00 - 7FFF	Reserved	Yes
8000	ORGANIZATION_EXTENSION_DO_NOT_PROPAGATE	No

8001	L1_SYNC	No
8002	PORT_COMMUNICATION_AVAILABILITY	No
8003	PROTOCOL_ADDRESS	No
8004	SLAVE_RX_SYNC_TIMING_DATA	No
8005	SLAVE_RX_SYNC_COMPUTED_DATA	No
8006	SLAVE_TX_EVENT_TIMESTAMPS	No
8007	CUMULATIVE_RATE_RATIO	No
8008	PAD	No
8009	AUTHENTICATION	No
800A - FFEF	Reserved	No
FFF0 - FFFF	Reserved	No

LengthField: The LengthField value is the number of bytes in the ValueField of the TLV. The ValueField value for MANAGEMENT TLVs includes the number of bytes for the ManagementID Field and the DataField. The LengthField contains an unsigned integer and is 16bits in length

ManagementID: The ManagementID Field value is used to define what function the MANAGEMENT TLV performs. If a Management Message is received with a ManagementID that is not supported or permitted the Management TLV is ignored or a Management Message is sent in response with a MANAGEMENT_ERROR_STATUS TLV attached. All ManagementID values are defined by the below table. The ManagementID Field contains an unsigned integer 16bits in length

Value (hex):	ManagementID Name:	Used By Management Messages:	PTP Port or PTP Clock?	Type of PTP Clock?
0000	NULLPTPMANAGEMENT	GET, SET, COMMAND	PTP Port	All PTP Clocks
0001	CLOCKDESCRIPTION	GET	PTP Port	All PTP Clocks
0002	USERDESCRIPTION	GET, SET	PTP Clock	All PTP Clocks
0003	SAVEINNONVOLATILESTORAGE	COMMAND	PTP Clock	All PTP Clocks
0004	RESETNONVOLATILESTORAGE	COMMAND	PTP Clock	All PTP Clocks
0005	INITIALIZE	COMMAND	PTP Clock	All PTP Clocks

0006	FAULTLOG	GET	PTP Clock	All PTP Clocks
0007	FAULTLOGRESET	COMMAND	PTP Clock	All PTP Clocks
0008-1FFF	Reserved			
2000	DEFAULT DATA SET	GET	PTP Clock	Ordinary And Boundary Clocks
2001	CURRENT DATA SET	GET	PTP Clock	Ordinary And Boundary Clocks
2002	PARENT DATA SET	GET	PTP Clock	Ordinary And Boundary Clocks
2003	TIMEPROPERTIES DATA SET	GET	PTP Clock	Ordinary And Boundary Clocks
2004	PORT DATA SET	GET	PTP Port	Ordinary And Boundary Clocks
2005	PRIORITY1	GET, SET	PTP Clock	Ordinary And Boundary Clocks
2006	PRIORITY2	GET, SET	PTP Clock	Ordinary And Boundary Clocks
2007	DOMAIN	GET, SET	PTP Clock	Ordinary And Boundary Clocks
2008	SLAVE ONLY	GET, SET	PTP Clock	Ordinary And Boundary Clocks

2009	LOGANNOUNCEINTERVAL	GET, SET	PTP Port	Ordinary And Boundary Clocks
200A	ANNOUNCERECEIPTTIMEOUT	GET, SET	PTP Port	Ordinary And Boundary Clocks
200B	LOGSYNCINTERVAL	GET, SET	PTP Port	Ordinary And Boundary Clocks
200C	VERSIONNUMBER	GET, SET	PTP Port	Ordinary And Boundary Clocks
200D	ENABLEPORT	COMMAND	PTP Port	Ordinary And Boundary Clocks
200E	DISABLEPORT	COMMAND	PTP Port	Ordinary And Boundary Clocks
200F	TIME	GET, SET	PTP Clock	Ordinary And Boundary Clocks
2010	CLOCKACCURACY	GET, SET	PTP Clock	Ordinary And Boundary Clocks
2011	UTCPROPERTIES	GET, SET	PTP Clock	Ordinary And Boundary Clocks
2012	TRACEABILITYPROPERTIES	GET, SET	PTP Clock	Ordinary And Boundary Clocks
2013	TIMESCALEPROPERTIES	GET, SET	PTP Clock	Ordinary And Boundary Clocks

2014	UNICASTNEGOTIATIONENABLE	GET, SET	PTP Clock	Ordinary And Boundary Clocks
2015	PATHTRACELIST	GET	PTP Clock	Ordinary And Boundary Clocks
2016	PATHTRACEENABLE	GET, SET	PTP Clock	Ordinary And Boundary Clocks
2017	GRANDMASTERCLUSTERTABLE	GET, SET	PTP Clock	Ordinary And Boundary Clocks
2018	UNICASTMASTERTABLE	GET, SET	PTP Port	Ordinary And Boundary Clocks
2019	UNICASTMASTERMAXTABLESIZE	GET	PTP Port	Ordinary And Boundary Clocks
201A	ACCEPTABLEMASTERTABLE	GET, SET	PTP Clock	Ordinary And Boundary Clocks
201B	ACCEPTABLEMASTERTABLE ENABLED	GET, SET	PTP Port	Ordinary And Boundary Clocks
201C	ACCEPTABLEMASTERMAXTABLE SIZE	GET	PTP Clock	Ordinary And Boundary Clocks
201D	ALTERNATEMASTER	GET, SET	PTP Port	Ordinary And Boundary Clocks
201E	ALTERNATETIMEOFFSETENABLE	GET, SET	PTP Clock	Ordinary And Boundary Clocks

201F	ALTERNATETIMEOFFSETNAME	GET, SET	PTP Clock	Ordinary And Boundary Clocks
2020	ALTERNATETIMEOFFSETMAXKEY	GET	PTP Clock	Ordinary And Boundary Clocks
2021	ALTERNATETIMEOFFSET PROPERTIES	GET, SET	PTP Clock	Ordinary And Boundary Clocks
2022-2FFF	Reserved			
3000	EXTERNALPORTCONFIGURATION ENABLED	GET, SET	PTP Clock	Ordinary And Boundary Clocks
3001	MASTERONLY	GET, SET	PTP Port	Ordinary And Boundary Clocks
3002	HOLDOVERUPGRADEENABLE	GET, SET	PTP Clock	Ordinary And Boundary Clocks
3003	EXTPORTCONFIGPORT DATA SET	GET, SET	PTP Port	Ordinary And Boundary Clocks
3004-3FFF	Reserved			
4000	TRANSPARENTCLOCKDEFAULT DATA SET	GET	PTP Clock	Transparent Clocks
4001	TRANSPARENTCLOCKPORT DATA SET	GET	PTP Port	Transparent Clocks
4002	PRIMARYDOMAIN	GET, SET	PTP Clock	Transparent Clocks
4003-5FFF	Reserved			

6000	DELAYMECHANISM	GET, SET	PTP Port	Ordinary, Boundary And Transparent Clocks
6001	LOGMINPDELAYREQINTERVAL	GET, SET	PTP Port	Ordinary, Boundary And Transparent Clocks
6002-BFFF	Reserved			
C000-DFFF	Custom ManagementID values to be operable between Clocks of the Manufacturer			
E000-FFFE	Used by an Alternate PTP Profile			
FFFF	Reserved			

DataField: The DataField is used to contain the specific ManagementID's data. The DataField is highly variable in the data types used and the length of the field. These are dependent on the ManagementID

MANAGEMENT_ERROR_STATUS TLV

Some Management PTP Messages will have a MANAGEMENT_ERROR_STATUS TLV attached. This is the format of the MANAGEMENT_ERROR_STATUS TLV:

Byte1	Byte2
TLVType	
LengthField	
ManagementErrorID	
ManagementID	
Reserved	
Reserved(cont)	
DisplayData	
Pad	

TLVType: The TLVType Field value indicates the type of TLV. For MANAGEMENT_ERROR_STATUS TLVs the value is 0002(hex). All TLVType values are defined by the next table. The TLVType Field contains an unsigned integer and is 16bits in length

Value (hex):	TLVType Name:	Propagation by Boundary Clock?
0000	Reserved	No
0001	MANAGEMENT	No
0002	MANAGEMENT_ERROR_STATUS	No
0003	ORGANIZATION_EXTENSION	No
0004	REQUEST_UNICAST_TRANSMISSION	No
0005	GRANT_UNICAST_TRANSMISSION	No
0006	CANCEL_UNICAST_TRANSMISSION	No
0007	ACKNOWLEDGE_CANCEL_UNICAST_TRANSMISSION	No
0008	PATH_TRACE	Yes
0009	ALTERNATE_TIME_OFFSET_INDICATOR	Yes
000A - 1FFF	Reserved	No
2000 - 2003	Reserved	No
2004 - 202F	Reserved	No
2030 - 3FFF	Reserved	No
4000	ORGANIZATION_EXTENSION_PROPAGATE	Yes
4001	ENHANCED_ACCURACY_METRICS	Yes

4002 - 7EFF	Reserved	Yes
7F00 - 7FFF	Reserved	Yes
8000	ORGANIZATION_EXTENSION_DO_NOT_PROPAGATE	No
8001	L1_SYNC	No
8002	PORT_COMMUNICATION_AVAILABILITY	No
8003	PROTOCOL_ADDRESS	No
8004	SLAVE_RX_SYNC_TIMING_DATA	No
8005	SLAVE_RX_SYNC_COMPUTED_DATA	No
8006	SLAVE_TX_EVENT_TIMESTAMPS	No
8007	CUMULATIVE_RATE_RATIO	No
8008	PAD	No
8009	AUTHENTICATION	No
800A - FFEF	Reserved	No
FFF0 - FFFF	Reserved	No

LengthField: The LengthField value is the number of bytes in the ValueField of the TLV. The ValueField value for MANAGEMENT_ERROR_STATUS TLVs includes the number of bytes for the ManagementErrorID Field, ManagementID Field, Reserved Field, DisplayData Field and the Pad Field. The LengthField contains an unsigned integer and is 16bits in length

ManagementErrorID: The ManagementErrorID Field value indicates the type of error. All ManagementErrorID values are defined by the next table. The ManagementErrorID contains an unsigned integer and is 16bits in length

Value (hex):	ManagementErrorID Name:	Description:
0000	Reserved	
0001	RESPONSE_TOO_BIG	One Response Message will not fit the request
0002	NO_SUCH_ID	Unknown ManagementID
0003	WRONG_LENGTH	The LengthField is not correct for the specified ManagementID
0004	WRONG_VALUE	One or more DataField values are not correct for the specified ManagementID and LengthField
0005	NOT_SETABLE	One or more DataField data set members requested by a SET Management Message are nonconfigurable
0006	NOT_SUPPORTED	The Requested Management Message operation is not possible to complete on this PTP Clock
0007	UNPOPULATED	The UNPOPULATED Response in the MANAGEMENT_ERROR_STATUS Message indicates a PTP Port in the TargetPortIdentity Message Field that is not currently in use at the time of the Request Management Message being received
0008-BFFF	Reserved	
C000-DFFF	Implementation specific	Custom ManagementErrorID values to be operable between Clocks of the Manufacturer
E000-FFFD	PTP Profile defined	Used by an Alternate PTP Profile
FFFE	GENERAL_ERROR	The GENERAL_ERROR is an error that is not specified by other ManagementErrorID errors
FFFF	Reserved	

ManagementID: The ManagementID Field value is used to define what type of MANAGEMENT TLV the MANAGEMENT_ERROR_STATUS TLV is responding to. All ManagementID values are defined by the below table. The ManagementID Field contains an unsigned integer and is 16bits in length

Value (hex):	ManagementID Name:	Used By Management Messages:	For the PTP Port or PTP Clock?	Type of PTP Clock?
0000	NULLPTPMANAGEMENT	GET, SET, COMMAND	PTP Port	All PTP Clocks
0001	CLOCKDESCRIPTION	GET	PTP Port	All PTP Clocks
0002	USERDESCRIPTION	GET, SET	PTP Clock	All PTP Clocks
0003	SAVEINNONVOLATILESTORAGE	COMMAND	PTP Clock	All PTP Clocks
0004	RESETNONVOLATILESTORAGE	COMMAND	PTP Clock	All PTP Clocks
0005	INITIALIZE	COMMAND	PTP Clock	All PTP Clocks
0006	FAULTLOG	GET	PTP Clock	All PTP Clocks
0007	FAULTLOGRESET	COMMAND	PTP Clock	All PTP Clocks
0008-1FFF	Reserved			
2000	DEFAULT DATA SET	GET	PTP Clock	Ordinary And Boundary Clocks
2001	CURRENT DATA SET	GET	PTP Clock	Ordinary And Boundary Clocks
2002	PARENT DATA SET	GET	PTP Clock	Ordinary And Boundary Clocks
2003	TIMEPROPERTIES DATA SET	GET	PTP Clock	Ordinary And Boundary Clocks

2004	PORT DATA SET	GET	PTP Port	Ordinary And Boundary Clocks
2005	PRIORITY1	GET, SET	PTP Clock	Ordinary And Boundary Clocks
2006	PRIORITY2	GET, SET	PTP Clock	Ordinary And Boundary Clocks
2007	DOMAIN	GET, SET	PTP Clock	Ordinary And Boundary Clocks
2008	SLAVE ONLY	GET, SET	PTP Clock	Ordinary And Boundary Clocks
2009	LOGANNOUNCEINTERVAL	GET, SET	PTP Port	Ordinary And Boundary Clocks
200A	ANNOUNCERECEIPTTIMEOUT	GET, SET	PTP Port	Ordinary And Boundary Clocks
200B	LOGSYNCINTERVAL	GET, SET	PTP Port	Ordinary And Boundary Clocks
200C	VERSIONNUMBER	GET, SET	PTP Port	Ordinary And Boundary Clocks
200D	ENABLEPORT	COMMAND	PTP Port	Ordinary And Boundary Clocks
200E	DISABLEPORT	COMMAND	PTP Port	Ordinary And Boundary Clocks

200F	TIME	GET, SET	PTP Clock	Ordinary And Boundary Clocks
2010	CLOCKACCURACY	GET, SET	PTP Clock	Ordinary And Boundary Clocks
2011	UTCPROPERTIES	GET, SET	PTP Clock	Ordinary And Boundary Clocks
2012	TRACEABILITYPROPERTIES	GET, SET	PTP Clock	Ordinary And Boundary Clocks
2013	TIMESCALEPROPERTIES	GET, SET	PTP Clock	Ordinary And Boundary Clocks
2014	UNICASTNEGOTIATIONENABLE	GET, SET	PTP Clock	Ordinary And Boundary Clocks
2015	PATHTRACELIST	GET	PTP Clock	Ordinary And Boundary Clocks
2016	PATHTRACEENABLE	GET, SET	PTP Clock	Ordinary And Boundary Clocks
2017	GRANDMASTERCLUSTER TABLE	GET, SET	PTP Clock	Ordinary And Boundary Clocks
2018	UNICASTMASTERTABLE	GET, SET	PTP Port	Ordinary And Boundary Clocks
2019	UNICASTMASTERMAXTABLE SIZE	GET	PTP Port	Ordinary And Boundary Clocks

201A	ACCEPTABLEMASTERTABLE	GET, SET	PTP Clock	Ordinary And Boundary Clocks
201B	ACCEPTABLEMASTERTABLE ENABLED	GET, SET	PTP Port	Ordinary And Boundary Clocks
201C	ACCEPTABLEMASTERMAXTABLE SIZE	GET	PTP Clock	Ordinary And Boundary Clocks
201D	ALTERNATEMASTER	GET, SET	PTP Port	Ordinary And Boundary Clocks
201E	ALTERNATETIMEOFFSET ENABLE	GET, SET	PTP Clock	Ordinary And Boundary Clocks
201F	ALTERNATETIMEOFFSETNAME	GET, SET	PTP Clock	Ordinary And Boundary Clocks
2020	ALTERNATETIMEOFFSETMAXKEY	GET	PTP Clock	Ordinary And Boundary Clocks
2021	ALTERNATETIMEOFFSET PROPERTIES	GET, SET	PTP Clock	Ordinary And Boundary Clocks
2022-2FFF	Reserved			
3000	EXTERNALPORTCONFIGURATION ENABLED	GET, SET	PTP Clock	Ordinary And Boundary Clocks
3001	MASTERONLY	GET, SET	PTP Port	Ordinary And Boundary Clocks

3002	HOLDOVERUPGRADE ENABLE	GET, SET	PTP Clock	Ordinary And Boundary Clocks
3003	EXTPORTCONFIGPORT DATA SET	GET, SET	PTP Port	Ordinary And Boundary Clocks
3004-3FFF	Reserved			
4000	TRANSPARENTCLOCKDEFAULT DATA SET	GET	PTP Clock	Transparent Clocks
4001	TRANSPARENTCLOCKPORT DATA SET	GET	PTP Port	Transparent Clocks
4002	PRIMARYDOMAIN	GET, SET	PTP Clock	Transparent Clocks
4003-5FFF	Reserved			
6000	DELAYMECHANISM	GET, SET	PTP Port	Ordinary, Boundary And Transparent Clocks
6001	LOGMINPDELAYREQINTERVAL	GET, SET	PTP Port	Ordinary, Boundary And Transparent Clocks
6002-BFFF	Reserved			
C000-DFFF	Custom ManagementID values to be operable between Clocks of the Manufacturer			
E000-FFFE	Used by an Alternate PTP Profile			
FFFF	Reserved			

Reserved: This Reserved Field for the MANAGEMENT_ERROR_STATUS TLV is 4bytes in length

DisplayData: The DisplayData Field value is a text of the specific error that has occurred. If there is no text available than the DisplayData Field should not be in the MANAGEMENT_ERROR_STATUS TLV. The DisplayData Field value may contain up to 50 characters. The DisplayData Field contains the special data type PTPText and is variable in length

Pad: The Pad Field is used simply to add an extra byte to the MANAGEMENT_ERROR_STATUS TLV if specified to do so. If the byte is added all bits contained in the Pad Field are to be zero. The Pad Field contains an unsigned integer and is either 0bits or 8bits in length

Special Data Types

As may have been guessed by the reader PTP uses many special data types that need to be defined in order to understand how the protocol operates.

TimeInterval

Integer64 TimeInterval;

TimeInterval is a one field special data type that indicates intervals of time in a particular format. It is a time value in nanoseconds multiplied by 2^{16}. It is a signed integer and is 64bits in length.

An example of the calculation to convert the time value to a format that can be stored in TimeInterval is:

Time Value:
10.5ns(dec)

Multiple the Time Value by 2^{16}:
$(0.000\ 000\ 010\ 5)*(2^{16}) = 0.000\ 688\ 128$(dec)

Represent the value without decimal points:
688,128(dec)

Convert to Hex:
0000 0000 000A 8000(hex)

SecondsField

UInteger48 SecondsField;

SecondsField is a one field special data type that indicates a positive time from the chosen epoch recorded in seconds. It is an unsigned integer 48bits in length.

NanosecondsField

UInteger32 NanosecondsField;

NanosecondsField is a one field special data type that indicates a positive time recorded in nanoseconds. The NanosecondField value is always less than 10^9. It is a unsigned integer 32bits in length.

Timestamp

```
Timestamp
{
UInteger48 SecondsField;
UInteger32 NanosecondsField;
};
```

Timestamp is a two field special data type that indicates a positive time that is relative to the chosen epoch. The first field of the Timestamp special data type is the SecondsField. The second field of the Timestamp special data type is the NanosecondsField.

An example of how to store a time value into a format that can be stored as a Timestamp special data type is:

Time Value:
10.000 000 005s(dec)

Separate the seconds from the Time Value:
SecondsField = 10(dec)

Separate the nanoseconds from the Time Value:
NanosecondsField = 5(dec)

ClockIdentity

Octet[8] ClockIdentity;

ClockIdentity is a one field special data type that indicates the PTP capable devices(a PTP Clock or Management Node) assigned identifying number within a PTP capable Network. The value of the ClockIdentity for each PTP Clock must be unique. It is an unsigned integer and is 8bytes in length.

Note: ClockIdentity can be the MAC Address of the Clock but this is not required

Note: ClockIdentity is not the protocol address

PortNumber

UInteger16 PortNumber;

PortNumber is a one field special data type that indicates a specific PTP Port on a PTP Clock. The 65,535 Logical PortNumber is used to specify all the Logical Ports on a specific Clock-this is typically used by PTP Management Messages and Signaling Messages. It is an unsigned integer and is 16bits in length.

PTP Messages when received by a Clock are sent to Logical Ports(Sockets):

PTP Message Types:	Logical Port(Socket) Number Used(dec):
PTP Event Messages(Sync, Delay_Req, Pdelay_Req and Pdelay_Resp	319
PTP General Messages(Announce, Follow_Up, Delay_Resp, Pdelay_Resp_Follow_Up, Management and Signaling)	320

PortIdentity

PortIdentity
{
Octet[8] ClockIdentity;
UInteger16 PortNumber;
};

PortIdentity is a two field special data type that indicates a particular PTP Port on the PTP capable Network. The first field of PortIdentity is the special data type ClockIdentity. The second field is the special data type PortNumber.

NetworkProtocol

UInteger16 NetworkProtocol;

NetworkProtocol is a one field special data type that indicates the Network Transport Protocol that is to be used. It is an unsigned integer 16bits in length. It is defined by the next table. For this book we will only be looking at Ethernet so the NetworkProtocol will be 0003(hex).

Value(hex):	NetworkProtocol:
0000	Reserved
0001	UDP/IPv4
0002	UDP/IPv6
0003	Ethernet(IEEE 802.3)
0004	DeviceNet
0005	ControlNet
0006	Profinet
0007-EFFF, FFFF	Reserved
F000-FFFD	PTP Profile specific
FFFE	Unknown Protocol

AddressLength

UInteger16 AddressLength;

AddressLength is a one field special data type that indicates the length of the address in octets and will be between 1-16. It is defined by the next table. For this book we will only be looking at Ethernet so the AddressLength value will be 6(dec). It is an unsigned integer and is 16bits in length.

NetworkProtocol:	Value(dec):
UDP/IPv4	4
UDP/IPv6	16
Ethernet(IEEE802.3)	6
DeviceNet	2
ControlNet	2
Profinet	6

AddressField

Octet[AddressLength] AddressField;

For Ethernet the AddressField is a one field special data type that indicates the MAC Address to be used by the PTP protocol. The values contained in the AddressField is defined by the NetworkProtocol special data type.

The AddressLength special data type defines how many octets the AddressField will be. Since we are using Ethernet as defined by the NetworkProtocol special data type we will be using MAC Addresses and therefore there will be six octets.

The AddressLength data type determines the length of the AddressField data type therefore the length is 6*8(octets) = 48bits

The AddressLength is an unsigned integer 48bits in length.

The AddressField value for Ethernet will always be the Source MAC Address Field of the Ethernet Header.

For Multicast PTP Messages the following table is adhered to for the AddressField special data type.

PTP Multicast Message Types:	IEEE 802.3 Ethernet Multicast MAC Address(hex):
Peer Delay Path Mechanism(used to measure the Peer-to-Peer Delay)	01-80-C2-00-00-0E
All PTP Messages(not including Peer Delay Path Mechanism Messages though)	01-1B-19-00-00-00

Note: Both of these Multicast MAC Addresses can be used for both types of PTP Messages but only if it is specified as such in the selected PTP Profile

Peer Delay Path Mechanism Messages will use for the Source MAC Address Field the Transmitting Devices MAC Address. Peer Delay Path Mechanism Messages with the Destination MAC Address Field will use value 01-80-C2-00-00-0E.

Peer Delay Path Mechanism Messages are not retransmitted by Peer-to-Peer Ports. Which is exactly the type of behavior you would want to keep the Peer Delay Path Mechanism Messages confined to their one Network Link they are attempting to measure the Link Delay Time of.

PortAddress

PortAddress
{
UInteger16 NetworkProtocol;
UInteger16 AddressLength;
Octet[AddressLength] AddressField;
};

PortAddress is a three field special data type that indicates the Network Transport Protocol(Ethernet) and the source MAC Address Field of the Ethernet Header. For Ethernet the PortAddress special data type is 10bytes in length.

When using Ethernet any data set member using the PortAddress special data type will have the following values:

UInteger16 NetworkProtocol;	0003(hex)
UInteger16 AddressLength;	6(dec)
Octet[AddressLength] AddressField;	Uses the same Source MAC Address value as the associated Ethernet Frame

ClockClass

UInteger8 ClockClass;

ClockClass is a one field special data type that indicates the traceability of the Time Signal to the International Atomic Time(TAI), anticipated distribution accuracy of time or frequency by a Master Clock and Synchronization status. The ClockClass of a Clock is one of the major values used when determining the best Master Clock using the BMCA. The lower the ClockClass value the better quality or more trusted the Clock is. It is defined by the next table. It is an unsigned integer and is 8bits in length.

ClockClass (dec):	Description:
0	Reserved
1-5	Reserved
6	A Clock Synchronized to a Primary Reference Time Source. Class 6 Clocks cannot be assigned as a Slave Clock in a PTP Domain
7	A previously Class 6 Clock but no longer has the capability to Synchronize to a Primary Reference Time Source and is in Holdover Mode. Class 7 Clocks cannot be assigned as a Slave Clock in a PTP Domain
8	Reserved
9-10	Reserved
11-12	Reserved
13	A Clock Synchronized to an Application Specific Time Source. Class 13 Clocks cannot be assigned as a Slave Clock in a PTP Domain
14	A previously Class 13 Clock but no longer has the capability to Synchronize to an Application Specific Time Source and is in Holdover Mode. Class 14 Clocks cannot be assigned as a Slave Clock in a PTP Domain
15-51	Reserved
52	A previously Class 7 Clock but no longer has the capability to Synchronize to a Primary Reference Time Source, is in Holdover Mode and is out of the designated allowed Holdover Period. Class 52 Clocks cannot be assigned as a Slave Clock in a PTP Domain
53-57	Reserved
58	A previously Class 14 Clock but no longer has the capability to Synchronize to an Application Specific Time Source, is in Holdover Mode and is out of the designated allowed Holdover Period. Class 58 Clocks cannot be assigned as a Slave Clock in a PTP Domain
59-67	Reserved

68-122	PTP Profile specific. Meant to be used by PTP Profiles that allow for the dispensation of frequency
123-127	Reserved
128-132	Reserved
133-170	PTP Profile specific. Meant to be used by PTP Profiles that allow for the dispensation of frequency
171-186	Reserved
187	A previously Class 7 Clock but no longer has the capability to Synchronize to a Primary Reference Time Source, is in Holdover Mode and is out of the designated allowed Holdover Period. Also specifies a Class for a Backup Master Clock to act as a Slave when a superior Master Clock is present but will take over as Master Clock if said superior Master Clock is lost
188-192	Reserved
193	A previously Class 14 Clock but no longer has the capability to Synchronize to an Application Specific Time Source, is in Holdover Mode and is out of the designated allowed Holdover Period. Class 193 Clocks can be assigned as a Slave Clock in a PTP Domain
194-215	Reserved
216-232	PTP Profile specific. Meant to be used by PTP Profiles to allow certain Clocks to be assigned a higher priority than other Clocks based on only the specifics of the PTP Profile.
233-247	Reserved
248	Default value if none of the other ClockClass descriptions are applicable
249-250	Reserved
251	Reserved
252-254	Reserved
255	SlaveOnly Clocks

Note: During start up a Clock is not expected to provide a ClockClass unless otherwise specified by a special event called the Powerup Event

Note: Holdover Mode is defined as when the Clock is not currently synchronized to a superior Time Signal and must retain its own accuracy using its own internal clock

ClockAccuracy

UInteger8 ClockAccuracy;

ClockAccuracy is a one field special data type that indicates the best estimate of the accuracy of a Clock. The estimate is based on the special data type TimeSource, the current Holdover Period and other Holdover details particular to the Clock. If these values are not provided than the ClockAccuracy value would be FE(hex) to specify as Unknown. The ClockAccuracy of a Clock is one of the major values when determining the best Master Clock using the BMCA. It is defined by the next table. It is an unsigned integer and is 8bits in length.

Value(hex):	Description(dec):
00-16	Reserved
17	Accurate to 1ps
18	Accurate to 2.5ps
19	Accurate to 10ps
1A	Accurate to 25ps
1B	Accurate to 100ps
1C	Accurate to 250ps
1D	Accurate to 1ns
1E	Accurate to 2.5ns
1F	Accurate to 10ns
20	Accurate to 25ns
21	Accurate to 100ns
22	Accurate to 250ns
23	Accurate to 1μs
24	Accurate to 2.5μs
25	Accurate to 10μs
26	Accurate to 25μs
27	Accurate to 100μs
28	Accurate to 250μs
29	Accurate to 1ms
2A	Accurate to 2.5ms
2B	Accurate to 10ms
2C	Accurate to 25ms
2D	Accurate to 100ms
2E	Accurate to 250ms
2F	Accurate to 1s
30	Accurate to 10s
31	Accurate to >10s
32-7F	Reserved

80-FD	PTP Profile specific
FE	Unknown
FF	Reserved

OffsetScaledLogVariance

UInteger16 OffsetScaledLogVariance;

OffsetScaledLogVariance is a one field special data type that indicates the stability of the Clock otherwise known as its inherent precision. It is determined by a calculation involving the stability of the internal clock and the errors created during the Timestamping of PTP Messages process. The OffsetScaledLogVariance of a Clock is one of the major values used when determining the best Master Clock using the BMCA. The max value is 65,534 and the minimum value is 0. It is an unsigned integer and is 16bits in length.

OffsetScaledLogVariance is a coded value. Deciphering the actual Variance value found in this data set member is found by the following example:

OffsetScaledLogVariance:
60,000(dec)

Subtract 32,768(dec) from the OffsetScaledLogVariance value:
60,000 - 32,768 = 27,232(dec)

Take the result divide it by 256(dec):
27,232 / 256 = 106.375(dec)

Perform the following calculation on the result:
$(2^{106.375}) = 1.052*(10^{32})$(dec)
Therefore the OffsetScaledLogVariance Variance value is:
$1.052*(10^{32})s^2$(dec)

Note: Other PTP documentation or guides may represent the OffsetScaledLogVariance in hexadecimal format as opposed to the decimal format presented above

ClockQuality

```
ClockQuality
{
UInteger8 ClockClass;
UInteger8 ClockAccuracy;
UInteger16 OffsetScaledLogVariance;
};
```

ClockQuality is a three field special data type that includes three other special data types that indicates the overall clock quality. The first field of ClockQuality is the ClockClass. The second field is ClockAccuracy. The third field is OffsetScaledLogVariance. The ClockQuality changes based on the changing status and environment of the individual PTP Clock. These statuses include but are not limited to starting up state, operating state, Holdover Mode and temperature. A rare option that could be implemented on your clock that could also affect the ClockQuality is the HoldoverUpgrade.

TLVType

UInteger16 TLVType;

TLVType is a one field special data type that indicates the type of TLV that is being used. All TLVType values are defined by the next table. It is an unsigned integer 16bits in length.

Value (hex):	TLVType Name:	Propagated by Boundary Clock?
0000	Reserved	No
0001	MANAGEMENT	No
0002	MANAGEMENT_ERROR_STATUS	No
0003	ORGANIZATION_EXTENSION	No
0004	REQUEST_UNICAST_TRANSMISSION	No
0005	GRANT_UNICAST_TRANSMISSION	No
0006	CANCEL_UNICAST_TRANSMISSION	No
0007	ACKNOWLEDGE_CANCEL_UNICAST_TRANSMISSION	No
0008	PATH_TRACE	Yes
0009	ALTERNATE_TIME_OFFSET_INDICATOR	Yes
000A - 1FFF	Reserved	No

2000 - 2003	Reserved	No
2004 - 202F	Reserved	No
2030 - 3FFF	Reserved	No
4000	ORGANIZATION_EXTENSION_PROPAGATE	Yes
4001	ENHANCED_ACCURACY_METRICS	Yes
4002 - 7EFF	Reserved	Yes
7F00 - 7FFF	Reserved	Yes
8000	ORGANIZATION_EXTENSION_DO_NOT_PROPAGATE	No
8001	L1_SYNC	No
8002	PORT_COMMUNICATION_AVAILABILITY	No
8003	PROTOCOL_ADDRESS	No
8004	SLAVE_RX_SYNC_TIMING_DATA	No
8005	SLAVE_RX_SYNC_COMPUTED_DATA	No
8006	SLAVE_TX_EVENT_TIMESTAMPS	No
8007	CUMULATIVE_RATE_RATIO	No
8008	PAD	No
8009	AUTHENTICATION	No
800A - FFEF	Reserved	No
FFF0 - FFFF	Reserved	No

LengthField

UInteger8 LengthField;
OR
UInteger16 LengthField;

Length Field is a one field special data type that indicates the length of the data type it is embedded in. It is an unsigned integer 8bits or 16bits in length as indicated by the special data type it is embedded into.

TLV

```
TLV
{
UInteger16 TLVType;
UInteger16 LengthField;
Octet [LengthField] ValueField;
};
```

TLV is a three field special data type and stands for Type, Length and Value. It is a generic data type and way of organizing data. The first field of TLV is the TLVType. The second field is LengthField. The third field is ValueField. ValueField is defined in both length, format and purpose by the specified TLVType.

TextField

Octet[LengthField] TextField;

TextField is a one field special data type and its length is determined by the LengthField value associated with it. The text contained therein is coded in UTF-8 characters and each character can be 1-4 octets in length. It is an unsigned integer and is variable in length.

PTPText

```
PTPText
{
UInteger8 LengthField;
Octet[LengthField] TextField;
};
```

PTPText is a two field special data type and contains text for certain PTP Messages. The first field of PTPText is LengthField, and the second field is TextField.

FaultRecordLength

UInteger16 FaultRecordLength;

FaultRecordLength is a one field special data type and contains a value that indicates the amount of octets used in the associated FaultRecord special data type minus two to account for the FaultRecordLength itself. It is an unsigned integer 16bits in length.

FaultTime

Timestamp FaultTime;

FaultTime is a one field special data type that contains and uses the Timestamp special data type that specifies the time when the fault occurred. If the value contained in the FaultTime Timestamp is all ones then the fault time of the associated FaultRecord was not obtained. It is a Timestamp special data type that is 10bytes in length.

SeverityCode

UInteger8 SeverityCode;

SeverityCode is a one field special data type that indicates the seriousness of the fault for the associated FaultRecord as defined in the next table. It is an unsigned integer 8bits in length.

SeverityCode Name	Description	Value(hex):
Emergency	Clock is inoperable	00
Alert	Clock requires immediate attention	01
Critical	Clock in extreme condition	02
Error	Clock error	03
Warning	Clock warning	04
Notice	Clock condition change	05
Informational	Clock information message	06
Debug	Clock debug message	07
Reserved	Reserved	08-FF

FaultName

PTPText FaultName;

FaultName is a one field special data type that uses the PTPText special data type and indicates the name of the fault for the associated FaultRecord. The FaultName value is usually dependent on the PTP Profile or is PTP Domain specific. FaultName may have not been used or included within the associated FaultRecord.

FaultValue

PTPText FaultValue;

FaultValue is a one field special data type that uses the PTPText special data type and indicates a value for that specific fault type for the associated FaultRecord. FaultValue may have not been used or included within the associated FaultRecord.

FaultDescription

PTPText FaultDescription;

FaultDescription is a one field special data type that uses the PTPText special data type and describes in further detail that specific fault type for the associated FaultRecord. FaultDescription may have not been used or included within the associated FaultRecord.

FaultRecord

FaultRecord
{
UInteger16 FaultRecordLength;
Timestamp FaultTime;
UInteger8 SeverityCode;
PTPText FaultName;
PTPText FaultValue;
PTPText FaultDescription;
};

FaultRecord is a six field special data type used to build error records. The first field of FaultRecord is FaultRecordLength. The second field is FaultTime. The third field is SeverityCode. The fourth field is FaultName. The fifth field is FaultValue. The sixth field is FaultDescription.

RelativeDifference

Integer64 RelativeDifference;

RelativeDifference is a one field special data type that indicates the difference between two values. The difference value stored in this special data type uses a special storage method. The actual difference value between two values is multiplied by 2^62 and removing the remaining decimal values. It is a signed integer 64bits in length.

Example of the calculation to convert the difference value to a format that can be stored in RelativeDifference is:

Difference Value: 0.000 000 005(dec)

$(0.000\ 000\ 005)*(2^{62})=$
23,058,430,092.13693952(dec)

Remove the decimal portion of value:
23,058,430,092(dec)

AcceptablePortIdentity

PortIdentity AcceptablePortIdentity;

AcceptablePortIdentity is a one field special data type that indicates the PortIdentity of a specific PTP Port on the Network that is included in a Slave Clocks AcceptableMasterTable entry. It is a PortIdentity special data type that is 10bytes in length.

AlternatePriority1

UInteger8 AlternatePriority1;

AlternatePriority1 is a one field special data type that indicates the Priority1 value of a specific Clock on the Network that is included in a Slave Clocks AcceptableMaster list entry. It is an unsigned integer 8bits in length.

AcceptableMaster

```
AcceptableMaster
{
PortIdentity AcceptablePortIdentity;
UInteger8 AlternatePriority1;
};
```

AcceptableMaster is a two field special data type that indicates the information of a PTP Port that the Slave PTP Port is allowed to Synchronize to. The first field of the AcceptableMaster special data type is the AcceptablePortIdentity. The second field of the AcceptableMaster special data type is the AlternatePriority1.

PTP Data Sets

There are numerous PTP data sets that define how PTP Clocks and their internal systems function and interact with each other. Different types of Clocks, services, options and hardware will have different data sets and the values contained in the data sets are how a specific implementation of PTP will function.

Ordinary Clocks

Ordinary Clocks will have the following data sets by default:
1. Default Data Set
2. Current Data Set
3. Parent Data Set
4. TimeProperties Data Set
5. Port Data Sets(Every PTP Port will have its own Port Data Set)
6. Optional Features that are enabled will also have the associated Data Set

Transparent Clocks

Transparent Clocks will have the following data sets by default:
1. Default Data Set
2. Port Data Set
3. Optional Features that are enabled will also have the associated Data Set

Boundary Clocks

Boundary Clocks will have the following data sets by default:
1. Default Data Set
2. Current Data Set
3. Parent Data Set
4. TimeProperties Data Set
5. Port Data Sets(Every PTP Port will have its own Port Data Set)
6. Optional Features that are enabled will also have the associated Data Set

Default Data Set

The Default Data Set is used by Ordinary Clocks, Boundary Clocks, End-to-End Transparent Clocks and Peer-to-Peer Transparent Clocks. It includes the following data set members.

Default Data Set Member:	Ordinary Clock:	Boundary Clock:	End-to-End Transparent Clock:	Peer-to-Peer Transparent Clock:
TwoStepFlag	deprecated member	deprecated member	NA	NA
ClockIdentity	required member	required member	optional member	required member
NumberPorts	required member	required member	optional member	required member
ClockQuality	required member	required member	NA	NA
Priority1	required member	required member	NA	NA
Priority2	required member	required member	NA	NA
Domain Number	required member	required member	required member	required member
SlaveOnly	required member	NA	NA	NA
CurrentTime	management member	management member	management member	management member
Instance Enable	optional member	optional member	NA	NA
ExternalPort Configuration Enabled	optional member	optional member	NA	NA
MaxSteps Removed	optional member	optional member	NA	NA
SdoID	required member	required member	required member	required member
Instance Type	management member	management member	management member	management member

Deprecated Member. Deprecated member means the feature is allowed to be used but is no longer required to be used. This is due to the newest standard indicating that a better option already must be used

Management Member: Management member means the data set member is not required in order to run PTP and the associated state machines but may be used for management functions

Optional Member: Optional member means the data set member is not required by the data set but may be required by the selected PTP Profile

Required Member: Required member means the data set member is required to be used by the data set

TwoStepFlag

Boolean TwoStepFlag;

TwoStepFlag is a data set member of the Default Data Set that indicates with a value of one if the Clock is a Two-Step Clock. One-Step or Two-Step status can be specified based on the individual PTP Port or based on the Clock itself. It is a boolean 1bit in length.

ClockIdentity

ClockIdentity ClockIdentity;

ClockIdentity is a data set member of the Default Data Set that uses the ClockIdentity special data type to indicate the PTP capable device's assigned number within a PTP capable Network. It is a ClockIdentity special data type 8bytes in length.

NumberPorts

UInteger16 NumberPorts;

NumberPorts is a data set member of the Default Data Set used to indicate the number of PTP Ports for the Clock. The value will usually be one for Ordinary Clocks. It is an unsigned integer 16bits in length.

ClockQuality

ClockQuality ClockQuality;

ClockQuality is a data set member of the Default Data Set that uses the ClockQuality special data type to indicate the current specifications of the Clock. It is a ClockQuality special data type 32bytes in length.

Priority1

UInteger8 Priority1;

Priority1 is a data set member of the Default Data Set that is set by the Network Professional and used in the BMCA. It is an unsigned integer 8bits in length.

Priority2

UInteger8 Priority2;

Priority2 is a data set member of the Default Data Set that is set by the Network Professional and used in the BMCA. It is an unsigned integer 8bits in length.

DomainNumber

UInteger8 DomainNumber;

DomainNumber is a data set member of the Default Data Set that is set by the Network Professional and used to indicate what PTP Domain the Clock belongs to. It is an unsigned integer 8bits in length.

SlaveOnly

Boolean SlaveOnly;

SlaveOnly is a data set member of the Default Data Set that indicates with a value of one if the Clock is a SlaveOnly Clock. It is a boolean 1bit in length.

CurrentTime

Timestamp CurrentTime;

CurrentTime is a data set member of the Default Data Set that uses the Timestamp special data type to indicate the current time of that specific Clock. When CurrentTime is management written to it will set the Clocks current time. Under normal operating circumstances the only Clock in a PTP capable Network that gets this management member written to is the GrandMaster Clock usually by an outside Time Signal such as from GPS. Otherwise if the CurrentTime of any other Clock besides the GrandMaster is written to it will be overwritten quickly by the normal operation of PTP. The only way to write to CurrentTime over the Network is through a Management Message and as Management Messages are not Event Messages and are not updated as they transit through the Network. They are not accurate and should not be used to Synchronize Clocks. It is a Timestamp special data type that is 10bytes in length.

InstanceEnable

Boolean InstanceEnable;

InstanceEnable is a data set member of the Default Data Set that indicates with a value of one if the Clock has PTP turned on. The default and usual value for InstanceEnable is one. As the InstanceEnable data set member is optional and if a Clock is designed without it PTP for the Clock would be automatically turned on. If InstanceEnable is zero indicating off and then written over with a one the Initialize PTP Event will start. If the InstanceEnable is one indicating that PTP is on and then written over with a zero the Clock will end all operation of PTP. It is a boolean 1bit in length.

ExternalPortConfigurationEnabled

Boolean ExternalPortConfigurationEnabled;

ExternalPortConfigurationEnabled is a data set member of the Default Data Set that indicates with a value of one if the Clock has the option to have its PTP Ports PortStates modified externally turned on. Under normal PTP each PTP Port on a Clock has its PortState modified by the BMCA. The default and usual value for ExternalPortConfigurationEnabled is zero. It is a boolean 1bit in length.

MaxStepsRemoved

UInteger8 MaxStepsRemoved;

MaxStepsRemoved is a data set member of the Default Data Set that indicates the largest StepsRemoved value an Announce Message can have. If the Clock receives an Announce Message that meets or exceeds this value it will ignore it and will not use it with the BMCA. A Clock can have option "e" in the BMCA disabled and the feature not in use. But when option "e" is used it can reduce Rogue(Looping) Announce Messages. The default value and if not in use the value for MaxStepsRemoved is 255. The value must be between 2 and 255. It is an unsigned integer 8bits in length.

SdoID

UInteger12 SdoID;

SdoID is a data set member of the Default Data Set that contains a value based on the selected PTP Profile of the PTP Domain. The possible values of SdoID and what the DomainNumber ranges are defined in the next table. It is an unsigned integer 12bits in length.

SdoID Value Range(hex):		DomainNumber values when PTP uses Ethernet as per IEEE 802(dec):	Notes:
Major SdoID:	Minor SdoID:		
From: 0	00	*0-127 are allowed *128-255 are reserved	*If using IEEE 1588-2008 or the PTP specifies as such
To: 0	00		
From: 0	01		*For use only with the IEEE 1588-2008 version, for backwards compatibility
To: 0	FF		
From: 1	00	*0-239 are allowed *240-255 are reserved	*If using IEEE 802.1 PTP Profiles
To: 1	00		
From: 1	01		*For use only with the IEEE 1588-2008 version, for backwards compatibility
To: 1	FF		
From: 2	00	*240-255 are reserved	*Used by IEEE 1588 Common MeanLinkDelay
To: 2	00		
From: 2	01	*reserved	*Used by IEEE 1588 Working Group
To: 2	FF		
From: 3	00	*0-239 are allowed *240-255 are reserved	*If using QSDOs PTP Profiles
To: F	FC		
From: F	FD	*0-239 are allowed *240-255 are reserved	*For temporary or testing
To: F	FE		
From: F	FF	*reserved	*Used by IEEE 1588 Working Group
To: F	FF		

InstanceType

UInteger8 InstanceType;

InstanceType is a data set member of the Default Data Set that indicates the type of PTP Clock the Clock is as defined in the next table. InstanceType is very similar to the ClockType found in Management Messages. It is an unsigned integer 8bits in length.

InstanceType Description:	Value(hex):
Ordinary Clock	00
Boundary Clock	01
Peer-to-Peer Transparent Clock	02
End-to-End Transparent Clock	03
Reserved	04-FF

Current Data Set

The Current Data Set is used by Ordinary Clocks and Boundary Clocks. It includes the following data set members.

Current Data Set Member:	Ordinary Clock:	Boundary Clock:	End-to-End Transparent Clock:	Peer-to-Peer Transparent Clock:
Steps Removed	required member	required member	NA	NA
Offset From Master	required member	required member	NA	NA
Mean Delay	required member	required member	NA	NA
Synchronization Uncertain	optional member	optional member	NA	NA

StepsRemoved

UInteger16 StepsRemoved;

StepsRemoved is a data set member of the Current Data Set that contains a value that indicates the number of Network Links between this Clock and the GrandMaster Clock. The initial value for StepsRemoved is zero. It is an unsigned integer 16bits in length.

OffsetFromMaster

TimeInterval OffsetFromMaster;

OffsetFromMaster is a data set member of the Current Data Set that contains a value that indicates the constant time difference between the Master Clock and the Slave Clock. This time difference is also called the Offset and is calculated by the Slave Clock. It is a TimeInterval special data type that is 64bits in length.

MeanDelay

TimeInterval MeanDelay;

MeanDelay is a data set member of the Current Data Set that contains a value that indicates either the MeanPathDelay, the MeanLinkDelay, Zero or the Mean Propagation Time calculated by the PTP Port. MeanDelay could be specified to be many different values and is defined in the next table. It is a TimeInterval special data type that is 64bits in length.

MeanDelay Value:	MeanDelay Description:
Zero	When a Clocks PTP Port that is in Slave or Uncalibrated PortStates is also configured Special or No_Mechanism. Or when all PTP Ports of a Clock are not in Slave or Uncalibrated PortStates.
Mean Propagation Time calculated by the PTP Port	The MeanDelay is calculated by the PTP Port when the PTP Port is in the Slave or Uncalibrated PortState.

MeanPathDelay	When the Delay Request-Response Mechanism is in use the MeanPathDelay is used.
MeanLinkDelay	When the Peer Delay Mechanism is in use the MeanLinkDelay is used.

SynchronizationUncertain

Boolean SynchronizationUncertain;

SynchronizationUncertain is a data set member of the Current Data Set that indicates with a value of zero if the Clocks transmitted Announce Messages use the SynchronizationUncertain Flag. Whether a Clock uses the SynchronizationUncertain Flag and thus has this data set member set as zero is dependent on the Clocks selected PTP Profile. However under the following circumstances the Flag will be one:

1. A received Announce Message from the Master Clock is one. But this value is stored in the data set member SynchronizationUncertain of the Parent Data Set
2. The receiving PTP Port is in the Uncalibrated PortState
3. The Clocks selected PTP Profile includes operational criteria that determines if the Clock is not functioning within specification

Besides the above given circumstances the value of SynchronizationUncertain data set member of the Current Data Set is to be determined by the Clocks selected PTP Profile receiving the Announce Message. The default value of SynchronizationUncertain is zero. It is a boolean 1bit in length.

Parent Data Set

The Parent Data Set is used by Ordinary Clocks and Boundary Clocks. It includes the following data set members.

Parent Data Set Member:	Ordinary Clock:	Boundary Clock:	End-to-End Transparent Clock:	Peer-to-Peer Transparent Clock:
Parent Port Identity	required member	required member	NA	NA
ParentStats	required member	required member	NA	NA
Observed Parent Offset Scaled Log Variance	optional member	optional member	NA	NA
Observed Parent Clock Phase Change Rate	optional member	optional member	NA	NA
Grandmaster Identity	required member	required member	NA	NA
Grandmaster ClockQuality	required member	required member	NA	NA
Grandmaster Priority1	required member	required member	NA	NA
Grandmaster Priority2	required member	required member	NA	NA
Protocol Address	optional member	optional member	NA	NA
Synchronization Uncertain	optional member	optional member	NA	NA

ParentPortIdentity

PortIdentity ParentPortIdentity;

ParentPortIdentity is a data set member of the Parent Data Set that contains the PortIdentity of the Master Clocks PTP Port that the Slave Clock is receiving Sync Messages from and is Synchronizing to. The initial value of ParentPortIdentity is zero. It is a PortIdentity special data type 10bytes in length.

ParentStats

Boolean ParentStats;

ParentStats is a data set member of the Parent Data Set that indicates with a value of one if the Clock has a PTP Port in the Slave PortState or has calculated reasonable values for the ObservedParentOffsetScaledLogVariance and ObservedParentClockPhaseChangeRate. Both ObservedParentOffsetScaledLogVariance and ObservedParentClockPhaseChangeRate are members of the Parent Data Set as well and are covered next. The initial value of ParentStats is zero. It is a boolean 1bit in length.

ObservedParentOffsetScaledLogVariance

UInteger16 ObservedParentOffsetScaledLogVariance;

ObservedParentOffsetScaledLogVariance is a data set member of the Parent Data Set that contains the calculated value of the difference in the phase between the Master Clock and the Slave Clock. The value is calculated by the Slave Clock. The initial value of ObservedParentOffsetScaledLogVariance is 65,535. If the ObservedParentOffsetScaledLogVariance value is not calculated then the ParentStats data set member value is zero. It is an unsigned integer 16bits in length.

ObservedParentClockPhaseChangeRate

Integer32 ObservedParentClockPhaseChangeRate;

ObservedParentClockPhaseChangeRate is a data set member of the Parent Data Set that contains the calculated value of the phase change rate between the Master Clock and the Slave Clock. The value is calculated by the Slave Clock. The initial value of ObservedParentClockPhaseChangeRate is 2,147,483,647. The 2,147,483,647 value is used to indicate that the value has not been calculated or the value is too large. 2,147,483,648 is also used to indicate the value is too large for the data type. When the Master Clocks phase rate change is greater than the Slave Clock than the value will be positive. If the ObservedParentClockPhaseChangeRate value is not calculated then the ParentStats data set member value is zero. The units used by ObservedParentClockPhaseChangeRate are determined by the selected PTP Profile. It is a signed integer 32bits in length.

GrandmasterIdentity

ClockIdentity GrandmasterIdentity;

GrandmasterIdentity is a data set member of the Parent Data Set that contains the Grandmaster Clocks ClockIdentity value. The initial value of GrandmasterIdentity is the value found in the ClockIdentity data set member of the Default Data Set. It is a ClockIdentity special data type 8bytes in length.

GrandmasterClockQuality

ClockQuality GrandmasterClockQuality;

GrandmasterClockQuality is a data set member of the Parent Data Set that contains the Grandmaster Clocks ClockQuality value. The initial value of the GrandmasterClockQuality is the value found in the ClockQuality data set member of the Default Data Set. It is a ClockQuality special data type 32bytes in length.

GrandmasterPriority1

UInteger8 GrandmasterPriority1;

GrandmasterPriority1 is a data set member of the Parent Data Set that contains the Grandmaster Clocks Priority1 value. The initial value of GrandmasterPriority1 is the value found in the Priority1 data set member of the Default Data Set. It is an unsigned integer 8bits in length.

GrandmasterPriority2

UInteger8 GrandmasterPriority2;

GrandmasterPriority2 is a data set member of the Parent Data Set that contains the Grandmaster Clocks Priority2 value. The initial value of GrandmasterPriority2 is the value found in the Priority2 data set member of the Default Data Set. It is an unsigned integer 8bits in length.

ProtocolAddress

PortAddress ProtocolAddress;

ProtocolAddress is a data set member of the Parent Data Set that contains the Master Clocks PTP Ports PortAddress that this Slave Clock is using to Synchronize to. The ProtocolAddress of the Parent Data Set that belongs to the Slave Clock needs to be the same value as the value from the ProtocolAddress of the DescriptionPort Data Set from the Master Clocks PTP Port that the Slave Clock is Synchronizing to. It is a PortAddress special data type 10bytes in length.

SynchronizationUncertain

Boolean SynchronizationUncertain;

SynchronizationUncertain is a data set member of the Parent Data Set that indicates the SynchronizationUncertain Flag value from the most recently received Announce Message from the Master Clock. The PTP Port that receives the Announce Message must be in the Slave or Uncalibrated PortState. If none of the Slave Clocks PTP Ports are in the Slave or Uncalibrated PortStates than the SynchronizationUncertain value will be set to zero. The initial value of the SynchronizationUncertain member of the Parent Data Set is zero. It is a boolean 1bit in length.

TimeProperties Data Set

The TimeProperties Data Set is used by Ordinary Clocks and Boundary Clocks. It includes the following data set members. The GrandMaster Clock updates these data set member values and then transmits the new values to the other Clocks.

TimeProperties Data Set Member:	Ordinary Clock:	Boundary Clock:	End-to-End Transparent Clock:	Peer-to-Peer Transparent Clock:
CurrentUTCOffset	required member	required member	NA	NA
CurrentUTCOffsetValid	required member	required member	NA	NA
Leap59	required member	required member	NA	NA
Leap61	required member	required member	NA	NA
TimeTraceable	required member	required member	NA	NA
FrequencyTraceable	required member	required member	NA	NA
PTPTimescale	required member	required member	NA	NA
TimeSource	required member	required member	NA	NA

CurrentUTCOffset

Integer16 CurrentUTCOffset;

CurrentUTCOffset is a data set member of the TimeProperties Data Set that indicates the value of DLS that was received from the GrandMaster Clock. Readers will remember from an earlier section that the DLS value is used to calculate the UTS time when TAI time is known with the formula:

UTC = TAI - DLS

If the CurrentUTCOffsetValid data set member of the TimeProperties Data Set is zero CurrentUTCOffset will not be used to calculate UTC time. The DLS value cannot be used to calculate the UTC time if the ARB timescale is selected. It is a signed integer 16bits in length.

CurrentUTCOffsetValid

Boolean CurrentUTCOffsetValid;

CurrentUTCOffsetValid is a data set member of the TimeProperties Data Set that indicates with a value of one if the CurrentUTCOffset and Leap59 values are understood to be accurate. It is a boolean 1bit in length.

Leap59

Boolean Leap59;

Leap59 is a data set member of the TimeProperties Data Set that when the PTP Timescale is selected indicates with a value of one that the last minute of the day will comprises only 59seconds. When the ARB Timescale is used the Leap59 value will be automatically set to zero. It is a boolean 1bit in length.

Leap61

Boolean Leap61;

Leap61 is a data set member of the TimeProperties Data Set that when the PTP Timescale is selected indicates with a value of one that the last minute of the day will comprise 61seconds. When the ARB Timescale is used the Leap61 value will be automatically set to zero. It is a boolean 1bit in length.

TimeTraceable

Boolean TimeTraceable;

TimeTraceable is a data set member of the TimeProperties Data Set that indicates with a value of one if the timescale can be traced back to a Primary Reference Time Source. It is a boolean 1bit in length.

FrequencyTraceable

Boolean FrequencyTraceable;

FrequencyTraceable is a data set member of the TimeProperties Data Set that indicates with a value of one if the frequency for the timescale can be traced back to a Primary Reference Time Source. It is a boolean 1bit in length.

PTPTimescale

Boolean PTPTimescale;

PTPTimescale is a data set member of the TimeProperties Data Set that indicates with a value of one if the GrandMaster Clock has the PTP Timescale selected. If the value is zero the GrandMaster Clock has the ARB Timescale selected. It is a boolean 1bit in length.

TimeSource

UInteger8 TimeSource;

TimeSource is a data set member of the TimeProperties Data Set that indicates the origin of the Time Signal used by the GrandMaster Clock. The next table indicates the different TimeSources and their associated values. It is an unsigned integer 8bits in length.

Value(hex):	TimeSource:
10	ATOMIC_CLOCK
20	GNSS
30	TERRESTRIAL_RADIO
39	SERIAL_TIME_CODE
40	PTP
50	NTP
60	HAND_SET
90	OTHER
A0	INTERNAL OSCILLATOR
F0-FE	PTP Profile Dependent
FF	Reserved

Description Data Set

The Description Data Set is used by Ordinary Clocks, Boundary Clocks, End-to-End Transparent Clocks and Peer-to-Peer Transparent Clocks. It includes the following data set members. The Description Data Set outlines information for the different Clock types.

Description Data Set Member:	Ordinary Clock:	Boundary Clock:	End-to-End Transparent Clock:	Peer-to-Peer Transparent Clock:
Manufacturer Identity	management member	management member	management member	management member
Product Description	management member	management member	management member	management member
Product Revision	management member	management member	management member	management member
User Description	management member	management member	management member	management member

ManufacturerIdentity

UInteger24 ManufacturerIdentity;

ManufacturerIdentity is a data set member of the Description Data Set that indicates the OUI or CID of the equipment manufacturer. It is an unsigned integer 24bits in length.

ProductDescription

PTPText ProductDescription;

ProductDescription is a data set member of the Description Data Set that indicates the ManufacturerName, ModelNumber and InstanceIdentifier. ManufacturerName, ModelNumber and InstanceIdentifier are described by the manufacturer in text and separated by semicolons. It is a PTPText special data type that is variable in length.

ProductRevision

PTPText ProductRevision;

ProductRevision is a data set member of the Description Data Set that indicates the Clocks hardware version, firmware version and software version. The Clocks hardware version, firmware version and software version are described by the manufacturer in text and separated by semicolons. It is a PTPText special data type that is variable in length.

UserDescription

PTPText UserDescription;

UserDescription is a data set member of the Description Data Set that indicates the Clock's name and the Clocks location. The Clock's name and location are described by the Network Professional and separated by semicolons. It is a PTPText special data type that is variable in length.

FaultLog Data Set

The FaultLog Data Set is used by Ordinary Clocks, Boundary Clocks, End-to-End Transparent Clocks and Peer-to-Peer Transparent Clocks. It includes the following data set members. The FaultLog Data Set outlines how to store fault information for PTP Clocks.

FaultLog Data Set Member:	Ordinary Clock:	Boundary Clock:	End-to-End Transparent Clock:	Peer-to-Peer Transparent Clock:
Number Of Fault Records	management member	management member	management member	management member
FaultRecord List	management member	management member	management member	management member
Reset	management member	management member	management member	management member

NumberOfFaultRecords

UInteger16 NumberOfFaultRecords;

NumberOfFaultRecords is a data set member of the FaultLog Data Set that indicates the total amount of fault records located in the FaultRecordList. It is an unsigned integer 16bits in length.

FaultRecordList

FaultRecord FaultRecordList;

FaultRecordList is a data set member of the FaultLog Data Set that is comprised of an array of elements of the NumberOfFaultRecords member. The most amount of elements contained in the FaultRecordList is based on the specific Clock. Each element of the FaultRecordList will use the FaultRecord special data type It is variable in length.

Reset

Boolean Reset;

Reset is a data set member of the FaultLog Data Set that is used to clear the FaultRecordList with a value of one. When the FaultRecordList is cleared with a Management Message the member data set NumberOfFaultRecords is also reset to zero. It is a boolean 1bit in length.

NonvolatileStorage Data Set

The NonvolatileStorage Data Set is used by Ordinary Clocks, Boundary Clocks, End-to-End Transparent Clocks and Peer-to-Peer Transparent Clocks. It includes the following data set members. The NonvolatileStorage Data Set stores nonvolatile storage configurations for PTP Clocks.

Nonvolatile Storage Data Set Member:	Ordinary Clock:	Boundary Clock:	End-to-End Transparent Clock:	Peer-to-Peer Transparent Clock:
Reset	management member	management member	management member	management member
Save	management member	management member	management member	management member

Reset

Boolean Reset;

Reset is a data set member of the NonvolatileStorage Data Set that is used to clear the nonvolatile memory that is read-write capable with a value of one. When enabled a Management Message can write to the Reset data set member with a one and this will clear a Clocks nonvolatile memory. Read-write capable data set members will return to their default values. It is a boolean 1bit in length.

Save

Boolean Save;

Save is a data set member of the NonvolatileStorage Data Set that is used to store the values residing in read-write capable data set members into nonvolatile memory with a value of one. When enabled a Management Message can write to the Save data set member with a one and this will save a Clocks read-write values into nonvolatile memory. It is a boolean 1bit in length.

Port Data Set

The Port Data Set is used by Ordinary Clocks, Boundary Clocks, End-to-End Transparent Clocks and Peer-to-Peer Transparent Clocks and includes the following data set members. Separate Port Data Sets are maintained for each PTP Port on a Clock.

Port Data Set Member:	Ordinary Clock:	Boundary Clock:	End-to-End Transparent Clock:	Peer-to-Peer Transparent Clock:
PortIdentity	required member	required member	optional member	required member
PortState	required member	required member	NA	NA
LogMinDelayReqInterval	required member	required member	required member	NA
MeanLinkDelay	required member	required member	NA	required member
LogAnnounceInterval	required member	required member	NA	NA
AnnounceReceiptTimeout	required member	required member	NA	NA
LogSyncInterval	required member	required member	NA	NA
DelayMechanism	required member	required member	NA	NA
LogMinPdelayReqInterval	required member	required member	NA	required member
VersionNumber	required member	required member	NA	required member
MinorVersionNumber	required member	required member	NA	required member
PortEnable	optional member	optional member	NA	NA
MasterOnly	optional member	optional member	NA	NA
DelayAsymmetry	required member	required member	required member	required member

PortIdentity

PortIdentity PortIdentity;

PortIdentity is a data set member of the Port Data Set that indicates the PortIdentity of that specific PTP Port. The PortIdentity data set member confusingly uses the PortIdentity special data type that has already been covered in an earlier section. Within each PortIdentity data set member is the ClockIdentity data set member. The ClockIdentity contains the value of the respective PTP Clock the PTP Port belongs to. Also within the PortIdentity is the specific PortNumber of that PTP Port belonging to that respective PTP Clock. It is a PortIdentity special data type 10bytes in length.

PortState

UInteger8 PortState;

PortState is a data set member of the Port Data Set that indicates the current PortState of that specific PTP Port. The different PortStates detailed below are used to configure the PTP Port to be what it needs to be in order for PTP to function on a Clock. It is an unsigned integer 8bits in length.

Value(hex):	PortState:
01	Initializing
02	Faulty
03	Disabled
04	Listening
05	Pre-Master
06	Master
07	Passive
08	Uncalibrated
09	Slave

LogMinDelayReqInterval

Integer8 LogMinDelayReqInterval;

LogMinDelayReqInterval is a data set member of the Port Data Set that indicates the MinDelayReqInterval value except in logarithm to the base of two format. It is a signed integer 8bits in length.

MinDelayReqInterval = $2^{\wedge}$(LogMinDelayReqInterval)

Note: MinDelayReqInterval is the least amount of time in seconds allowed between consecutive Delay_Req Messages. The MinDelayReqInterval and LogMinDelayReqInterval are only relevant to Multicast PTP Messages

MeanLinkDelay

TimeInterval MeanLinkDelay;

MeanLinkDelay is a data set member of the Port Data Set that indicates the PTP Ports Peer Delay Path Mechanism's Link Delay Time. Peer Delay Path Mechanism is explained more in a later section. The MeanLinkDelay data set member stores the most recent one way Link Delay Time between this PTP Port and the PTP Port of another Clock it is communicating with. If the DelayMechanism Port data set member is designated as End-to-End, No_Mechanism or Special the MeanLinkDelay data set member's value will be zero. It is a timeInterval special data type that is 64bits in length.

LogAnnounceInterval

Integer8 LogAnnounceInterval;

LogAnnounceInterval is a data set member of the Port Data Set that indicates the AnnounceInterval value except in logarithm to the base of two format. It is a signed integer 8bits in length.

AnnounceInterval = $2^{\wedge}$(LogAnnounceInterval)

Note: AnnounceInterval is the least amount of time in seconds allowed between consecutive Announce Messages. The AnnounceInterval and LogAnnounceInterval are only relevant to Multicast PTP Messages

AnnounceReceiptTimeout

UInteger8 AnnounceReceiptTimeout;

AnnounceReceiptTimeout is a data set member of the Port Data Set that indicates the total amount of AnnounceIntervals that must occur without receiving an Announce Message. When this time period has elapsed the PTP Event AnnounceReceiptTimeoutExpires is activated. PTP Events are covered in a later section. It is an unsigned integer 8bits in length.

LogSyncInterval

Integer8 LogSyncInterval;

LogSyncInterval is a data set member of the Port Data Set that indicates the SyncInterval value except in logarithm to the base of two format. It is a signed integer 8bits in length.

SyncInterval = 2^(LogSyncInterval)

Note: SyncInterval is the least amount of time in seconds allowed between consecutive Sync Messages. The SyncInterval and LogSyncInterval are only relevant to Multicast PTP Messages

DelayMechanism

UInteger8 DelayMechanism;

DelayMechanism is a data set member of the Port Data Set that indicates the Path Delay Mechanism that is to be used by that specific PTP Port. The different values below indicate the DelayMechanism the PTP Port is configured for. It is an unsigned integer 8bits in length.

Value(hex):	DelayMechanism:	DelayMechanism Description:
01	End-to-End	Delay Request-Response Path Mechanism is used
02	Peer-to-Peer	Peer Delay Path Mechanism is used
FE	No_Mechanism	No Path Mechanism is used
03	Common_P2P	Common Mean Link Delay Service is used
04	Special	A special Path Mechanism is used

LogMinPdelayReqInterval

Integer8 LogMinPdelayReqInterval;

LogMinPdelayReqInterval is a data set member of the Port Data Set that indicates the MinPdelayReqInterval value except in logarithm to the base of two format. It is a signed integer 8bits in length.

MinPdelayReqInterval = $2^{(LogMinPdelayReqInterval)}$

Note: MinPdelayReqInterval is the least amount of time in seconds allowed between consecutive Pdelay_Req Messages

VersionNumber

UInteger4 VersionNumber;

VersionNumber is a data set member of the Port Data Set that indicates what version of PTP the PTP Port is using. It is an unsigned integer 4bits in length.

PortEnable

Boolean PortEnable;

PortEnable is a data set member of the Port Data Set that indicates with a value of one if the PTP Port has PTP turned on. PortEnable can also be a management member of the Port Data Set. When allowed for a Management Message can write the PortEnable member with a one and the Designated_Enabled PTP Event is activated. When allowed for a Management Message can write the PortEnable member with a zero and the Designated_Disabled PTP Event is activated. It is a boolean 1bit in length.

MasterOnly

Boolean MasterOnly;

MasterOnly is a data set member of the Port Data Set that indicates with a value of one if the PTP Port will be configured for MasterOnly mode. A MasterOnly PTP Port can never be set to the Slave or Passive PortStates. It is a boolean 1bit in length.

DelayAsymmetry

TimeInterval DelayAsymmetry;

DelayAsymmetry is a data set member of the Port Data Set that indicates the PTP Port's DelayAsymmetry value. DelayAsymmetry is when the Transit Time for a Packet is not the same transmitting to Clock2 from Clock1 as transmitting to Clock1 from Clock2. It is a TimeInterval special data type that is 64bits in length.

TimestampCorrectionPort Data Set

The TimestampCorrectionPort Data Set is not required to be used by the PTP Ports of the four types of PTP Clocks. Rather the TimestampCorrectionPort Data Set is completely optional to the PTP Ports of Ordinary Clocks, Boundary Clocks, End-to-End Transparent Clocks and Peer-to-Peer Transparent Clocks. The TimestampCorrectionPort Data Set allows for the alteration of PTP related Timestamps.

Timestamp Correction Port Data Set Member:	Ordinary Clock:	Boundary Clock:	End-to-End Transparent Clock:	Peer-to-Peer Transparent Clock:
EgressLatency	optional member	optional member	optional member	optional member
IngressLatency	optional member	optional member	optional member	optional member

EgressLatency

TimeInterval EgressLatency;

EgressLatency is a data set member of the TimestampCorrectionPort Data Set that indicates the interval of time between the generation of the Timestamp for a transmitting PTP Message and when the Message is actually transmitted. The EgressLatency when the TimestampCorrectionPort Data Set is enabled accounts for this miniscule time period. It is a TimeInterval special data type that is 64bits in length.

IngressLatency

TimeInterval IngressLatency;

IngressLatency is a data set member of the TimestampCorrectionPort Data Set that indicates the time interval between when the PTP Message is received and when the Timestamp is generated. The IngressLatency when the TimestampCorrectionPort Data Set is enabled accounts for this miniscule time period. It is a TimeInterval special data type that is 64bits in length.

AsymmetryCorrectionPort Data Set

The AsymmetryCorrectionPort Data Set is not required to be used by the PTP Ports of the four types of PTP Clocks. Rather the AsymmetryCorrectionPort Data Set is completely optional to the PTP Ports of Ordinary Clocks, Boundary Clocks, End-to-End Transparent Clocks and Peer-to-Peer Transparent Clocks. The AsymmetryCorrectionPort Data Set allows for the alteration of the DelayAsymmetry data set member of the Port Data Set.

Asymmetry Correction Port Data Set Member:	Ordinary Clock:	Boundary Clock:	End-to-End Transparent Clock:	Peer-to-Peer Transparent Clock:
ConstantAsymmetry	optional member	optional member	optional member	optional member
ScaledDelayCoefficient	optional member	optional member	optional member	optional member
Enable	optional member	optional member	optional member	optional member

ConstantAsymmetry

TimeInterval ConstantAsymmetry;

ConstantAsymmetry is a data set member of the AsymmetryCorrectionPort Data Set that indicates an unchanging asymmetry value used to perform minor modifications to the DelayAsymmetry data set member of the Port Data Set. It is a TimeInterval special data type that is 64bits in length.

ScaledDelayCoefficient

RelativeDifference ScaledDelayCoefficient;

ScaledDelayCoefficient is a data set member of the AsymmetryCorrectionPort Data Set that indicates the DelayCoefficient used to adjust the DelayAsymmetry data set member of the Port Data Set. It is a RelativeDifference special data type that is 64bits in length.

Enable

Boolean Enable;

Enable is a data set member of the AsymmetryCorrectionPort Data Set that indicates with a one if the DelayAsymmetry data set member of the Port Data Set is calculated on this PTP Port. It is a boolean 1bit in length.

DescriptionPort Data Set

The DescriptionPort Data Set is used by Ordinary Clocks, Boundary Clocks, End-to-End Transparent Clocks and Peer-to-Peer Transparent Clocks and includes the following data set members. Separate DescriptionPort Data Sets are maintained for each PTP Port on a Clock.

Description Port Data Set Member:	Ordinary Clock:	Boundary Clock:	End-to-End Transparent Clock:	Peer-to-Peer Transparent Clock:
Profile Identifier	management member	management member	management member	management member
Protocol Address	optional member	optional member	management member	management member

ProfileIdentifier

UInteger48 ProfileIdentifier;

ProfileIdentifier is a data set member of the DescriptionPort Data Set that indicates the PTP Profile used on the PTP Port. It is an unsigned integer that is 48bits in length.

ProtocolAddress

PortAddress ProtocolAddress;

ProtocolAddress is a data set member of the DescriptionPort Data Set that indicates the source address by the network transport protocol used by this PTP Port. PTP Ports belonging to the same Clock may use different ProtocolAddresses from each other. It is a PortAddress special data type 10bytes in length.

UnicastNegotiationPort Data Set

The UnicastNegotiationPort Data Set is not required to be used by the PTP Ports of Ordinary Clocks and Boundary Clocks. This data set is only applicable to the Unicast Message Negotiation Mechanism an optional feature and only applies to Ordinary Clocks and Boundary Clocks PTP Ports.

Unicast Negotiation Port Data Set Member:	Ordinary Clock:	Boundary Clock:	End-to-End Transparent Clock:	Peer-to-Peer Transparent Clock:
Enable	optional member	optional member	NA	NA

Enable

Boolean Enable;

Enable is a data set member of the UnicastNegotiationPort Data Set that indicates with a one if the Unicast Message Negotiation Mechanism optional feature is to be used on this PTP Port. It is a boolean 1bit in length.

AlternateMasterPort Data Set

The AlternateMasterPort Data Set is not required to be used. Rather the AlternateMasterPort option is completely optional to Ordinary Clocks and Boundary Clocks. The AlternateMasterPort allows PTP Ports that are not in the Master PortState to nonetheless transmit Announce Messages to other PTP Ports on the same Network. The other PTP Ports will also gather the transmission path characteristics of every AlternateMasterPort PTP Ports.

Alternate Master Port Data Set Member:	Ordinary Clock:	Boundary Clock:	End-to-End Transparent Clock:	Peer-to-Peer Transparent Clock:
Number Of Alternate Masters	required member	required member	NA	NA
Transmit Alternate Multicast Sync	required member	required member	NA	NA
Log Alternate Multicast Sync Interval	required member	required member	NA	NA

NumberOfAlternateMasters

UInteger8 NumberOfAlternateMasters;

NumberOfAlternateMasters is a data set member of the AlternateMasterPort Data Set that indicates the total allowable PTP Ports not in the Master PortState that are permitted to transmit Announce Messages as AlternateMasterPorts. These Multicast Announce Messages are to have their AlternateMasterFlag set to one. It is an unsigned integer 8bits in length.

TransmitAlternateMulticastSync

Boolean TransmitAlternateMulticastSync;

TransmitAlternateMulticastSync is a data set member of the AlternateMasterPort Data Set that indicates with a value of one if the AlternateMasterPort PTP Port is currently transmitting Sync Messages and if required the associated Follow_Up Messages as well. It is a boolean 1bit in length.

LogAlternateMulticastSyncInterval

Integer8 LogAlternateMulticastSyncInterval;

LogAlternateMulticastSyncInterval is a data set member of the AlternateMasterPort Data Set that indicates the AlternateMulticastSyncInterval value except in logarithm to the base of two format. It is a signed integer 8bits in length.

AlternateMulticastSyncInterval = 2^(LogAlternateMulticastSyncInterval)

Note: AlternateMulticastSyncInterval is the least amount of time in seconds allowed between consecutive Sync Messages transmitted by AlternateMasterPort PTP Ports

UnicastDiscoveryPort Data Set

The UnicastDiscoveryPort Data Set is not required to be used. Rather the UnicastDiscoveryPort option is completely optional to Ordinary Clocks and Boundary Clocks. UnicastDiscoveryPort allows PTP Ports to try to use Unicast Messages to communicate with other predetermined PTP Clocks. The UnicastDiscoveryPort Data Set is turned on when the Unicast Discovery Mechanism is enabled so too is the Unicast Negotiation option.

Unicast Discovery Port Data Set Member:	Ordinary Clock:	Boundary Clock:	End-to-End Transparent Clock:	Peer-to-Peer Transparent Clock:
MaxTableSize	required member	required member	NA	NA
LogQueryInterval	required member	required member	NA	NA
ActualTableSize	required member	required member	NA	NA
PortAddress	required member	required member	NA	NA

MaxTableSize

UInteger16 MaxTableSize;

MaxTableSize is a data set member of the UnicastDiscoveryPort Data Set that indicates the total allowable PTP Port PortAddresses that can be stored for use for the Unicast Discovery Mechanism. It is an unsigned integer 16bits in length.

LogQueryInterval

Integer8 LogQueryInterval;

LogQueryInterval is a data set member of the UnicastDiscoveryPort Data Set that indicates the QueryInterval value except in logarithm to the base of two format. It is a signed integer 8bits in length.

QueryInterval = 2^(LogQueryInterval)

Note: QueryInterval is the least amount of time in seconds allowed between requests from a Slave Clock for a Unicast Announce Message

ActualTableSize

UInteger16 ActualTableSize;

ActualTableSize is a data set member of the UnicastDiscoveryPort Data Set that indicates the total PTP Port PortAddresses that are currently stored in the PortAddress data set member for use for the Unicast Discovery Mechanism. It is an unsigned integer 16bits in length.

PortAddress

PortAddress PortAddress;

PortAddress is a data set member of the UnicastDiscoveryPort Data Set that is comprised of an array of elements of the PortAddress special data type. The size of the array is determined by the ActualTableSize data set member. Each element of the PortAddress will use the PortAddress special data type 10bytes in length.

AcceptableMasterTable Data Set

AcceptableMasterTable Data Set is not required to be used. Rather the Acceptable Master Table is completely optional to Ordinary Clocks and Boundary Clocks. The Acceptable Master Table option when enabled restricts PTP Ports in the Slave PortState to only be able to Synchronize to PTP Ports that are in the Acceptable Master Table.

Acceptable Master Table Data Set Member:	Ordinary Clock:	Boundary Clock:	End-to-End Transparent Clock:	Peer-to-Peer Transparent Clock:
MaxTableSize	required member	required member	NA	NA
ActualTableSize	required member	required member	NA	NA
List	required member	required member	NA	NA

MaxTableSize

UInteger16 MaxTableSize;

MaxTableSize is a data set member of the AcceptableMasterTable Data Set that indicates the total allowable PTP Ports that can be stored for use for the Acceptable Master Table. It is an unsigned integer 16bits in length.

ActualTableSize

UInteger16 ActualTableSize;

ActualTableSize is a data set member of the AcceptableMasterTable Data Set that indicates the total PTP Ports that are currently stored in the List data set member for use for the Acceptable Master Table. It is an unsigned integer 16bits in length.

List

AcceptableMaster List;

List is a data set member of the AcceptableMasterTable Data Set that is comprised of an array of elements of the AcceptableMaster special data type. The size of the array is determined by the ActualTableSize data set member. Each element of the List will use the AcceptableMaster special data type that is 11bytes length.

CommunicationCapabilitiesPort Data Set

CommunicationCapabilitiesPort Data Set contains four data set members that indicates a PTP Ports available communication modes. The CommunicationCapabilitiesPort Data Set is used by Ordinary Clocks and Boundary Clocks. Separate CommunicationCapabilitiesPort Data Sets are maintained for each PTP Port on a Clock.

Communication Capabilities Port Data Set Member:	Ordinary Clock:	Boundary Clock:	End-to-End Transparent Clock:	Peer-to-Peer Transparent Clock:
Multicast Capable	required member	required member	NA	NA
Unicast Capable	required member	required member	NA	NA
Unicast Negotiation Capable	required member	required member	NA	NA
Unicast Negotiation Required	required member	required member	NA	NA

MulticastCapable

Boolean MulticastCapable;

MulticastCapable is a data set member of the CommunicationCapabilitiesPort Data Set that indicates with a value of one if the PTP Port is able to transmit Multicast PTP Messages. It is a boolean 1bit in length.

UnicastCapable

Boolean UnicastCapable;

UnicastCapable is a data set member of the CommunicationCapabilitiesPort Data Set that indicates with a value of one if the PTP Port is able to transmit Unicast PTP Messages. It is a boolean 1bit in length.

UnicastNegotiationCapable

Boolean UnicastNegotiationCapable;

UnicastNegotiationCapable is a data set member of the CommunicationCapabilitiesPort Data Set that indicates with a value of one if the PTP Port is able to arrange Unicast PTP Messages using the Unicast Message Negotiation option. It is a boolean 1bit in length.

UnicastNegotiationRequired

Boolean UnicastNegotiationRequired;

UnicastNegotiationRequired is a data set member of the CommunicationCapabilitiesPort Data Set that indicates with a value of one if the PTP Port is required to arrange Unicast PTP Messages using the Unicast Message Negotiation option. It is a boolean 1bit in length.

PTP Domains and Subdomains

A PTP Domain(or Subdomain) is a group of connected Clocks on the same Network that have been Synchronized to each other. PTP Domains are defined by the two data set members: SdoID and DomainNumber.

SdoID is a data set member of the Default Data Set that is 12bits in length and is broken down into two parts. MajorSdoID is the most significant 4bits of SdoID and MinorSdoID is the least significant 8bits of SdoID. MajorSdoID and MinorSdoID are contained in the Common PTP Message Header specified in an earlier section. The values contained in MajorSdoID and MinorSdoID are from the Transmitting Clocks SdoID value.

SdoID is used primarily to separate Clocks with one PTP Profile from other Clocks of different PTP Profiles. It also specifies which DomainNumber values are permissible. SdoID is contained in the Default Data Set. The SdoID value is defined by the next table

SdoID Value Range(hex):		DomainNumber values when PTP uses Ethernet as per IEEE 802(dec):	Description:
Major SdoID:	Minor SdoID:		
From: 0	00	*0-127 are allowed *128-255 are reserved	*If using IEEE 1588-2008 or the PTP specifies as such
To: 0	00		
From: 0	01		*For use only with the IEEE 1588-2008 version, for backwards compatibility
To: 0	FF		
From: 1	00	*0-239 are allowed *240-255 are reserved	*If using IEEE 802.1 PTP Profiles
To: 1	00		
From: 1	01		*For use only with the IEEE 1588-2008 version, for backwards compatibility
To: 1	FF		

From:		*240-255 are reserved	*Used by IEEE 1588 Common MeanLinkDelay
2	00		
To:			
2	00		
From:		*reserved	*Used by IEEE 1588 Working Group
2	01		
To:			
2	FF		
From:		*0-239 are allowed	*If using QSDOs PTP Profiles
3	00	*240-255 are reserved	
To:			
F	FC		
From:		*0-239 are allowed	*For temporary or testing
F	FD	*240-255 are reserved	
To:			
F	FE		
From:		*reserved	*Used by IEEE 1588 Working Group
F	FF		
To:			
F	FF		

RelativeDifference is a special data type that indicates the difference between two values. The difference value stored in this special data type uses a special storage method. The actual difference value between two values is multiplied by 2^62 and removing the remaining decimal values. It is a signed integer 64bits in length

A specific PTP Domain will decide almost every configurable setting or reliant protocol that there is for PTP. Each PTP Domain must be assigned a value of between 0-255(dec).

It is rare and not advised(except for Boundary Clocks) but a specialized Clock can belong to more than one PTP Domain. In such cases the Clock must have increased hardware requirements in order to support communications on both PTP Domains at the same time. Without the correct hardware Synchronization performance will be degraded.

In PTP version IEEE 1588-2002 Clocks were assigned to a respective Subdomain by use of the value contained in the "Subdomain name" found in the PTP Message Header. In PTP version IEEE 1588-2008 and IEEE 1588-2019 version Clocks are assigned to a respective Subdomain by use of the value contained in the "DomainNumber" found in the PTP Message Header.

Note: PTP version IEEE 1588-2002 is not compatible with any other major versions. IEEE 1588-2008 and IEEE 1588-2019 are compatible under certain conditions. This topic is covered in a later section

Each PTP Domain will maintain its time separately from other PTP Domains. However multiple PTP Domains can exist on the same Network. All PTP Messages must contain a designation of what Domain or Subdomain they belong to. A PTP Domain may be impaired if forced to share the same Network or Transparent Clocks with another PTP Domain. For the best Synchronization times between Clocks do not overlap PTP Domains.

The PTP Domain can be restricted from overlapping with another PTP Domain by limiting the retransmission of Messages. As well the segregation of two PTP Domains can be done physically or logically(Router Table Configuration or VLANs).
Ethernet Networks are naturally composed of Ethernet Switches and Routers. These Network Devices will or will not support the PTP protocol depending on the selected model. As mentioned before Ethernet Switches that do support PTP are called Transparent Clocks.

Not to be worried certain types of PTP will still work even if the Ethernet Switch is a NonTransparent Clock and not equipped to handle PTP Event Messages separately. However the Synchronization time between Clocks will suffer heavily for it.

Note: Boundary Clocks can be used to separate and communicate between PTP Domains

PTP Messages Not In The Same Domain

A PTP Message received by an Ordinary Clock or a Boundary Clock will be dropped and not processed if the PTP Message does not have the same Domain Number or MajorSdoID value as the Receiving Clock.

A PTP Message's Domain Number and MajorSdoID value will also need to be checked by Transparent Clocks. This is not to check if the PTP Message belongs to the same Domain/MajorSdoID value as the specific Transparent Clock. But rather so if there is a pair of PTP Messages that need each other as with the Sync and Follow_Up Messages that they do actually belong to each other. The Transparent Clock will need to know which Follow_Up Message belongs to which Sync Message to properly update the Follow_Up Message's CorrectionField. If the Sync Message is flagged as a One-Step Sync Message this check does not necessarily need to be performed by the Transparent Clock.

Note: The PTP standard does have provisions for messaging between PTP Clocks in separate PTP Domains but this option is rarely utilized

Serving Time To Multiple PTP Domains On the Same Network

There are two different methods of serving time to multiple PTP Domains that inhabit the same Network. The first is using two or more independent external Time Sources. This is usually achieved by using GrandMaster Clocks or Boundary Clocks configured to serve time to their respective Domains. Two Domains serviced by separate GrandMaster Clocks using the same PTP capable Network this is outlined below.

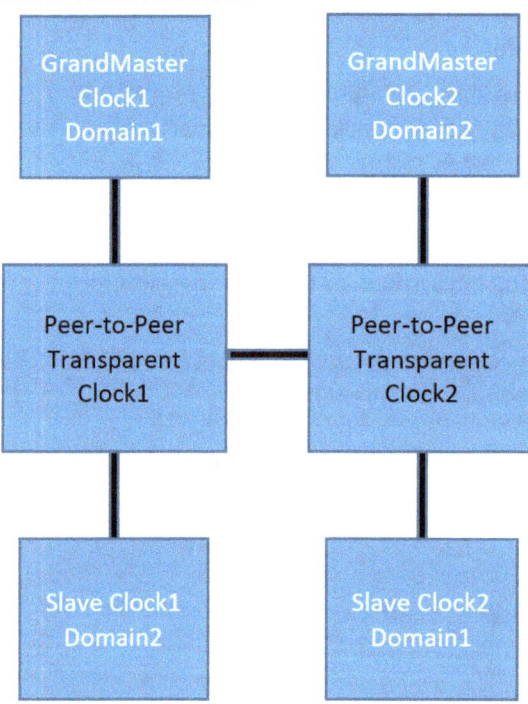

The second method is to use a single shared external Time Source. This is done by using a single GrandMaster Clock or Boundary Clock that will serve time to each separate PTP Domain. The single GrandMaster Clock or Boundary Clock can serve time to multiple PTP Domains using either different Physical Ports for each Domain or each Domain can be served time using the same Physical Port.

In the below example the two PTP Domains are served time using the same GrandMaster Clock through the same GrandMaster Physical Port and each Domains PTP Messages are transmitted to the Slave Clocks using the same PTP capable Network. This is outlined below.

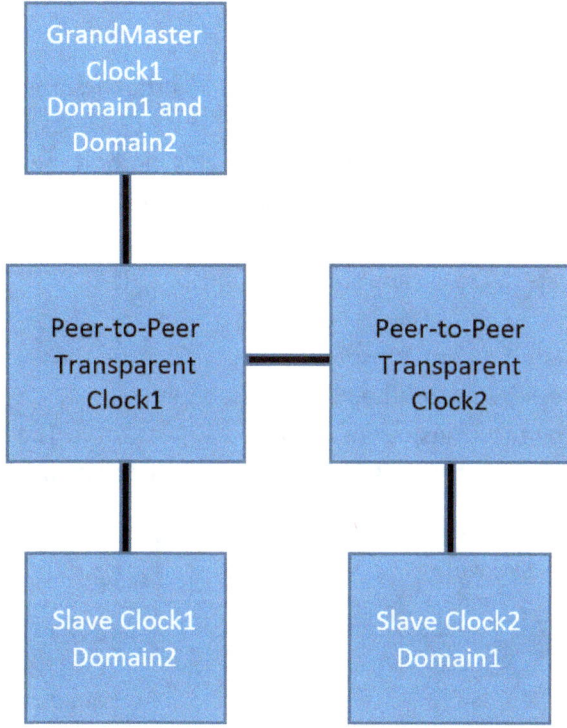

Once again utilizing the same Network to serve time to more than one domain is not recommended as Synchronization performance will suffer as a result.

Path Delay Mechanisms

There is two ways of calculating the Path Delay(or Propagation Delay, Propagation Time) of a Sync Message between a Master and Slave Clock: Delay Request-Response Mechanism and Peer Delay Mechanism.

The Delay Request-Response Mechanism calculates the End-to-End Delay. The End-to-End Delay is the method by which the time it takes for the PTP Message to travel between the Master and Slave Clock is determined. This method uses the Sync, Delay_Req, Delay_Resp and Follow_Up Messages. However the Delay Request-Response Mechanism is further broken down into two subtypes of Path Delay Mechanisms: with Transparent Clocks and with NonTransparent Clocks.

The only difference between them is when Transparent Clocks are used the ResidenceTime that the Sync Message spends being processed by the Transparent Clock is calculated by the Transparent Clock and adjusts for it. The Delay Request-Response Mechanism with Transparent Clock is outlined below.

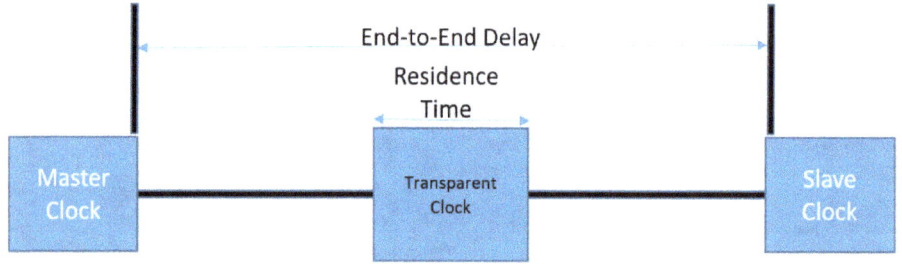

ResidenceTime: Time spent being processed by a NonTransparent CLock, Transparent Clock or Boundary Clock

When NonTransparent Clocks are used with the Delay Request-Response Mechanism the ResidenceTime is not calculated and therefore this method is the least accurate of the Path Delay Mechanisms. The Delay Request-Response Mechanism with NonTransparent Clocks is outlined below.

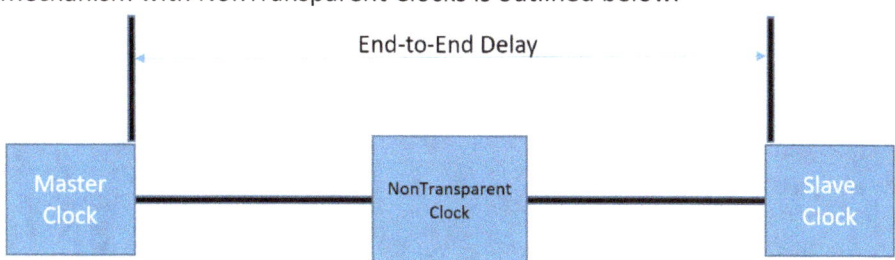

The Peer Delay Path Mechanism calculates the Peer-to-Peer Delay. The Peer-to-Peer Delay is the method by which each Network Link is measured(Peer-to-Peer Delay1 and Peer-to-Peer Delay2) as well as the ResidenceTime in each Transparent Clock. The Peer Delay Mechanism can only be used when all PTP Ports in a Domain are set to Peer-to-Peer. This method uses the Pdelay_Req, Pdelay_Resp and Pdelay_Resp_Follow_Up Messages to determine each Link Delay Time. The Sync Message(and possibly the associated Follow_Up Message) is also still used for the Peer Delay Mechanism.

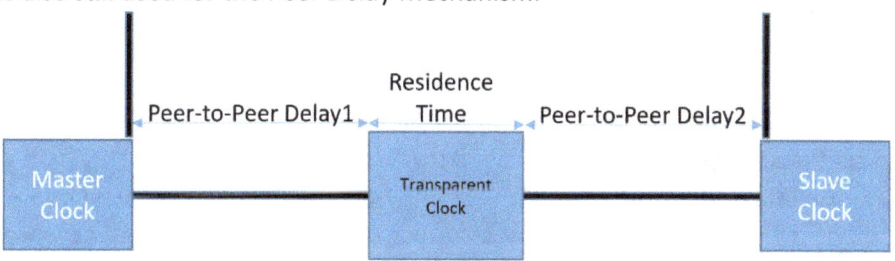

Note: The Different Path Delay Mechanisms(Delay Request-Response and Peer Delay) cannot use the same PTP Ports, Transparent Clocks, Master Clocks, etc.

The Delay Request-Response Mechanism and the Peer Delay Mechanism can be used by the Ports of Boundary Clocks and Ordinary Clocks. Peer-to-Peer Transparent Clock Ports will only use the Peer Delay Mechanism. End-to-End Transparent Clock Ports can only participate in a PTP capable Network using the Delay Request-Response Mechanism. NonTransparent Clock Ports can only participate in a PTP capable Network using the Delay Request-Response Mechanism.

Any Network employing PTP is advised to only use Clocks that employ either Delay Request-Response Mechanism or Peer Delay Mechanism as the two Mechanisms will not working correctly with each other unless separated by a suitable Boundary Clock.

Transparent Clocks Basic Functions and Design

PTP version IEEE 1588-2008 introduced Transparent Clocks as an improvement or alternative to Boundary Clocks, regular Ethernet Switches, Bridges and even Routers when it comes to PTP. A Transparent Clock will receive a PTP Event Message on an Ingress Port, separate it from the regular Network Traffic and will forward it out the Egress Port. However unlike regular Ethernet Switches- Transparent Clocks will measure the time it takes to perform this work and update the CorrectionField accordingly.
The time it takes for the Transparent Clock to process a PTP Event Message(mostly Sync Messages) is called the ResidenceTime. The ResidenceTime value is the Egress Timestamp minus the Ingress Timestamp.

Manufacturers have created two different ways of updating the Event Messages ResidenceTime in a Transparent Clock: Two-Step and One-Step Operation.

Two-Step Transparent Clock

A Two-Step Transparent Clock will measure the ResidenceTime of the Sync Message and will forward it with its Timestamp value unaltered. The associated Follow Up Message follows the Sync Message shortly afterwards. The ResidenceTime and possibly the Network Link Delay of the Sync Message that was just recorded is added to the CorrectionField of the Follow_Up Message.

For a Two-Step Transparent Clock if an One-Step Sync Message is received and the Two-Step Flag is therefore not set it will need to be set before being forwarded as a Two-Step Sync Message. As well the Sync Messages ResidenceTime and possibly the Sync Messages Network Link Delay will need to be added to the CorrectionField of a newly created Follow_Up Message that will need to be transmitted after the Sync Message.

One-Step Transparent Clock

For a One-Step Transparent Clock the Sync Message has its CorrectionField updated right before it is transmitted. The ResidenceTime and possibly the Network Link Delay is added to the CorrectionField of the Sync Message.

Note: There are other methods of updating the Sync Message to reflect the time it spent being processed by the Transparent Clock(ResidenceTime). This will usually involve updating both the OriginTimestamp as well as the CorrectionField of the Sync Message.

Much like Boundary Clocks Transparent Clocks also have an internal Multiplexer that divides Network Traffic between PTP and Non-PTP Packets. Non-PTP Packets are treated in the same manner as with any other Ethernet Switch or Router. While PTP Packets are sent to separate PTP hardware that controls the PTP functions.

One-Step And Two-Step Ports And Clocks

PTP Clocks and PTP Ports can be divided into two groups based on if they are One-Step(1S) or Two-Step(2S) Clocks or PTP Ports. Usually Master Ports belong to Master Clocks and Slave Ports belong to Slave Clocks. Boundary Clocks will have both Master Ports and Slave Ports. Transparent Clocks and NonTransparent Clocks do not have Master or Slave Ports.

If a Master PTP Port is a One-Step Port it will only transmit out a One-Step Sync Message. If a Master PTP Port is a Two-Step Port it will transmit out a Two-Step Sync Message and then transmit out an associated Follow_Up Message.

If a One-Step Transparent Clock receives a One-Step Sync Message it will update its CorrectionField and retransmit the One-Step Sync Message out. If a Two-Step Transparent Clock receives a One-Step Sync Message it will retransmit the Sync Message out as a Two-Step Sync Message. Then it will create, update the CorrectionField and transmit out a brand new associated Follow_Up Message.

If a One-Step Transparent Clock receives a Two-Step Sync Message it will, update the CorrectionField and retransmit the Two-Step Sync Message out. When the associated Follow_Up Message is received the One-Step Transparent Clock will retransmit out the associated Follow_Up Message unaltered. If a Two-Step Transparent Clock receives a Two-Step Sync Message it will retransmit the Sync Message out as a Two-Step Message. When the associated Follow_Up Message is received the Two-Step Transparent Clock will update the Follow_Up Message's CorrectionField and then retransmit it out.

End-to-End Transparent Clock Associating PTP Messages

For an End-to-End Transparent Clock the following PTP Messages will be checked for association to one another:

Sync	Follow_Up

Delay_Req	Delay_Resp

An End-to-End Transparent Clock will only match up these associated PTP Messages if the following conditions are true:

1. The associated PTP Messages must have the same DomainNumber, SdoID and SequenceID Field values

2. The SourcePortIdentity Field values must be the same for the Sync Message and its associated Follow_Up Message

3. The SourcePortIdentity Field value of the Delay_Req Message must be the same as the RequestingPortIdentity Field value of the Delay_Resp Message

Note: DomainNumber, SdoID and SequenceID Field values do not need to be tested on One-Step Sync Messages because they have no associated Follow_Up Message

Note: Msg is a shortened version of the word Message. 1S is a shortened version of One-Step. 2S is a shortened version of Two-Step

End-to-End One-Step Transparent Clock Processing a Sync Message

How an End-to-End One-Step Transparent Clock processes a Sync Message is outlined below.

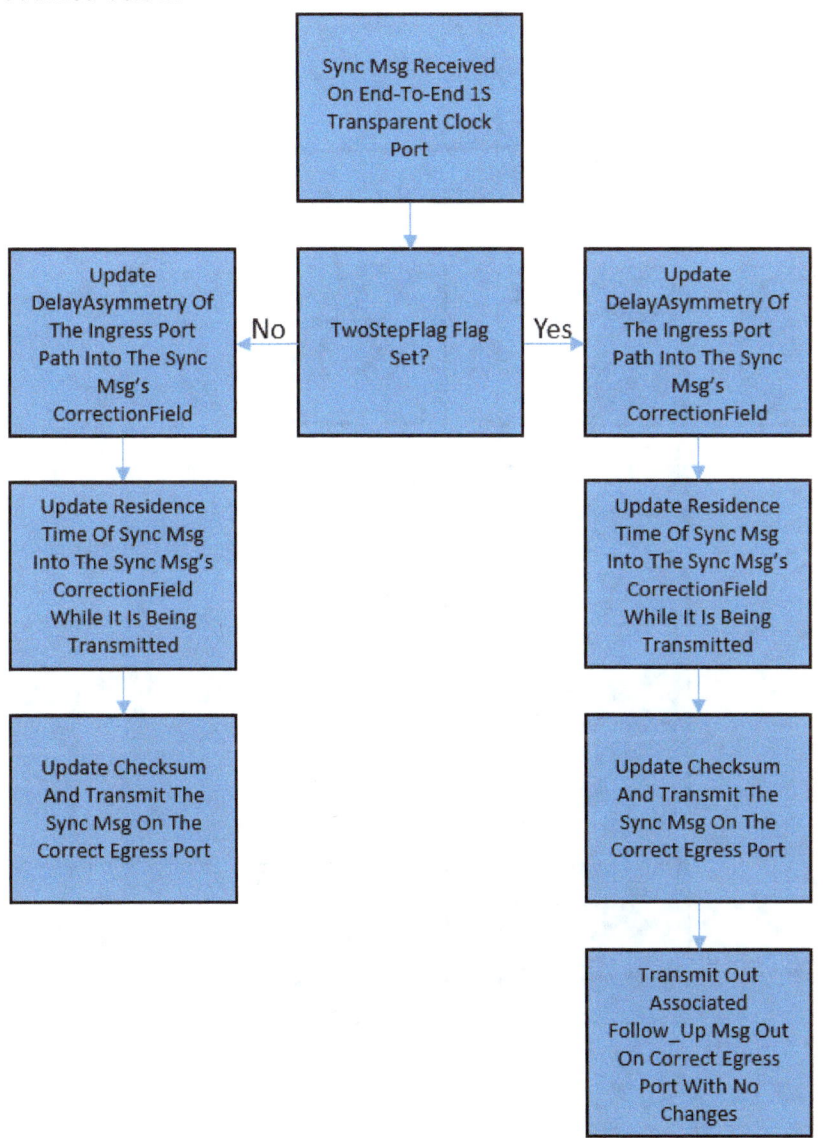

End-to-End Two-Step Transparent Clock Processing a Sync Message

How an End-to-End Two-Step Transparent Clock processes a Sync Message is outlined below.

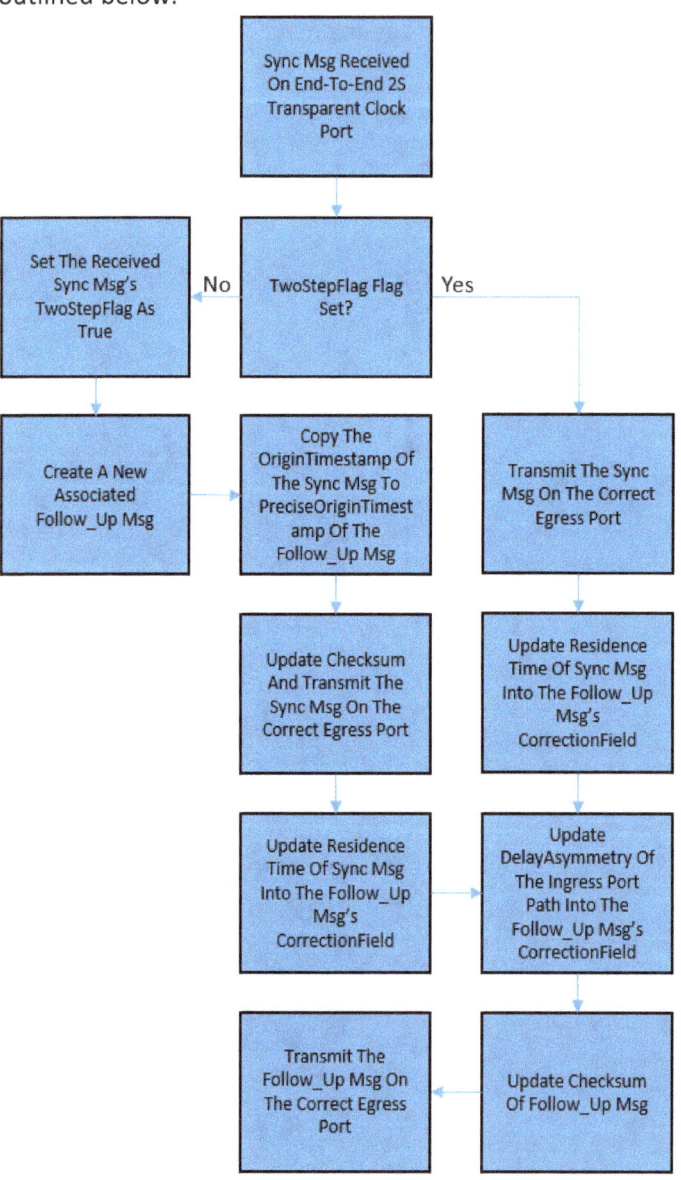

End-to-End One-Step Transparent Clock Processing a Delay_Req Message

How an End-to-End One-Step Transparent Clock processes a Delay_Req Message is outlined below.

```
┌─────────────────────┐
│  Delay_Req Msg      │
│  Received On End-   │
│  To-End 1S          │
│  Transparent Clock  │
│  Port               │
└──────────┬──────────┘
           ▼
┌─────────────────────┐
│  Update             │
│  DelayAsymmetry Of  │
│  The Egress Port Path│
│  Into The Delay_Req │
│  Msg's              │
│  CorrectionField    │
└──────────┬──────────┘
           ▼
┌─────────────────────┐
│  Update Residence   │
│  Time Of Delay_Req  │
│  Msg Into The       │
│  Delay_Req Msg's    │
│  CorrectionField    │
│  While It Is Being  │
│  Transmitted        │
└──────────┬──────────┘
           ▼
┌─────────────────────┐
│  Update Checksum    │
│  And Transmit The   │
│  Delay_Req Msg On   │
│  The Correct Egress │
│  Port               │
└─────────────────────┘
```

End-to-End Two-Step Transparent Clock Processing a Delay_Req Message

How an End-to-End Two-Step Transparent Clock processes a Delay_Req Message is outlined below.

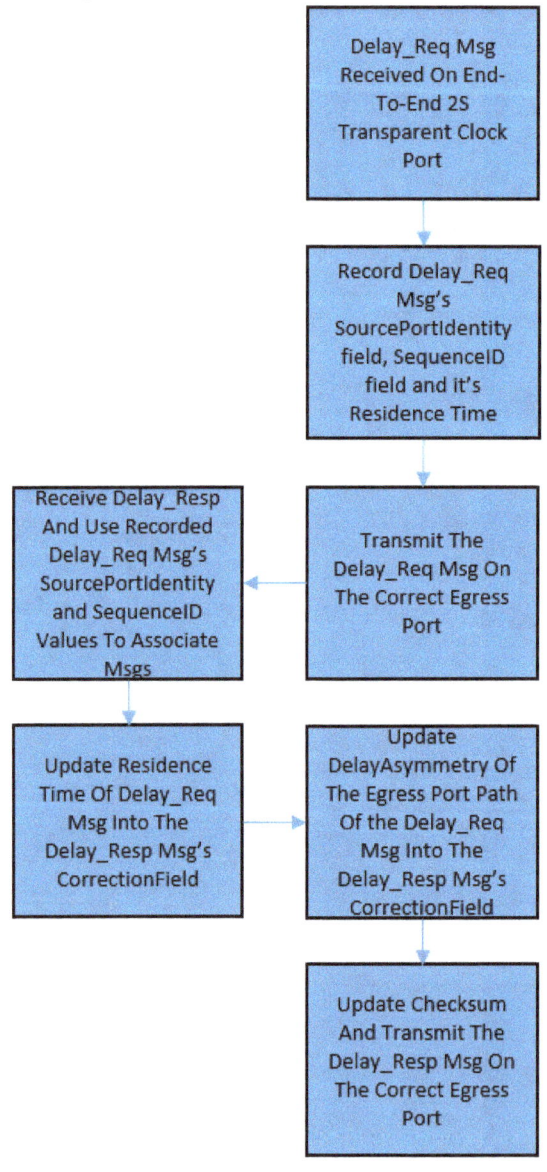

End-to-End Transparent Clock Processing Pdelay_Req, Pdelay_Resp and Pdelay_Resp_Follow_Up Messages

Pdelay_Req, Pdelay_Resp and Pdelay_Resp_Follow_Up PTP Messages are used only for the Peer Delay Path Mechanism. They are never supposed to be received or transmitted by End-to-End Transparent Clocks. End-to-End Transparent Clocks and Peer-to-Peer Transparent Clocks should never be used on the same Network and if they must be they need to be separated by a capable Boundary Clock.

Peer-to-Peer Transparent Clock Associating PTP Messages

For a Peer-to-Peer Transparent Clock the following PTP Messages will be checked for association to one another:

Sync	Follow_Up

Pdelay_Req	Pdelay_Resp	Pdelay_Resp_Follow_Up

A Peer-to-Peer Transparent Clock will only match up these associated PTP Messages if the following conditions are true:

1. The associated PTP Messages must have the same DomainNumber, SdoID and SequenceID Field values

2. The SourcePortIdentity Field values must be the same for the Sync Message and its associated Follow_Up Message

3. The SourcePortIdentity Field value of the Pdelay_Req Message must be the same as the RequestingPortIdentity Field value of the Pdelay_Resp Message(and if required Pdelay_Resp_Follow_Up Message)

Peer-to-Peer One-Step Transparent Clock Processing a Sync Message

How a Peer-to-Peer One-Step Transparent Clock processes a Sync Message is outlined below.

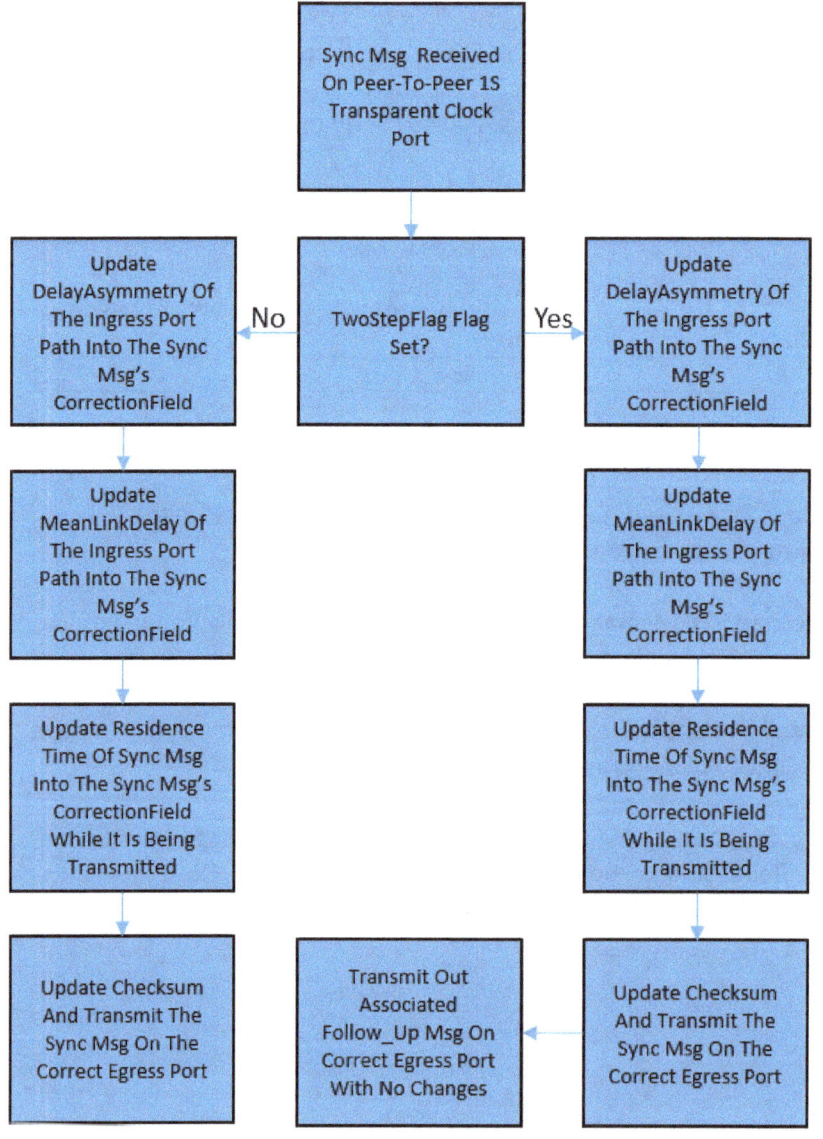

Peer-to-Peer Two-Step Transparent Clock Processing a Sync Message

How a Peer-to-Peer Two-Step Transparent Clock processes a Sync Message is outlined below.

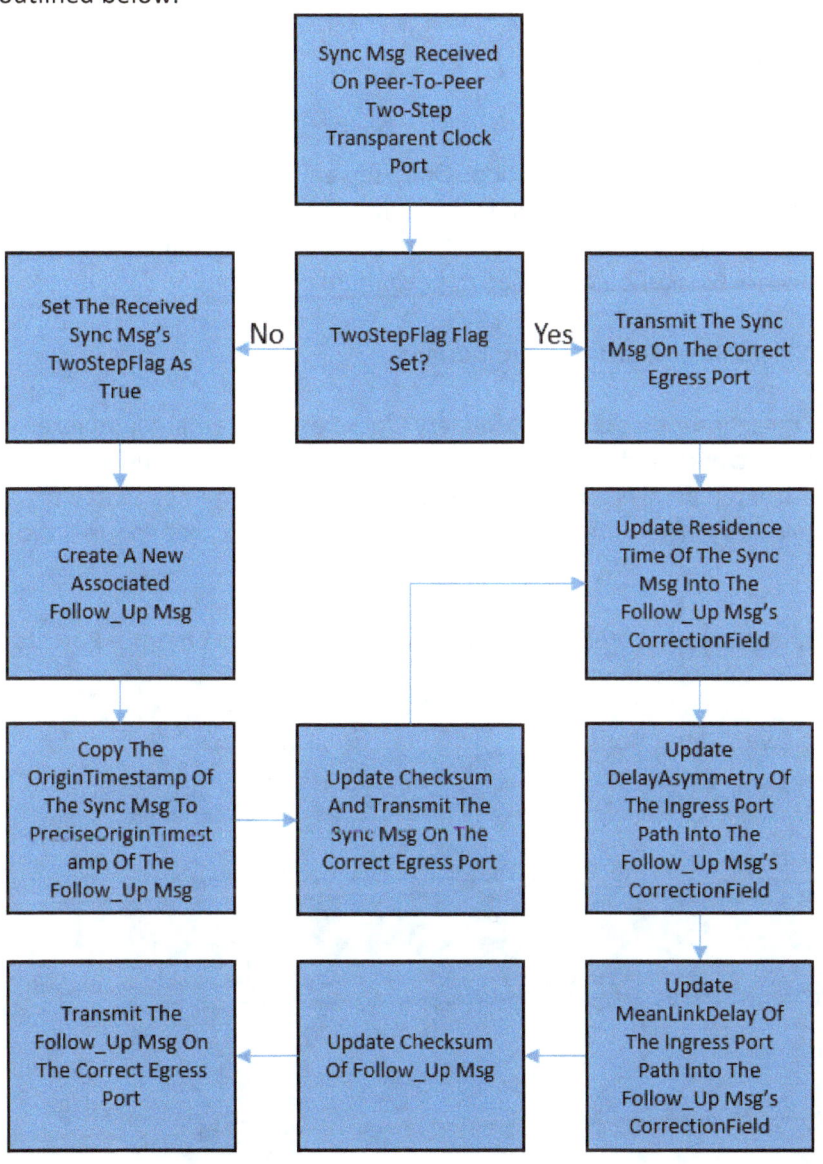

One-Step and Two-Step Clocks or PTP Ports On The Same PTP Network?

A point of contention when building a PTP capable Network is the question: Can One-Step Clocks and Two-Step Clocks work together?

The answer is a resounding:
Usually!

As indicated by the just covered sections One-Step and Two-Step Clocks can usually work together and can adjust to accommodate each other. However mixing One-Step and Two-Step Clocks is still not recommended and if it must be done a Boundary Clock should be used to keep them separated.

Boundary Clocks Basic Functions and Design

Similar to Transparent Clocks each Boundary Clock has an internal Multiplexer that divides Network Traffic between PTP and Non-PTP Packets. Non-PTP Packets are treated in the same manner as with any other Ethernet Switch or Router. While PTP Packets are sent to separate PTP hardware that controls the PTP functions.

See the diagram below of a Boundary Clock with four Physical Ethernet Ports to see a simplistic diagram of how this works:

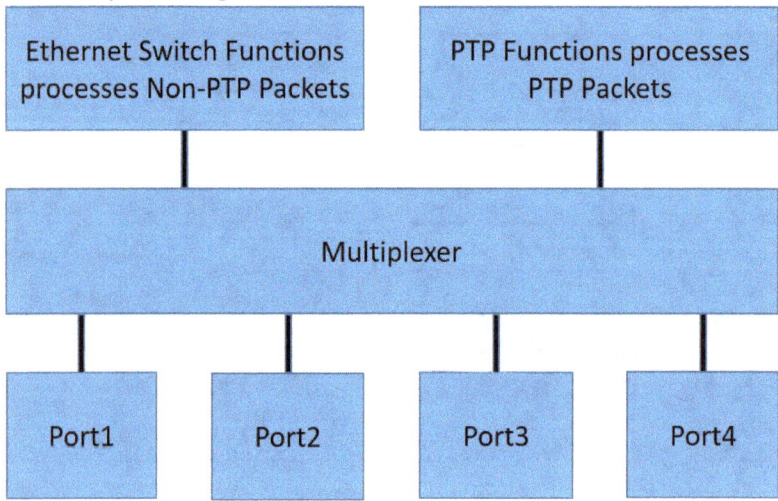

The PTP hardware will manage each of the separate PTP Ports(each Physical Ports will have at least one Logical PTP Port) separately allowing for them to be in various distinct states(Master, Slave or Passive). The Boundary Clocks PTP hardware will ordinarily only have one internal clock shared between each Physical Port that is currently employing PTP.

When a Boundary Clocks PTP Port is assigned to the Slave PortState status(Meaning it is receiving the best possible PTP Time Signal from a Master Clock) it will Synchronize the Boundary Clocks internal clock to that PTP Time Signal. From there all its other PTP Ports will be assigned to either the Master or Passive PortState and will Synchronize to the Boundary Clocks internal clock.

Be aware that Boundary Clocks can also be selected as a GrandMaster Clock by the BMCA. Where Network Slave Clocks will Synchronize to the Boundary Clocks and its internal clock. The BMCA will rarely select a Boundary Clock as the GrandMaster Clock since Network Professionals will often use dedicated GrandMaster Clocks instead and will configure each Clock based on this decision

Boundary Clocks will not forward any received PTP Synchronization related Messages(Sync, Follow_Up, Delay_Req, Delay_Resp). The PTP Ports of a Boundary Clock appear as belonging to an Ordinary Clock to other Clocks connected to them. The Boundary Clock will generate new PTP Sync Messages and transmit them as usual but the Timestamps are based on the internal clock of the Boundary Clock. This is done in order to administer a PTP Time Signal to a large amount of Clocks and to make a larger Network scalable.

Management Messages however received by a Boundary Clock are then retransmitted/forwarded out. These Management Messages will only be forwarded a limited number of times however.

Note: Specialized Boundary Clocks can often be set to communicate between the different PTP versions(IEEE 1588-2002, IEEE 1588-2008 or PTP version IEEE 1588-2019)

More on Boundary Clocks

An Announce Message received by a Boundary Clock PTP Port that originated from that same Boundary Clock except from a different PTP Port can happen if both PTP Ports are attached to the same Network Segment. In this instance the Boundary Clock is to place all affected PTP Ports into the Passive PortState with the exception of the PTP Port with the lowest PortNumber. This is done until the Boundary Clock's BMCA determines the correct PortState assignment of each of its PTP Ports.

Ordinary and Boundary Clock Startup

Ordinary Clocks(that are not SlaveOnly Clocks) and Boundary Clocks when starting up will wait a predetermined amount of time to listen for Announce Messages transmitted by Master Clocks. After that time has passed and if no Announce Messages have been received than the Ordinary Clock(that is not a SlaveOnly Clock) or Boundary Clock will decide it is the Master Clock. Afterwards if an Announce Message is received from a Clock that has better Clock properties than it does as determined by the BMCA it will relegate its self to a Slave Clock.

Best Master Clock Algorithm: Master, Slave or Passive

The Best Master Clock Algorithm(BMCA) will first decide which Clock is the GrandMaster Clock(and if required any other Master Clocks) in the local Network. It will also decide if any newly introduced potential GrandMaster Clocks are superior than the currently selected GrandMaster Clock. Each PTP Port of Ordinary Clocks and Boundary Clocks will run BMCA constantly and at set intervals will transmit Announce Messages out. Announce Messages as discussed publish the original transmitting Clock's properties out to other Clocks on the Network. The BMCA allows each Clock to rapidly accommodate any changes to the Network Topology or the loss of the Preferred GrandMaster Clock.

The GrandMaster Clock and any other Master Clocks are settled based on:

1. Clock Quality
2. Clock Accuracy of the Clocks Time Base
3. Quality of the Clocks internal Oscillator
4. Master Clock closest to the GrandMaster

The BMCA can be broken down into two distinct algorithms:

1. Data Set Comparison Algorithm
2. State Decision Algorithm

Each Clock running BMCA will run a Data Set Comparison Algorithm and will receive the Data Sets of each other Clock running on that PTP Domain. The GrandMaster Clock and any other Master Clocks will be settled. The Data Set members in order of importance:

1. Priority1: Priority1(or Clock Priority) is a data set member of the Default Data Set and is a value from 0 to 255(dec) to be allocated by a Networking Professional. Keep in mind that lower values have a higher priority. The default value will depend on the Clock Type and the selected PTP Profile being used. Though 120(dec) is the most common default value

2. ClockClass: ClockClass is the first field of the ClockQuality data set member of the Default Data Set and is used to define which Class of Clock this PTP Clock belongs to. Different Classes will have better or worse priority

3. ClockAccuracy: ClockAccuracy is the second field of the ClockQuality data set member of the Default Data Set and is used to indicate the accuracy of the internal clock of the PTP Clock

4. OffsetScaledLogVariance: OffsetScaledLogVariance(or Variance) is the third field of the ClockQuality data set member of the Default Data Set and is used to indicate the variability or stability of the internal clock of the PTP Clock

5. Priority2: Priority2 is a data set member of the Default Data Set and is used to indicate a value from 0 to 255(dec) determined after taking into account all the other above data set members. Lower values have a higher priority. Priority2 allows for the specific ranking of PTP Clocks that are in all other ways the same. The default value will depend on the Clock Type and the selected PTP Profile being used. Though 128(dec) is the most common default value

6. ClockIdentity: ClockIdentity(or Unique Identifier) is a data set member of the Default Data Set and is used to indicate a 64bit Extended Unique Identifier(EUI) that is a distinctive value for that PTP Clock. It is also used as the final deciding value for the ranking of PTP Clocks

The Data Set Comparison Algorithm for a particular Slave Clock(or Slave Port on a Boundary Clock) also evaluates the amount of hops between itself and the GrandMaster Clock. This is useful when two Announce Messages arrive to the same Slave Port that originated from the same GrandMaster Clock. Two Announce Messages from the same GrandMaster Clock arriving to the same Slave Port is rare but it can happen when Network Loops(or Cyclic Paths) form. The number of Hops of the Announce Message is found in its StepsRemoved Field. In this way the StepsRemoved Field helps the Data Set Comparison Algorithm choose which Master Clock is topologically superior.

Based on this data the Clocks PTP Ports are put into Passive, Slave or Master PortState by the State Decision Algorithm. However Transparent Clock PTP Ports will not enter any PortState. When a Transparent Clock PTP Port receives a PTP Message it will retransmit that Message through one or more PTP enabled Ports depending on the underlying Network Transport Protocol.

Master Port: Master Ports are a source of time and transmit Sync Messages

Slave Port: Slave Ports Synchronize to a selected Master Clock or GrandMaster Clock using received Sync Messages

Passive Port: Passive Ports do not transmit Sync Messages and will not Synchronize to a Master Clock or GrandMaster Clock

BMCA also stops Clocks from having to negotiate with each other as well as always assigning a correct number of Master and GrandMasters to a Network. BMCA runs continuously meaning if another GrandMaster Clock that has just been plugged into the Network has superior attributes the Slave Clocks will Synchronize to it instead of the current GrandMaster Clock. The current GrandMaster Clock will move into a backup listening state.

Note: PTP Profiles can specify a BMCA that operates differently than the default BMCA-this is important. All custom varieties of BMCA are not covered by this document

In review, each PTP Clock runs the BMCA algorithm and it is broken up into two parts: The Data Set Comparison Algorithm and the State Decision Algorithm:

1. The Data Sets(contained in Announce Messages) from each Clock on a PTP Domain will be received. Master and GrandMaster Clocks will be determined. This is called the Data Set Comparison Algorithm

2. Each PTP Port is recommended to be moved to a particular PortState that it is to transition to: Master, Slave or Passive. This is called the State Decision Algorithm

BMCA: Network Topology

After determining the GrandMaster Clock and any other Master Clocks the second step to the BMCA(Best Master Clock Algorithm) is to assess the Network Topology. Which is done by looking at each Announce Messages number of Network links the Packet traversed before arriving at this particular Port-this is called the StepsRemoved. The SenderPortIdentity and the ReceiverPortIdentity values are also gathered.

MasterOnly PTP Port

In rare circumstances an Ordinary Clock or Boundary Clock may have the ability to configure or is designed to have one of its PTP Ports to be a MasterOnly Port. A MasterOnly Port can never be set to the Slave PortState or Passive PortState.

Other PTP PortStates

PTP Ports can exist in multiple different kinds of PTP PortStates and each Ports status is defined in their PortState data set member. The main PTP PortStates are Master, Slave and Passive as discussed earlier. However there are other transitory and less used PortStates. The next table describes each PTP PortState.

PortState:	PortState Description:
Initializing	A PTP Port can be placed in the Initializing PortState due to the events: Powerup, Initialize, Designated_Enabled or Fault_Cleared. In this PortState the Port is initializing its hardware and PTP Port Data Sets
Faulty	A PTP Port can be placed in the Faulty PortState due to it being faulted. A PTP Port placed in the Faulty PortState will not transmit any PTP Messages except required Management Messages. For a Boundary Clock a Faulty PTP Port is not to affect the other PTP Ports. If the Faulty PTP Port does affect other PTP Ports on the same Boundary Clock all PTP Ports are to be moved to the Faulty State. When the Faulty PortState is removed the PTP Port will move to the Initializing PortState
Disabled	A PTP Port can be placed in the Disabled PortState by a Network Professional. A PTP Port placed in the Disabled PortState will not transmit any PTP Messages except required Management Messages. All PTP Messages except for PTP Management Messages are to be dropped. For a Boundary Clock a Disabled PTP Port is not to affect other PTP Ports
Listening	A PTP Port can be placed in the Listening PortState when awaiting an Announce Message from a Master Clock or when waiting for the AnnounceReceiptTimeout to timeout. The Listening PortState is important as it allows the organized inclusion of newly added Clocks to the Master-Slave Hierarchy. A PTP Port in the Listening PortState will not transmit PTP Messages except for Management, Signaling, Pdelay_Req, Pdelay_Resp, and Pdelay_Resp_Follow_Up Messages
Pre-Master	A PTP Port can be placed in the Pre-Master PortState where it will act as if it were in the Master PortState however it will not transmit PTP Messages except for Management, Signaling, Pdelay_Req, Pdelay_Resp, and Pdelay_Resp_Follow_Up Messages
Master	A PTP Port can be placed in the Master PortState where it will act as a Master Clock. A PTP Port in the Master PortState will transmit all PTP Messages that it is required to in order to perform its functions as a Master Clock

Passive	A PTP Port can be placed in the Passive PortState and will not transmit any PTP Messages except for Management, Signaling, Pdelay_Req, Pdelay_Resp, and Pdelay_Resp_Follow_Up Messages
Uncalibrated	A PTP Port can be placed in the temporary Uncalibrated PortState when a new Master Clock has been discovered in the same PTP Domain. The PTP Port has chosen the correct Master Clock to Synchronize to and is preparing to do so. PTP Messages associated with the Uncalibrated State or a Management Mechanism will be transmitted a response
Slave	A PTP Port can be placed in the Slave PortState where it will act as a Slave Clock. PTP Ports in the Slave PortState will implement the BMCA and Synchronize to the best available Master Clock. A PTP Port in the Slave PortState will transmit all PTP Messages that it is required to in order to perform its functions as a Slave Clock

Note: The PortStates Faulty, Disabled, Listening, Pre-Master and Uncalibrated are found through the variables: PF, PD, PL, PP and PU

ForeignMasterList Optional Feature

The ForeignMasterList is an optional feature turned on by the selected PTP Profile or is enabled by default by the Clock manufacturer. The optional feature allows Manufacturers or PTP Profiles to indicate a smaller available number of PTP PortStates and whether the optional ForeignMasterList is to be used or not. ForeignMasterList is usually enabled by default.

The FMD attribute is what determines if the ForeignMasterList optional feature is to be used or not. The FMD value is decided by the selected PTP Profile. As well the FMD determines how an Announce Message is processed by the intended receiving PTP Port.

ForeignMasterList Table Entries

When the feature ForeignMasterList is turned on each PTP Port will construct its own ForeignMasterList table. This table is created in order to check Announce Messages and assist the Best Master Clock Algorithm. Each Foreign Master will have its own entry in the ForeignMasterList. The ForeignMasterList is to at least have five Foreign Master entries. Each entry will contain the following three data set members:

Data Set Members:	Description:
ForeignMasterPortIdentity	ForeignMasterPortIdentity is the SourcePortIdentity field value from the Announce Message transmitted by the Foreign Master
ForeignMasterAnnounceMessages	ForeignMasterAnnounceMessages is the amount of Announce Messages received from that particular Foreign Master within the time period determined by the ForeignMasterTimeWindow
MostRecentAnnounceMessage	MostRecentAnnounceMessage is an optional data set member that contains the latest Announce Message's information that updated this Foreign Master entry's values

New Foreign Master Clock Entries

New Foreign Masters are judged acceptable for entry into the ForeignMasterList based on the condition of ForeignMasterThreshold being activated. ForeignMasterThreshold is activated when two Announce Messages are received in the time period determined by the ForeignMasterTimeWindow. ForeignMasterTimeWindow is defined as four of the data set member AnnounceInterval.

Note: ForeignMasterList optional feature can be disabled by setting ForeignMasterThreshold to zero

ForeignMasterList PTP PortStates

In default PTP the Disabled, Faulty, Listening, Pre-Master and Uncalibrated PortStates are turned on. However a PTP Profile may turn them off. If the following variables are turned off than the associated PortState cannot be used.

Variable:	Description:
PF	PortState Faulty cannot be used
PD	PortState Disabled cannot be used
PL	PortState Listening cannot be used
PU	PortState Uncalibrated cannot be used
PP	PortState Pre-Master cannot be used

PTP Events

PTP Clocks are affected by PTP Events that will start a change in their state machine. PTP Events can affect one or more PTP Ports. The next table describes each PTP Event:

PTP Event:	Description:
Powerup	When the Clock is turned on or reset the Powerup PTP Event is started
Initialize	The Initialize PTP Event is started when the InstanceEnable data set member goes from False to True. The Initialize PTP Event is also started when the data set member InstanceType is modified but only if the Management Write of the data set member is allowed. The InstanceEnable data set member denotes if the Clock is allowed to run PTP
Designated_Enabled	The Designated_Enabled PTP Event is started when the PortEnable data set member goes from False to True. When the PortEnable data set member is True the Port in question is now enabled for PTP
Designated_Disabled	The Designated_Disabled PTP Event is started when the PortEnable data set member goes from True to False. When the PortEnable data set member is False the Port in question is now disabled for PTP
Fault_Cleared	The Fault_Cleared PTP Event is started when a PTP Port is no longer faulted or the PTP Port is now operating correctly
Fault_Detected	The Fault_Detected PTP Event is started when the PTP Port is faulted or is not operating correctly
Initialization_Complete	The Initialization_Complete PTP Event is started when the Initialize PTP Event has finished
State_Decision_Event	The State_Decision_Event PTP Event is started when an Announce Message is received or it activated based on the AnnounceInterval. This PTP Event is used to decide which PTP Clock is Master or GrandMaster Clock. This PTP Event is also used to start the process to decide if each PTP Port needs to change PortState as determined by the BMCA. Ports in PortStates Disabled, Faulty or Initializing shall not compute the BMCA and change their PortState
Recommended_State	The Recommended_State PTP Event is started when the State_Decision_Event PTP Event is completed

Qualification _Timeout _Expires	The Qualification_Timeout_Expires PTP Event is started when the timer qualificationTimeoutInterval in done timing. The timer qualificationTimeoutInterval is the length of time the Clock can remain in the Pre-Master State
Announce _Receipt _Timeout _Expires	The AnnounceReceiptTimeout_Expires PTP Event is started when the timer AnnounceReceiptTimeoutInterval is done timing. The timer AnnounceReceiptTimeoutInterval for a PTP Port will start or restart when: 1. At the timeout of the current AnnounceReceiptTimeoutInterval 2. A PTP Port is in the Uncalibrated or Slave PortStates and it receives an Announce Message from a Master Clock 3. A PTP Port moves to the Slave, Passive, Listening, or Uncalibrated PortStates 4. A PTP Port is in the Passive PortState and it receives an Announce Message from the same Clock that prompted the PTP Port to be in the Passive PortState The timer AnnounceReceiptTimeoutInterval for a PTP Port will be stopped and cannot be restarted when the PTP Port enters the Initializing, Pre-Master, Master, Disabled or Faulty PortStates
Synchronization _Fault	The Synchronization_Fault PTP Event is started when a PTP Port is in the Slave PortState and determines that the PTP Port needs to return to the Uncalibrated PortState and restart that part of the process
Master _Clock _Selected	The Master_Clock_Selected PTP Event is started when a PTP Port is in the Uncalibrated PortState and determines that the PTP Port has met all the conditions to allow for Synchronization while in the Slave PortState

PTP Events For Boundary Clocks

PTP Events affecting Boundary Clock Ports and a change in their state machines are specified below:

PTP Event:	PTP Ports Affected:
Powerup	All Boundary Clock PTP Ports
Initialize	All Boundary Clock PTP Ports
Designated_Enabled	A specific Boundary Clock PTP Port
Designated_Disabled	A specific Boundary Clock PTP Port
Fault_Cleared	All Boundary Clock PTP Ports impacted by the fault
Fault_Detected	All Boundary Clock PTP Ports impacted by the fault
Initialization_Complete	All Boundary Clock PTP Ports
State_Decision_Event	All Boundary Clock PTP Ports
Recommended _State	All Boundary Clock PTP Ports
Qualification_Timeout _Expires	A specific Boundary Clock PTP Port
AnnounceReceiptTimeoutExpires	A specific Boundary Clock PTP Port
Synchronization_Fault	A specific Boundary Clock PTP Port
Master_Clock_Selected	A specific Boundary Clock PTP Port

PTP Process

The PTP Process occurs in two steps:
1. Creating the Master-Slave Hierarchy
2. Synchronization of the PTP Clocks

For Step Two this book covers three different Path Delay Mechanisms used in the Synchronization process:
1. Request-Response Mechanism with a NonTransparent Clock
2. Request-Response Mechanism with an End-to-End Transparent Clock
3. Peer Delay Mechanism with Peer-to-Peer Transparent Clocks

Step One: Creating the Master-Slave Hierarchy

As mentioned earlier all Ordinary Clocks are divided into two groups: Master Clocks and Slave Clocks(Boundary Clocks have PTP Ports assigned to both PortStates though). The first step of the PTP protocol is to elect a GrandMaster Clock(or Preferred GrandMaster Clock) and to create a Master-Slave Hierarchy of all participating Clocks. This is done using the Best Master Clock Algorithm(BMCA or BMC). The GrandMaster Clock is the principal distributor of Time Signals within an Ethernet Network or PTP Domain. All Clocks within the same Domain can trace their time back to the sole GrandMaster Clock.

The PTP Clocks will arrange themselves into a Master-Slave Hierarchy with the GrandMaster Clock with the best quality and top priority at the top. If there are any Boundary Clocks are placed in the middle. Slave Clocks are found at the bottom of the Hierarchy.

BMCA: The Best Master Clock Algorithm(BMCA) will determine what Clocks will be GrandMaster Clocks and what Clocks will be designated Slave Clocks

Boundary Clocks as mentioned above act as both a Master Clock and a Slave Clock. They take the best Time Signal available to them on a Slave Port and distribute that Time Signal to downstream Slave Clocks using a Master Port.

Transparent Clocks and NonTransparent Clocks are unnoticed by the Master-Slave Hierarchy and will simply forward PTP Messages. They will not Synchronize to the PTP Time Signal of a GrandMaster Clock.

Master Clock PTP Ports including Boundary Clock Master PTP Ports will transmit out Announce Messages. These Announce Messages will include the data set member values(Priority1, ClockClass, ClockAccuracy, OffsetScaledLogVariance, Priority2, ClockIdentity, etc.) of the PTP Clock that transmitted them. The Announce Messages is received by each Ordinary Clock and Boundary Clock on the PTP Domain. The Data Set of each received Announce Message is assessed by each PTP Clock and using the BMCA it will determine the best Master Clock to Synchronize to. As well each Ordinary and Boundary Clock PTP Port will auto sort themselves into three different PTP PortStates: Master, Slave or Passive. The next diagram is a Typical Ethernet Network:

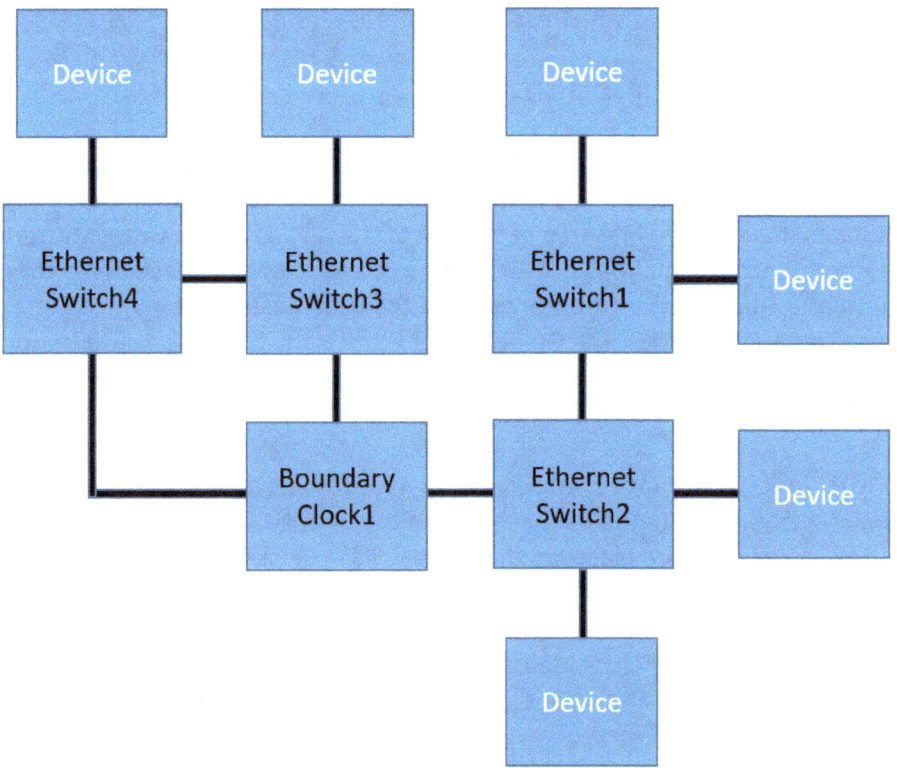

The next diagram is how PTP sees the same Typical Ethernet Network:

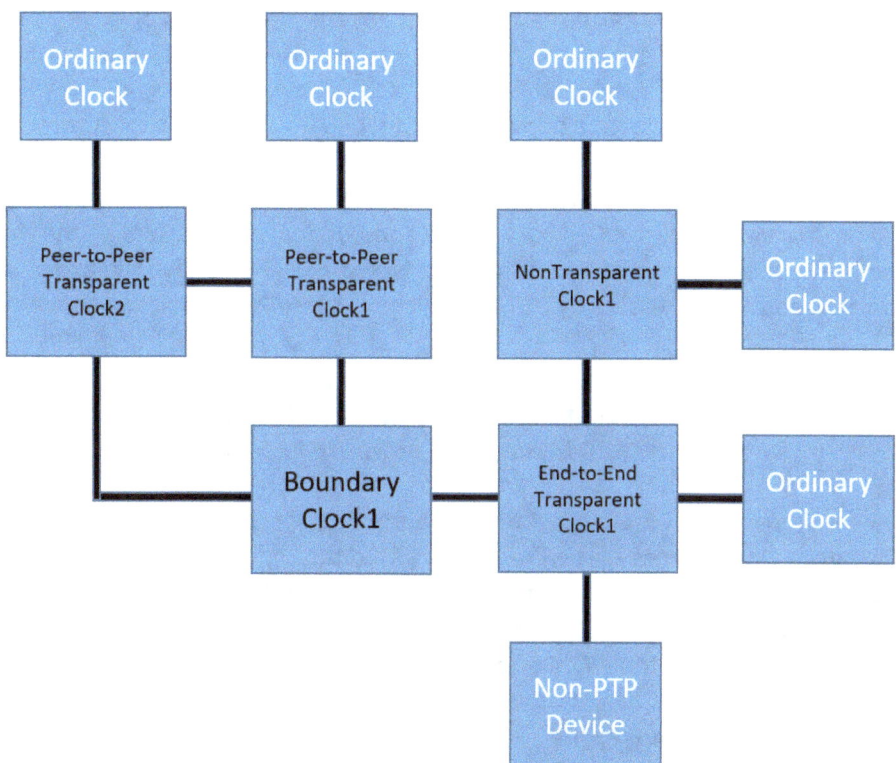

As mentioned Ethernet Switch1 disappears entirely from PTP's perspective. The Non-PTP Ethernet Switch1 will Multicast PTP Packets to all its active Ports, essentially acting as if it's not there from PTP's perspective. We will label it NonTransparent Clock1. However Ethernet Switch2 does not disappear-PTP will see it as a Transparent Clock. In this case it is an End-to-End Transparent Clock. We will re-label it End-to-End Transparent Clock1.

Boundary Clocks and Transparent Clocks will nearly always have more than one PTP capable Port. Ordinary Clocks will usually have just one PTP capable Port(unless Parallel Redundancy Protocol is employed for the Network in question).

Note: PTP allows for the use of Multicast or Unicast. Some PTP Profiles will restrict the Clock configuration to one or the other

Now we will label all participating Ports either Passive, Slave, Master, Disabled or we won't label them at all if they belong to a Transparent Clock or NonTransparent Clock.

PTP employs a variation of Spanning Tree Protocol(STP) and it uses this protocol to cut back unnecessary Network Links that it will not need to use. The PTP Ports of Ordinary Clocks and Boundary Clocks will be assigned to the Master, Slave or Passive PortStates. Ordinary Clocks and Boundary Clocks serving the same Network segment with more than one Network Link will have the extra Ports marked as unnecessary by PTP and will have these Ports assigned to the Passive PortState.

In this example one PTP Port of the Boundary Clock will be assigned to the Master PortState to serve PTP Messages to downstream Slave Clocks.

However Transparent Clocks operate differently. PTP Messages received on a Transparent Clock ingress Port will be transmitted through all other PTP enabled Ports(dependent on the rules of the Network Transport Protocol). As well in our example below the Network Professional has also wisely disabled PTP for the Port connected to the Non-PTP Device.

The next diagram are the results of the above labeling, trimming and setting changes to our Typical Ethernet Network:

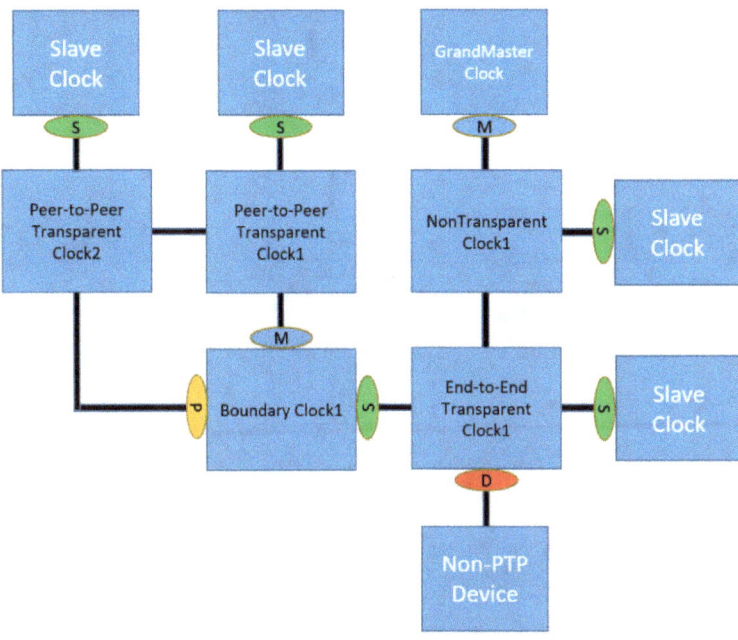

Take note that Boundary Clock1 puts its PTP Port connected to Peer-to-Peer Transparent Clock2 into the Passive PortState. Its PTP Port connected to End-to-End Transparent Clock1 is put into the Slave PortState as it will receive Sync Messages from the GrandMaster Clock. Its last PTP Port connected to Peer-to-Peer Transparent Clock1 is assigned to the Master PortState. This last PTP Port will distribute Sync Messages downstream to the rest of the Network on behalf of the GrandMaster Clock.

However what if there are two actively operating Grandmaster Clocks separated by a Boundary Clock? Having two GrandMaster Clocks is entirely possible especially if they are separated by at least one Boundary Clock(or if the PTP Profile allows for it). PTP will further prune the PTP Topology. We will make a Slave Clock a GrandMaster Clock instead.

The next diagram is the results of the introduction of a new active GrandMaster Clock to our Typical Ethernet Network:

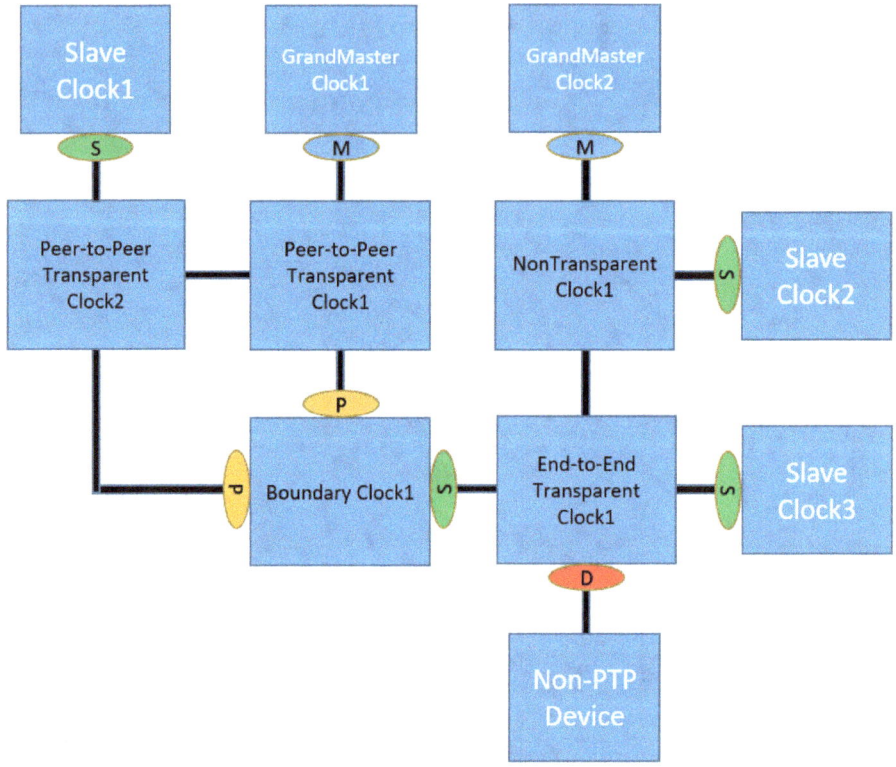

As you can see from the resulting PTP Topology the PTP capable Network is now divided up between GrandMaster Clock1 and GrandMaster Clock2. The Network Professional can have two separate PTP Domains. Because of this Boundary Clock1 will select the best GrandMaster Clock to Synchronize to and put its other PTP Ports receiving PTP Messages from a separate PTP Domain into the Passive PortState.

If GrandMaster Clock1 and GrandMaster Clock2 were on the same Network and were not separated by at least one Boundary Clock the one with the least priority/worst quality will realize this, stop transmitting Announce Messages and put its PTP Port(s) into the Passive PortState. It would in affect become a Backup GrandMaster Clock(or Alternate GrandMaster Clock). The Backup GrandMaster Clock will keep running the BMCA and if it detects it has become the best Master Clock on the Network it will start transmitting PTP Messages associated with the Synchronization process.

Some PTP Profiles or options allow for multiple active GrandMaster Clocks on the same PTP Domain with the Slave Clocks selecting the best GrandMaster Time Signal.

Received Announce Message Algorithm

Announce Messages are critical to how PTP forms the Master-Slave Hierarchy on an Ethernet Network. How a received Announce Message is processed by a PTP Port is outlined below.

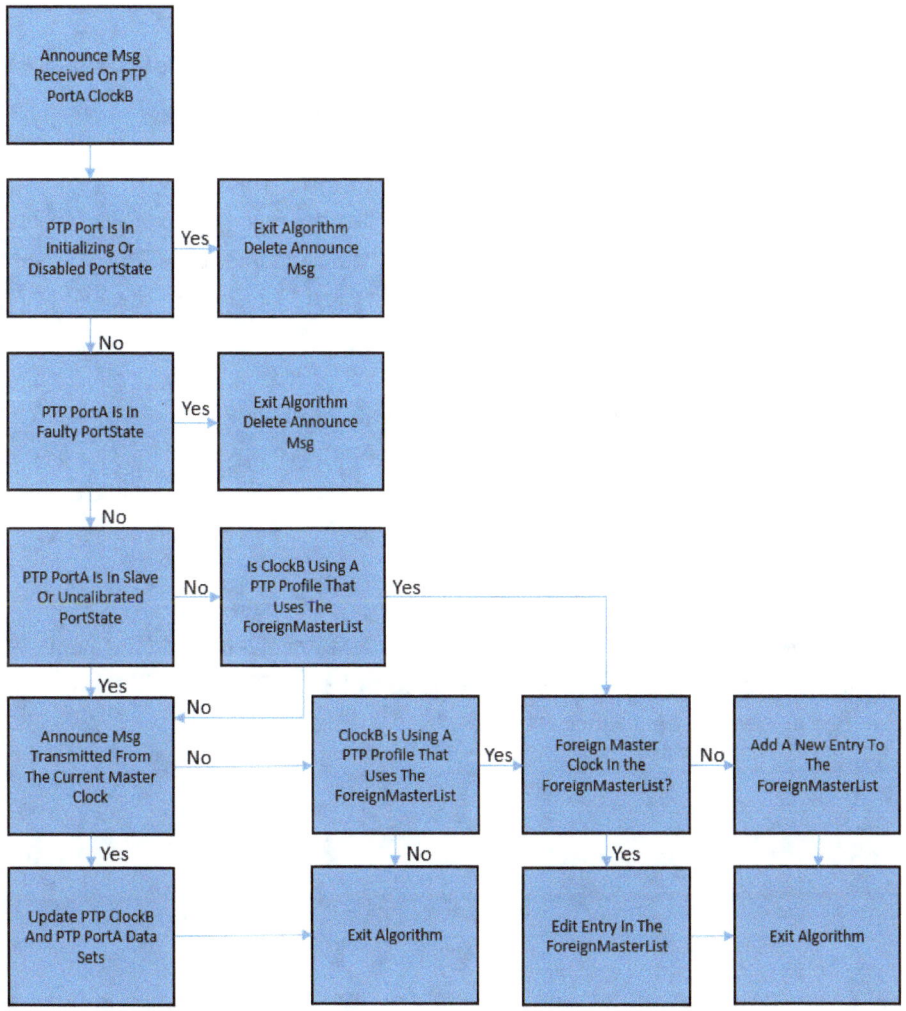

A State_Decision_Event and the BMCA may be triggered to start by either the receiving of an Announce Message or it may be based on the AnnounceInterval. Some PTP Profile or manufacturers may only start a State_Decision_Event under different cases not covered by this guide.

If however no State_Decision_Event is started the Announce Message is stored and processed with all other received Announce Messages the next time the State_Decision_Event is activated.

State_Decision_Event

When an Announce Message is received by an Ordinary Clock or Boundary Clock the State_Decision_Event may be started. This PTP Event is what starts the BMCA and uses the Data Sets in received Announce Messages to decide which Master Clock or Master PTP Port to Synchronize to. After the State_Decision_Event occurs, the PTP Clock will decide which PortState each of its PTP Ports should be changed to. This PTP Event occurs in each PTP Clock separately and each separate PTP Clock decides which PTP Clock in the PTP Domain is the Master or GrandMaster Clock.

The State_Decision_Event will occur at the same time on all PTP Ports of a PTP Clock. The State_Decision_Event will occur at minimum once per AnnounceInterval. If all the PTP Ports of a PTP Clock are in the Initializing PortState the State_Decision_Event will not occur.

Each PTP Clock that starts the State_Decision_Event will have each of its PTP Ports each separately decide on their own their Best Received Clock Data Set. Once all PTP Ports on a PTP Clock have decided this the PTP Clock will then decide on the Overall Best Clock Data Set.

How the default State_Decision_Event operates and how the default BMCA runs at the highest level is outlined below.

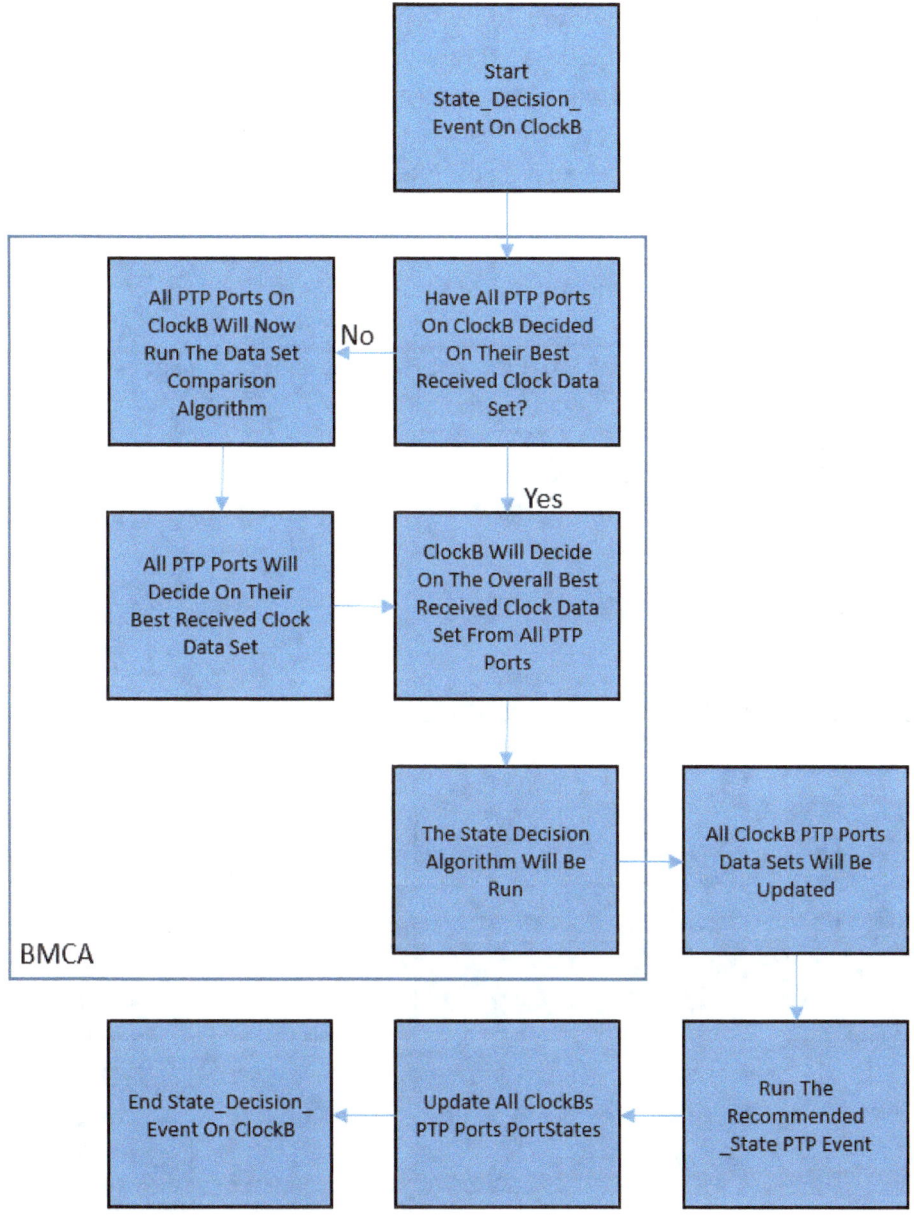

Data Set Comparison Algorithm

The Data Set Comparison Algorithm is used by each PTP Port on a PTP Clock to compare every Received Clock Data Set received on that PTP Port. The Received Clock Data Sets are transmitted using Announce Messages from the other PTP Clocks on the PTP Domain. Each PTP Port on a PTP Clock decides which of the received Data Sets it has received is its best Received Clock Data Set.

As the reader knows each PTP Clock has a Data Set and the Data Sets of other Clocks are delivered to it using Announce Messages. Each PTP Port separately runs the Data Set Comparison Algorithm that compares all received Clock Data Sets and makes its decision on what its Best Received Clock Data Set is. This algorithm is outlined below.

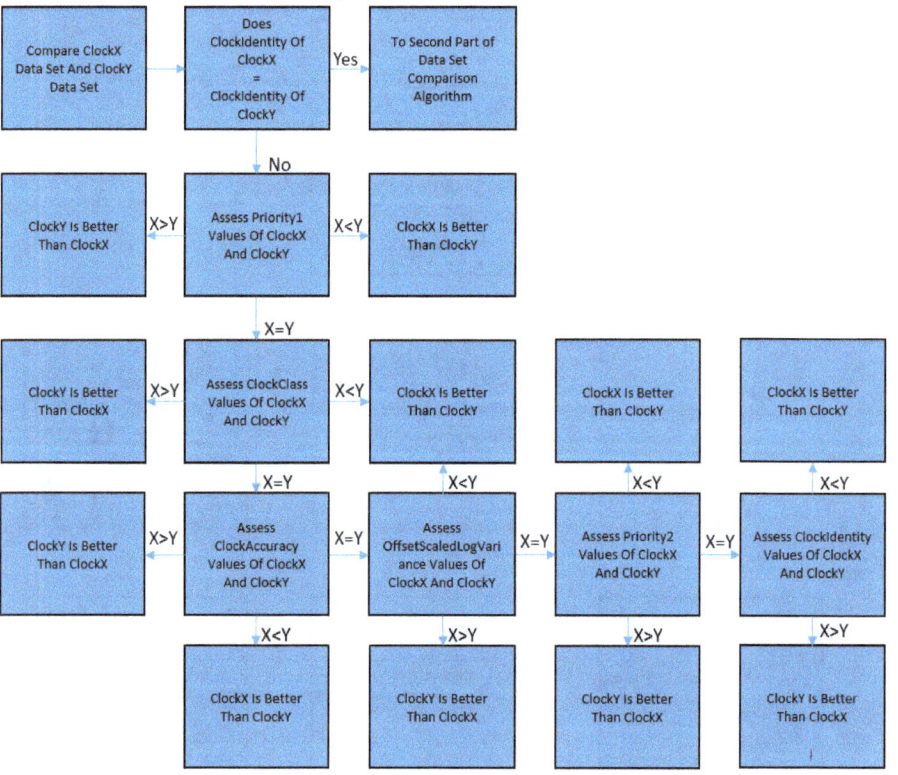

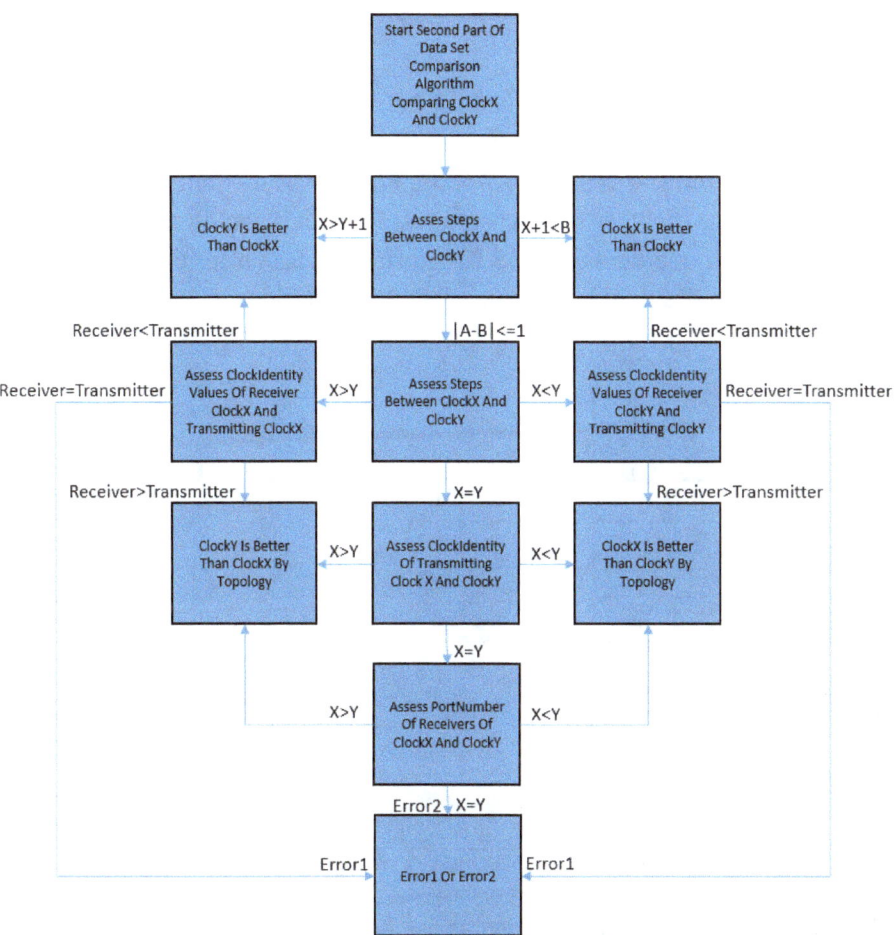

Error1 signifies that the Announce Message was received by the same PTP Clock that transmitted it and the Announce Message is not to be considered by the State Decision Algorithm. Error2 signifies that the Announce Messages are copies from the same GrandMaster or Master Clock or they are from the same GrandMaster or Master Clock just separated by time. Error1 and Error2 are not used in the State Decision Algorithm and are instead used for error logging and discovery.

State Decision Algorithm

After each PTP Port has decided on its Best Received Clock Data Set and the PTP Clock has decided on its Overall Best Received Clock Data Set the State Decision Algorithm will be run. The second part of the BMCA is as mentioned the State Decision Algorithm. The PTP Clock will run the State Decision Algorithm for each of its PTP Ports and update each of its PTP Ports Data Sets after the State Decision Algorithm has finished. How each PTP Port decides its PortState is outlined below.

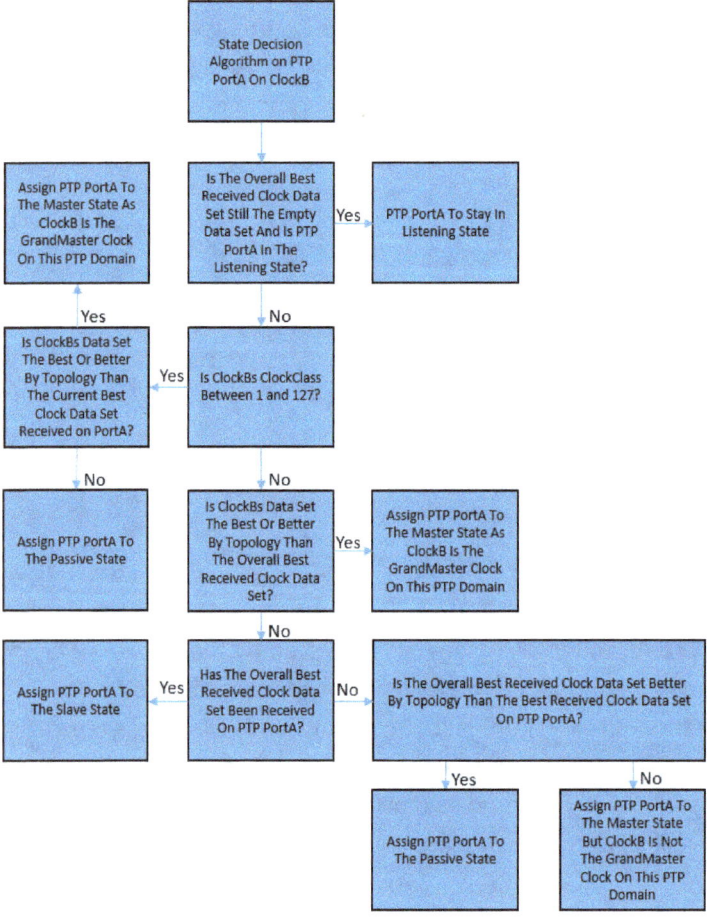

Note: Erbest and Ebest could be terms encountered by the reader when reading PTP related literature. Erbest is the Best Received Clock Data Set received on that specific PTP Port. Ebest is the Best Overall Clock Data Set received by that PTP Clock on all its PTP Ports and its own Data Set

Step Two: Synchronization Delay Request-Response Mechanism with a NonTransparent Clock

Once the Master-Slave Hierarchy has been created Step Two-Synchronization will begin. PTP needs to precisely measure the Total Transit Time between the Master Clock and the Slave Clock. There are three ways of performing this measurement: Peer Delay Mechanism(Peer-to-Peer), Request-Response Mechanism with NonTransparent Clocks and Request-Response Mechanism with Transparent Clocks.

We will pull apart our above Typical Ethernet Network to illustrate the Synchronization between GrandMaster Clock2 and Slave Clock2 using the Delay Request-Response Mechanism with NonTransparent Clock1 by measuring the End-to-End Delay(The delay between GrandMaster and Slave).

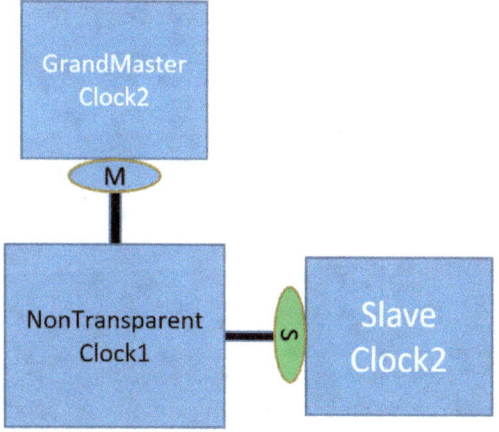

NonTransparent Clock1 is ignored due to it being an Ethernet Switch that is not equipped to separately handle PTP Messages from normal Network Traffic. From PTP's perspective, it does not exist.

GrandMaster Clock2 will transmit a Sync Message to Slave Clock2.

t1: t1 is defined as the time of transmission of the Sync Message by GrandMaster Clock2

t2: t2 is defined as the time that the Sync Message is received by Slave Clock2

Offset: The constant time difference between the Master and Slave Clock
Offset = [Time of Slave Clock2] – [Time of GrandMaster Clock2]

MeanPathDelay: The time it takes for the Sync Message to travel between the Master and Slave. Also known as Propagation Delay or Path Delay

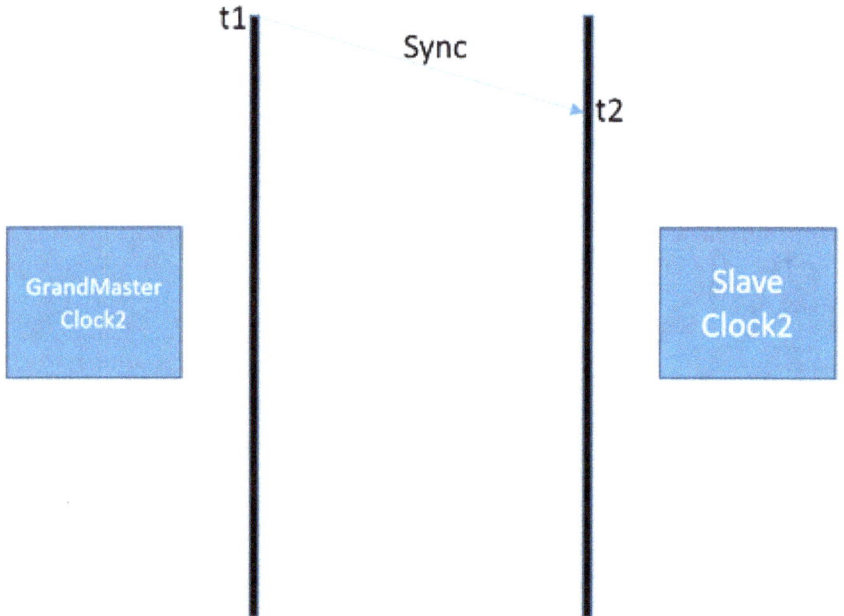

Slave Clock2 will receive the Sync Message at t2 and records the time done so as Timestamp t2. If the Sync Message is a One-Step Sync Message the Timestamp t1 will be contained in the Sync Message. The CorrectedSyncCorrectionField is calculated from the values stored in the Sync's CorrectionField. The calculation for the Offset of an End-To-End One-Step Sync Message is:

Offset = t2 - t1 - MeanPathDelay

Some of the variables of this formula have official IEEE 1588 variable names:

Offset: OffsetFromMaster
t2: SyncEventIngressTimestamp
t1: OriginTimestamp

Otherwise if the Sync Message is a Two-Step Sync Message it will be followed by an associated Follow_Up Message. The Follow_Up Message will contain the Timestamp of when the Sync Message was transmitted originally called here Timestamp t1.

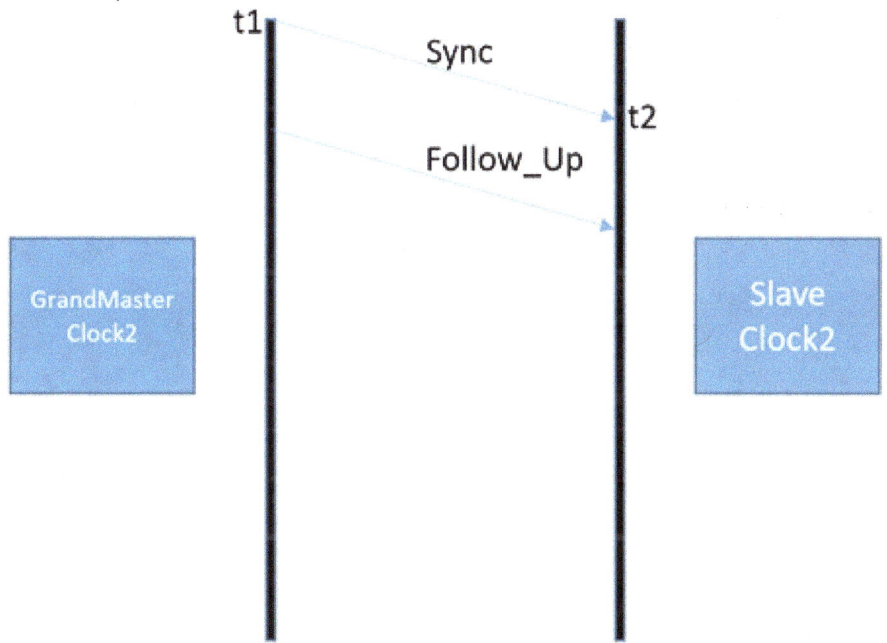

For an End-To-End Two-Step Sync Message Slave Clock2 now has the Timestamp of when the Sync Message was transmitted(t1) from the associated Follow_Up Message. It has the Timestamp of when it received the Sync Message(t2). The calculation for the Offset of an End-To-End Two-Step Sync Message is:

Offset = t2 - t1 - MeanPathDelay

Some of the variables of this formula have official IEEE 1588 variable names:

Offset: OffsetFromMaster
t2: SyncEventIngressTimestamp
t1: PreciseOriginTimestamp

Note: In this example NonTransparentClock1 is not equipped to update the Sync or associated Follow_Up Message's CorrectionField and as such the CorrectionField is not included into any formulas

You would think that having Timestamps t1 and t2 would be enough for Slave Clock2 to accurately Synchronize but it is not! We still need to somehow calculate the MeanPathDelay otherwise known as the Transit Time or Mean Transit Time.

A new process called the Request-Response Mechanism is initiated by Slave Clock2 to calculate the MeanPathDelay from itself(Slave Clock2) back to GrandMaster Clock2. Slave Clock2 will transmit a Delay_Req Message to GrandMaster Clock2 to begin this next step.

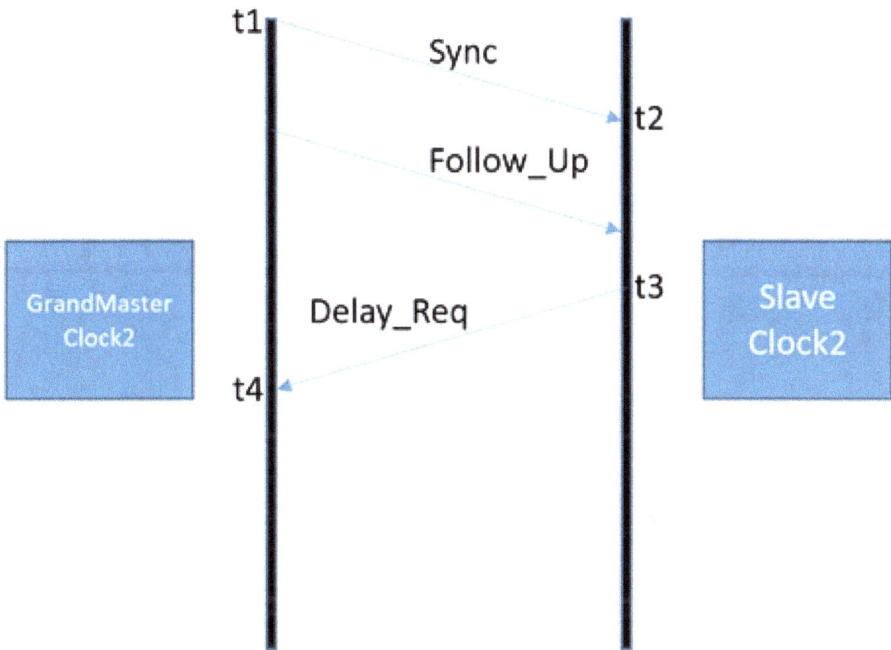

The Timestamp of when the Delay_Req Message was transmitted by Slave Clock2 we will designate t3. The Timestamp of when GrandMaster Clock2 receives the Delay_Req Message we will specify as t4.

GrandMaster Clock2 will now transmit a Delay_Resp Message to Slave Clock2 containing the Timestamp of t4.

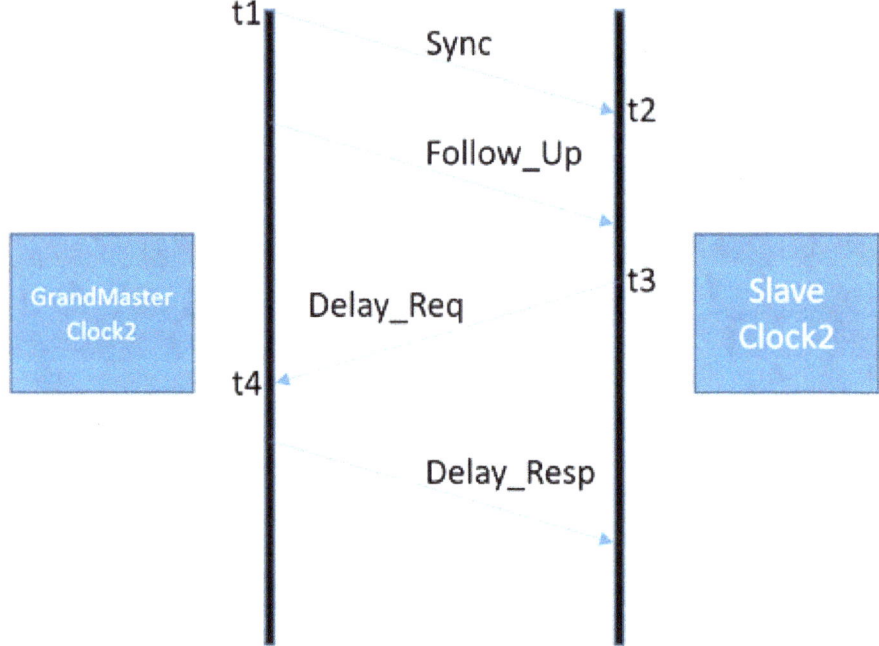

Slave Clock2 will receive the Delay_Resp Message and now has Timestamp t4. We can create a new simple formula resulting from this process:

One-Step and Two-Step Sync Message MeanPathDelay formula:

MeanPathDelay = [(t2 - t3) + (t4 - t1)]/2

The MeanPathDelay value shall be stored in the MeanDelay data set member of the Current Data Set of Slave Clock2.

Now that Slave Clock2 has the MeanPathDelay the Offset can be calculated and Slave Clock2 can accurately Synchronize itself to GrandMaster Clock2 from the below formula:

Offset = t2 - t1 - MeanPathDelay

So to review the Sync, Delay_Req, Delay_Resp and optional Follow_Up Messages give Slave Clock2 the timestamps values necessary to calculate the MeanPathDelay and Offset between GrandMaster Clock2 and Slave Clock2.

Slave Clock2 will use a combination of the Offset, MeanPathDelay, Network Propagation Delays, Slave Clock2's internal crystal temperature and the crystals aging impact to update its internal time to agree with GrandMaster Clock2.

The above example of the Synchronization Delay Request-Response Mechanism is very simple and does not include any Transparent Clocks. NonTransparent Clock1 is ignored by the PTP protocol as if it doesn't exist.

Sync Messages are transmitted on average about every 1-2(dec) seconds from the GrandMaster Clock. The Delay_Req Message is first transmitted when it is first needed and subsequently is transmitted at a period defined by either the Network Professional, the PTP Profile or after a Sync Message is received. A common practice is to transmit the Delay_Req Message every minute.

Step Two: Synchronization Delay Request-Response Mechanism with an End-to-End Transparent Clock

Synchronization using the Delay Request-Response Mechanism with an End-to-End Transparent Clock included is exactly the same as with just the NonTransparent Clock with the one exception. The End-to-End Transparent Clock will update the Sync(or optional Follow_Up) and Delay_Req Messages CorrectionField with the total time(Residence Time) the Sync Message spent being processed by that End-to-End Transparent Clock.

We will pull apart our above Typical Ethernet Network to illustrate the Synchronization between GrandMaster Clock2 and Slave Clock3 using the Delay Request-Response Mechanism with End-to-End Transparent Clock1 by measuring the End-to-End Delay(The delay between the GrandMaster Clock and Slave Clock).

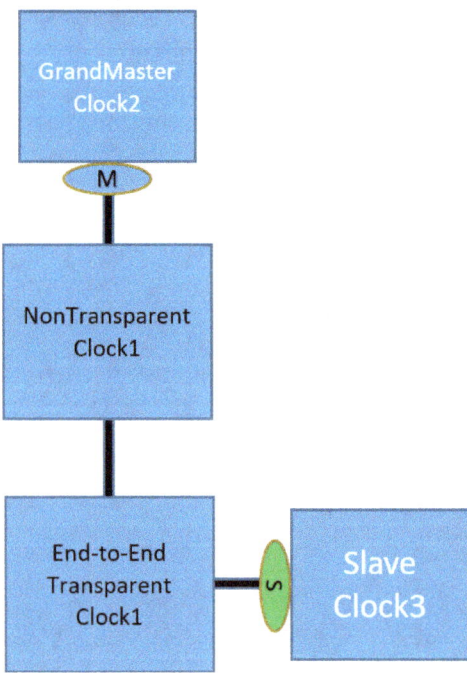

End-to-End Transparent Clock1 is important due to it being an Ethernet Switch that is equipped to separately handle PTP Messages from normal Network Traffic. NonTransparent Clock1 is still almost completely ignored by PTP.

GrandMaster Clock2 will transmit a Sync Message to Slave Clock3.

t1: t1 is defined as the time of transmission of the Sync Message by GrandMaster Clock2

t2: t2 is defined as the time that the Sync Message is received by Slave Clock3

Offset = [Time of Slave Clock3] – [Time of GrandMaster Clock2]

MeanPathDelay: The time it takes for the Sync Message to travel between the Master Clock and Slave Clock. Also known as Propagation Delay or Path Delay

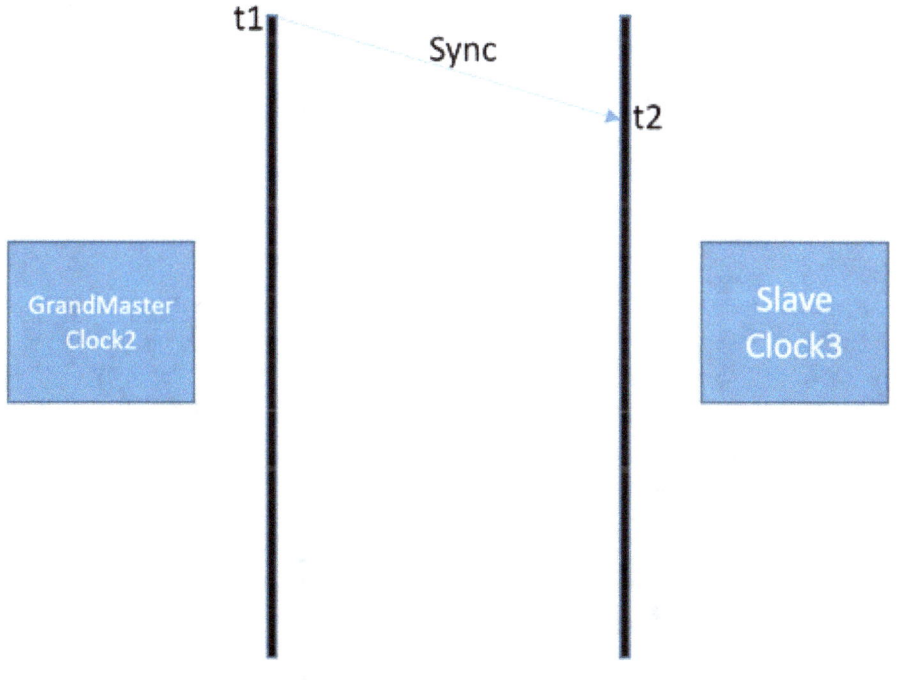

Slave Clock3 will receive the Sync Message at t2 and records the time done so as Timestamp t2. If the Sync Message is a One-Step Sync Message the Timestamp t1 will be contained in the Sync Message. The CorrectedSyncCorrectionField is calculated from the values stored in the Sync's CorrectionField. The calculation for the Offset of an End-To-End One-Step Sync Message is:

Offset = t2 - t1 - MeanPathDelay - CorrectedSyncCorrectionField

Some of the variables of this formula have official IEEE 1588 variable names:
Offset: OffsetFromMaster
t2: SyncEventIngressTimestamp
t1: OriginTimestamp

Otherwise if the Sync Message is a Two-Step Sync Message it will be followed by an associated Follow_Up Message. The Follow_Up Message will contain the Timestamp of when the Sync Message was transmitted originally called here Timestamp t1 and may contain additional Sync Message corrections.

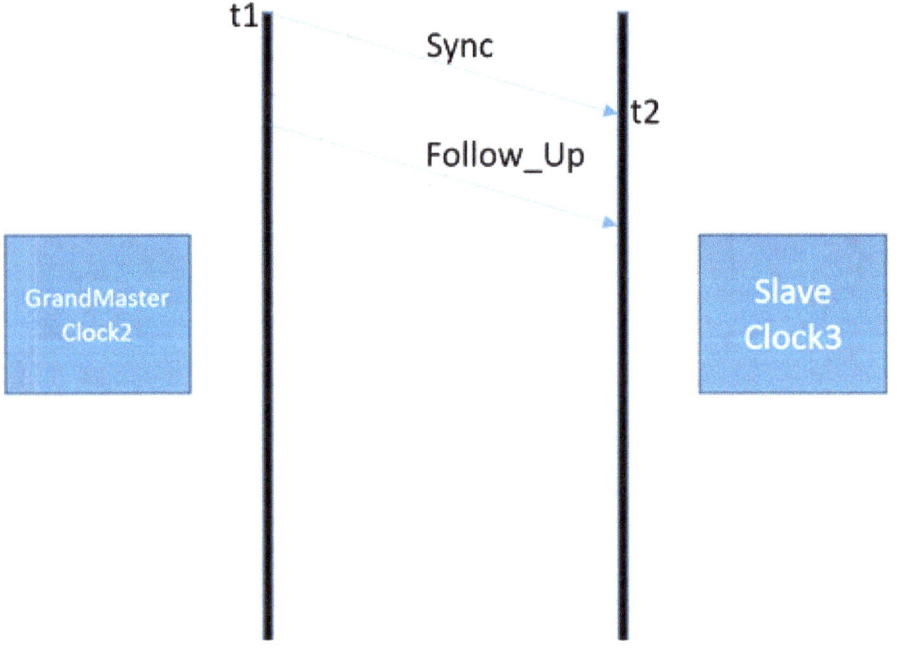

For an End-To-End Two-Step Sync Message Slave Clock3 now has the Timestamp of when the Sync Message was transmitted(t1) from the associated Follow_Up Message. It has the Timestamp of when it received the Sync Message(t2) as well as the CorrectionFields of the Sync Message and associated Follow_Up Message. The calculation for the Offset of an End-To-End Two-Step Sync Message is:

Offset = t2 - t1 - MeanPathDelay - CorrectedSyncCorrectionField - Follow_UpCorrectionField

Some of the variables of this formula have official IEEE 1588 variable names:

Offset: OffsetFromMaster
t2: SyncEventIngressTimestamp
t1: PreciseOriginTimestamp

Note: The CorrectedSyncCorrectionField is calculated from the values stored in the Sync's CorrectionField

In this example TransparentClock1 will update the Sync or the associated Follow_Up Message's CorrectionFields therefore the CorrectionFields are important to constructing the Offset formulas

You would think that having Timestamps t1 and t2 as well as the Sync CorrectionField and if required the Follow_Up CorrectionField would be enough for Slave Clock3 to accurately Synchronize but it is not!

We still need to somehow calculate the MeanPathDelay otherwise known as the Transit Time or Mean Transit Time.

A new process called the Request-Response Mechanism is initiated by Slave Clock3 to calculate the MeanPathDelay from itself(Slave Clock3) back to GrandMaster Clock2. Slave Clock3 will transmit a Delay_Req Message to GrandMaster Clock2 to begin.

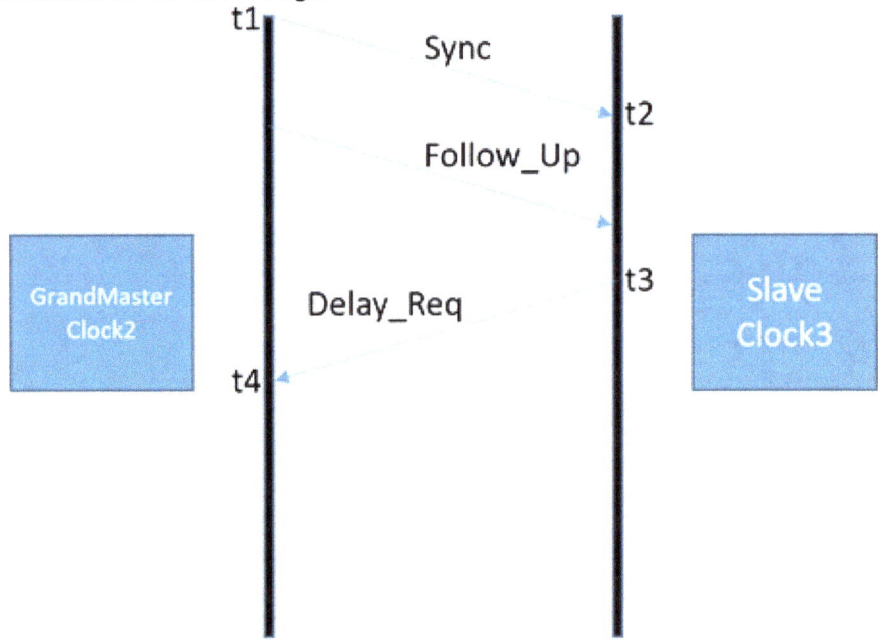

The Timestamp of when the Delay_Req Message was transmitted by Slave Clock3 we will designate t3. The Timestamp of when GrandMaster Clock2 receives the Delay_Req Message we will specify as t4.

GrandMaster Clock2 will now transmit a Delay_Resp Message to Slave Clock3 containing the Timestamp of t4.

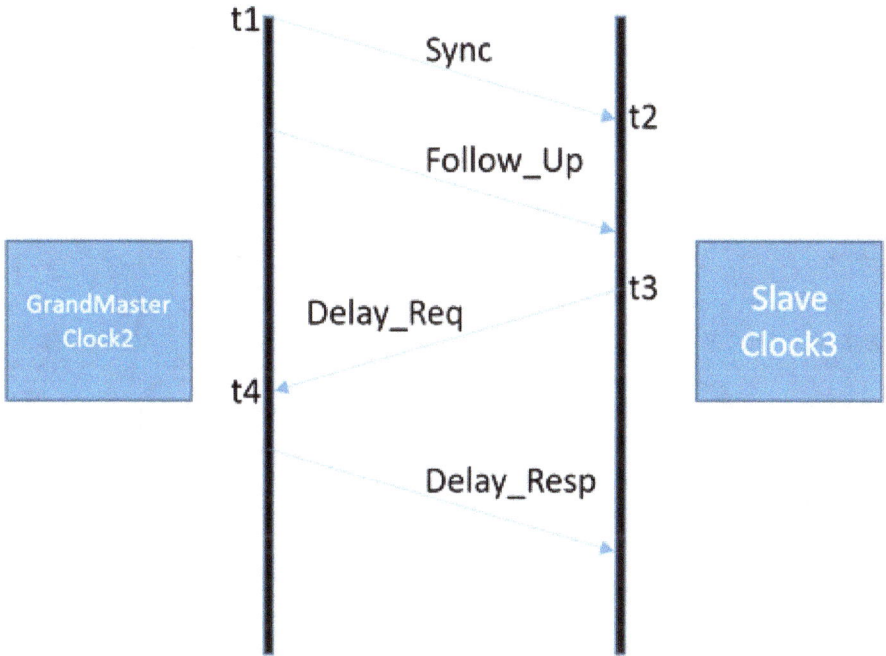

Slave Clock3 will receive the Delay_Resp Message and now has Timestamps t3 and t4. We can create a new simple formula resulting from this process:

One-Step Sync Message formula:

MeanPathDelay = [(t2 - t3) + (t4 - t1) - CorrectedSyncCorrectionField - Delay_RespCorrectionField]/2

Two-Step Sync Message formula:

MeanPathDelay = [(t2 - t3) + (t4 - t1) - CorrectedSyncCorrectionField - Follow_UpCorrectionField - Delay_RespCorrectionField]/2

The MeanPathDelay value shall be stored in the current Slave Clock3 Data Set.

Now that Slave Clock3 has the MeanPathDelay the Offset can be calculated from the One-Step Offset formula or Two-Step Offset formula.

End-To-End One-Step Sync Message Offset formula:

Offset = t2 - t1 - MeanPathDelay - CorrectedSyncCorrectionField

End-To-End Two-Step Sync Message Offset formula:

Offset = t2 - t1 - MeanPathDelay - CorrectedSyncCorrectionField - Follow_UpCorrectionField

Now that Slave Clock3 has the Offset value calculated it can accurately Synchronize itself to GrandMaster Clock2.

So to review the Sync, Delay_Req, Delay_Resp and optional Follow_Up Messages give Slave Clock3 the Timestamps and correction values necessary to calculate the MeanPathDelay and Offset between GrandMaster Clock2 and Slave Clock3.

Slave Clock3 will use a combination of the Offset, MeanPathDelay, Network Propagation Delays, Slave Clock3's internal crystal temperature and the crystals aging impact to update its internal time to agree with GrandMaster Clock2.

The above example of the Synchronization Delay Request-Response includes only one Transparent Clock and the one NonTransparent Clock is again mostly ignored by the PTP protocol as if it does not exist.

Sync Messages are transmitted on average about every 1-2(dec) seconds from the GrandMaster. The Delay_Req Message is first transmitted when it is first needed and subsequently is transmitted at a period defined by either the Network Professional, the PTP Profile or after a Sync Message is received. A common practice is to transmit the Delay_Req Message every minute.

As a reminder when End-to-End Transparent Clock1 receives the Sync Message that was forwarded from NonTransparent Clock1 on behalf of GrandMaster Clock2 it will record its ResidenceTime that the Message spent being processed. And as the Sync Message is about to be transmitted to Slave Clock3 the CorrectionField will be updated with that ResidenceTime. Alternatively, if this process is Two-Step the optional Follow_Up Message comes after and it will have its CorrectionField updated with the Sync Messages total ResidenceTime in the End-to-End Transparent Clock1. Asymmetry Delays are also updated in the Message's CorrectionFields. The Delay_Req Message would also have its CorrectionField updated by End-to-End Transparent Clock1 in the same manner.

Delay Request-Response Mechanism Assumptions

Of course this Synchronization process using the Delay Request-Response Mechanism assumes a few things. The first being that the Transit Time is the same going from Slave Clock2 to GrandMaster Clock2 as going from GrandMaster Clock2 to Slave Clock2. Any difference in Transit Times will introduce an error in the Offset and thus also the Mean Transit Time as well. This type of error is called an Asymmetry Delay Error(DelayAsymmetry).

The second assumption is that the Offset value is constant since it is such a short period of time that these processes take place over.

The third assumption is that the Slave Clock and GrandMaster Clock can both correctly measure the time that they receive and transmit an Event PTP Message.

The fourth assumption is that Network Propagation Delays will remain constant.

The fifth assumption is that other local conditions such as Temperature will gradually fluctuate over time.

The sixth assumption is that when there is multiple paths between Master and Slave that the PTP Messages(especially Sync Messages) will transit the same path as from the Master to Slave as Slave to Master.

Step Two: Synchronization Peer Delay Mechanism with Peer-to-Peer Transparent Clocks

The alternative and almost always(not always though!) superior way of Synchronizing a Slave Clock is to use the Peer Delay Mechanism with Peer-to-Peer Transparent Clocks. Once the Master-Slave Hierarchy has been created step two-Synchronization will begin. We will once again make use of our above example of a Typical Ethernet Network except we will observe the Synchronization process between GrandMaster Clock1 and Slave Clock1 using Peer-to-Peer Transparent Clock1 and Peer-to-Peer Transparent Clock2 to explain Peer Delay Mechanism.

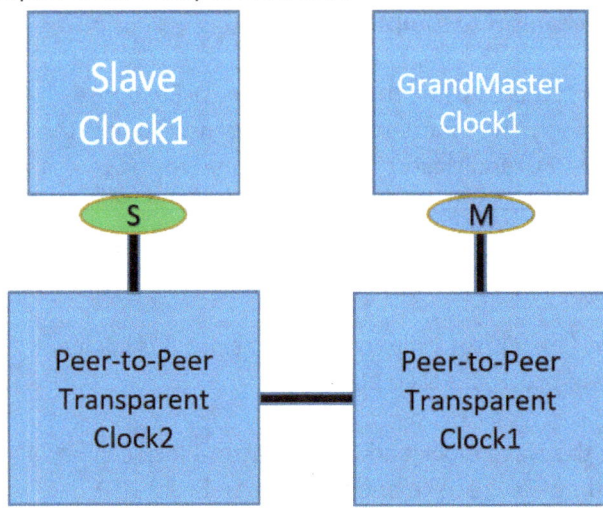

Each Network Link Delay between Peer-to-Peer Ports will be calculated using the Peer Delay Mechanism. In the direct above Typical Ethernet Network image the Path between GrandMaster Clock1 and Slave Clock1 includes the Links between:

1. GrandMaster Clock1 and Peer-to-Peer Transparent Clock1
2. Peer-to-Peer Transparent Clock1 to GrandMaster Clock1
3. Peer-to-Peer Transparent Clock1 to Peer-to-Peer Transparent Clock2
4. Peer-to-Peer Transparent Clock2 to Peer-to-Peer Transparent Clock1
5. Peer-to-Peer Transparent Clock2 to Slave Clock1
6. Slave Clock1 to Peer-to-Peer Transparent Clock1

Note: For Ordinary or Boundary Clocks the Peer Delay Mechanism operates separately from whether the PTP Port is configured to be in Master or Slave PortState

Each of the above Network Links will have its delay measured. This measured delay is called the MeanLinkDelay.

MeanLinkDelay: MeanLinkDelay(or Link Delay) is the Propagation Time between two Peer-to-Peer PTP Ports that share the same link

As you can see from the above list all Peer Delay Ports will measure their associated MeanLinkDelay independently. Each separate Network Link will be measured by both connected Ports therefore each separate Network Link will be measured twice. When the Network is changed in its configuration each affected Peer Delay PTP Port will recalculate its MeanLinkDelay. Thus the overall new Path Delay between Master Port and Slave Port will be automatically recalculated.

The steps to how each Peer-to-Peer PTP Port calculates its Link Delay is shown below.

Port1 is the Delay Requestor and will transmit a Pdelay_Req Message to Port2 the Delay Responder. The Timestamp of when the Pdelay_Req Message was transmitted by Port1 we will designate t1. The Timestamp of when Port2 receives the Pdelay_Req Message we will specify as t2.

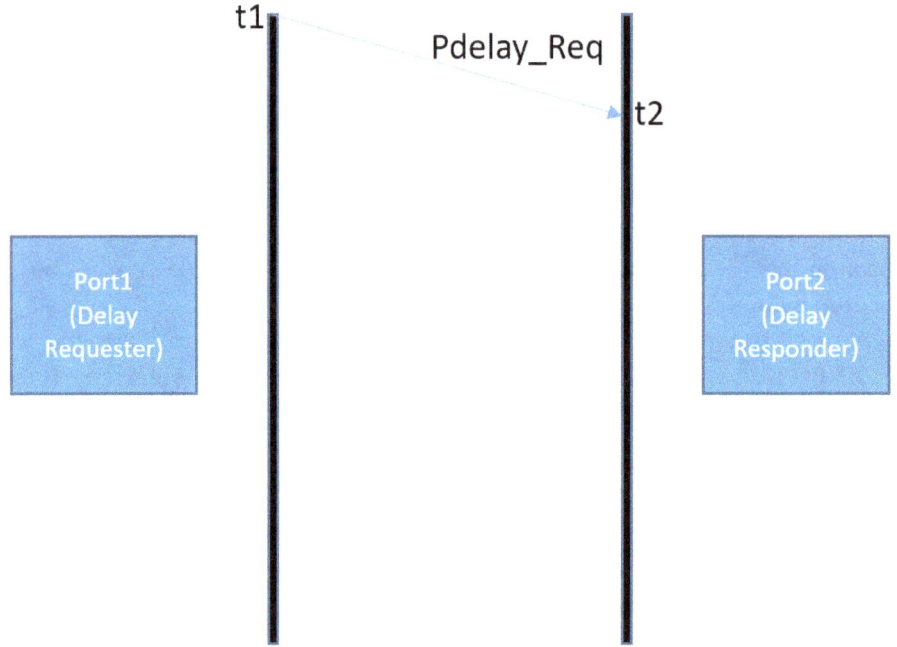

Port2 is the Delay Responder and will transmit a Pdelay_Resp Message to Port1 the Delay Requestor as soon as possible to reduce the Turnaround Time(t3-t2) and resulting inaccuracies. The Timestamp of when Port2 transmits the Pdelay_Resp Message we will specify as t3. The Pdelay_Resp Message will contain the information that contains Timestamps t2 and t3.

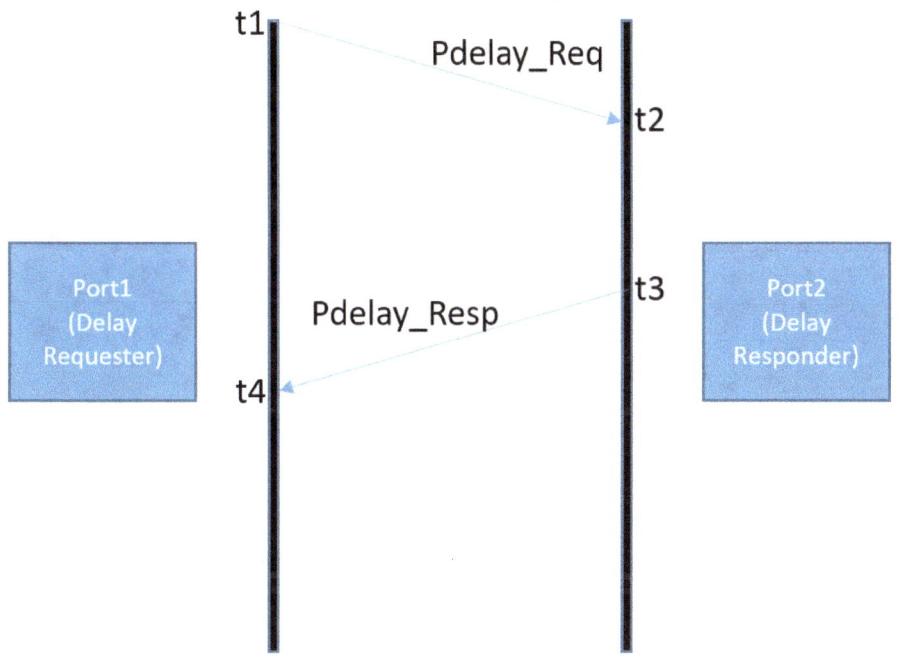

If Port2 is unable to support the insertion of the t3 value into the Pdelay_Resp Message as the Message is being transmitted, a Two-Step option may be employed. Where by a Pdelay_Resp_Follow_Up Message(containing the t3 Timestamp) is transmitted by Port2 after Pdelay_Resp has already been sent.

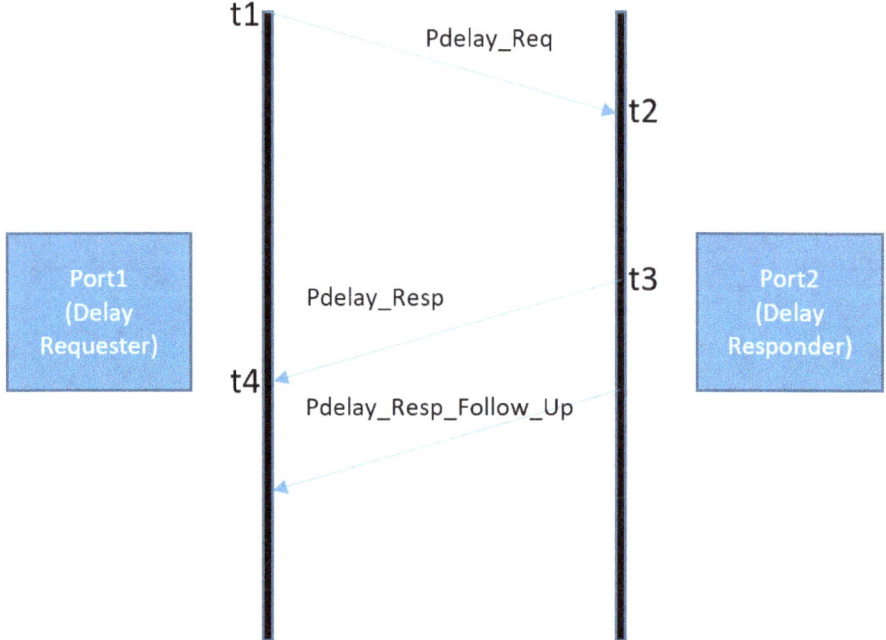

Port1 the Delay Requester will receive the Pdelay_Resp Message and generate Timestamp t4. Soon after if the Delay Responder Port2 was a Two-Step PTP Port Port1 will also have received the optional Pdelay_Resp_Follow_Up Message and now has Timestamps t1, t2, t3 and t4. We can proceed with solving for some of our variables.

A simple explanation for how to calculate the MeanLinkDelay is directly below.

$t2 - t1 = $ Offset $+$ MeanLinkDelay

$t4 - t3 = $ -Offset $+$ MeanLinkDelay

From the two equations we have created we can combine them and solve for the MeanLinkDelay variable:

MeanLinkDelay $= (t4 - t3 + t2 - t1)/2$

However the real world method of calculating the MeanLinkDelay is a little more complicated. The first variable to solve for is a new variable called the CorrectedPdelayRespCorrectionField which is found by adding the Delay Requestor Port's DelayAsymmetry plus the CorrectionField of the just received Pdelay_Resp Message:

CorrectedPdelayRespCorrectionField = DelayAsymmetry + Pdelay_RespCorrectionField

Now that we have calculated the CorrectedPdelayRespCorrectionField we can calculate the One-Step MeanLinkDelay or Two-Step MeanLinkDelay.

Peer-to-Peer One-Step Message MeanLinkDelay formula:

MeanLinkDelay = [(t4 - t1) - CorrectedPdelayRespCorrectionField]/2

Peer-to-Peer Two-Step Message MeanLinkDelay formula:

MeanLinkDelay = [(t4 - t1) - (ResponseOriginTimestamp – RequestReceiptTimestamp) - CorrectedPdelayRespCorrectionField - Pdelay_Resp_Follow_UpCorrectionField]/2

The MeanLinkDelay is calculated by each Peer Delay PTP Port and is then used for Sync and Follow_Up Messages to update their CorrectionFields. The updating of the CorrectionFields of the Sync or Follow_Up Message is done whenever this Peer Delay Mechanism Transparent Clock is about to re-transmit the Message.

The CorrectionField of the Sync or Follow_Up Message is updated with the MeanLinkDelay, the ResidenceTime values. Each Peer-to-Peer Transparent Clock encountered by a Sync or optional Follow_Up Message transiting through the Network would have its Messages CorrectionField updated in this manner.

With Peer Delay Mechanism GrandMaster Clock1 will transmit a Sync Message to Slave Clock1(and possibly the optional Follow_Up Message as well).

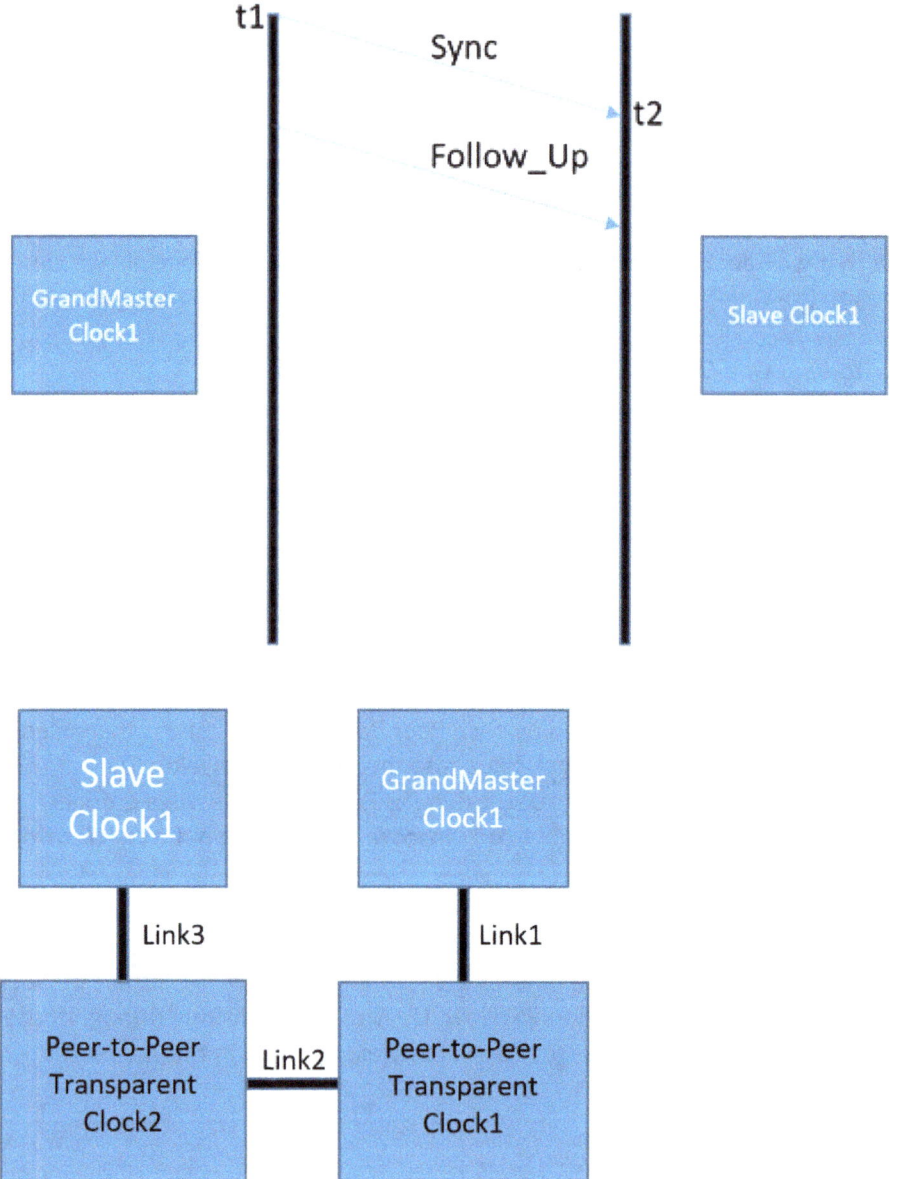

The Sync and optional Follow_Up Messages would be received by Slave Clock1.

The CorrectionField of the Sync(or optional Follow_Up) Message will have been first updated by Transparent Clock1 with MeanLinkDelay1 as well as the Transparent Clock1 ResidenceTime. The CorrectionField would second have been updated by Transparent Clock2 with MeanLinkDelay2 as well as the Transparent Clock2 ResidenceTime. The CorrectionField would thirdly have been updated by Slave Clock1 with MeanLinkDelay3.

For all three instances the MeanLinkDelay for each Network Link and the ResidenceTime in the two Transparent Switches are used to update the CorrectionField of the Synch(or optional Follow_Up) Message.

Slave Clock1 now has t1, t2, and the CorrectionField values from the Sync or Follow_Up Message and will now determine the Offset.

$t2 - t1 - CorrectionField = Offset$

Peer Delay Mechanism has the advantage over Request-Response Mechanism in that it is not affected by topology or path alterations nearly as much as each separate Sync Message's delay is determined as it traverses the Ethernet Network. The Total Transit Time that the Sync Message experienced is enclosed in the CorrectionField of itself or its trailing optional Follow_Up Message if it is a Two-Step Sync Message.

Peer Delay Mechanism also has the additional advantage in that the GrandMaster will have less work to perform. The GrandMaster will not need to receive any Delay_Req Messages sent back to it from each individual Slave Clock. This can be a huge advantage when there are many Slave Clocks on an Ethernet Network.

Transmitting Pdelay_Req Message By A Peer-to-Peer Delay Requestor PTP Port Algorithm

Pdelay_Req Messages are critical to how the Peer Delay Path Mechanism functions. The logic to how a Pdelay_Req Message is transmitted by a Peer-to-Peer(PtoP) Delay Requestor PTP Port is outlined below.

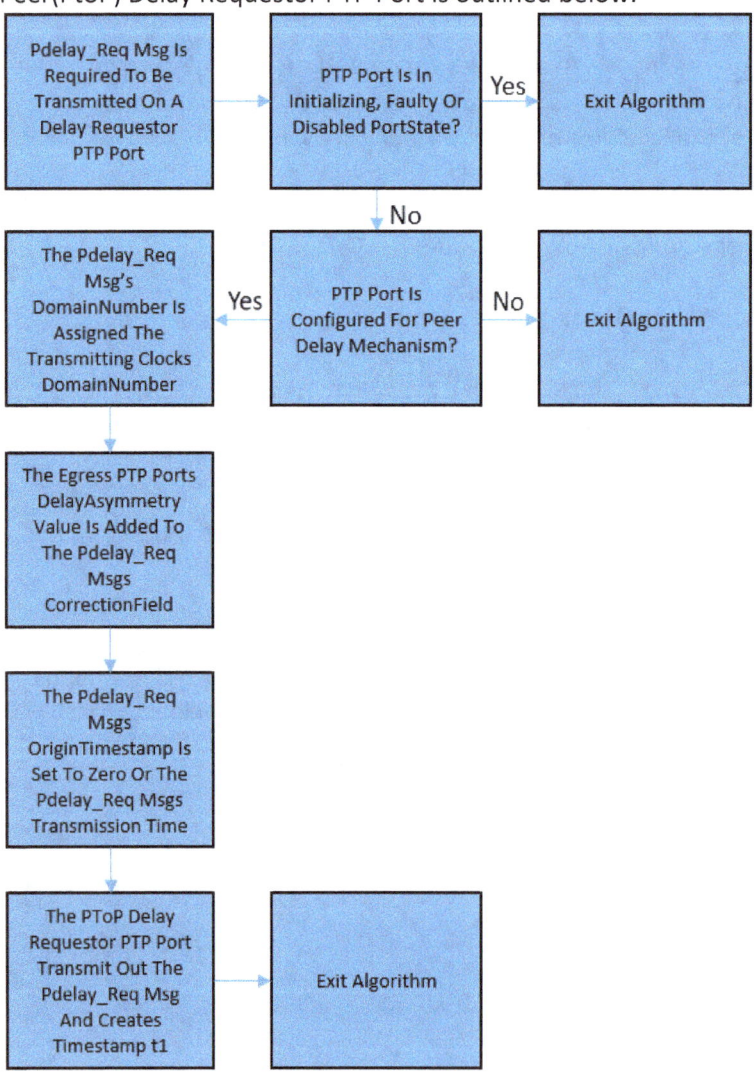

Transmitting Pdelay_Resp Message By A One-Step Peer-to-Peer Delay Responder PTP Port Algorithm

Pdelay_Resp Messages are critical to how the One-Step Peer Delay Path Mechanism functions and will need to be transmitted reasonably quickly after receiving a Pdelay_Req Message. The logic to how a Pdelay_Resp Message is transmitted by a One-Step(1S) Peer-to-Peer(PtoP) Delay Responder PTP Port is outlined below.

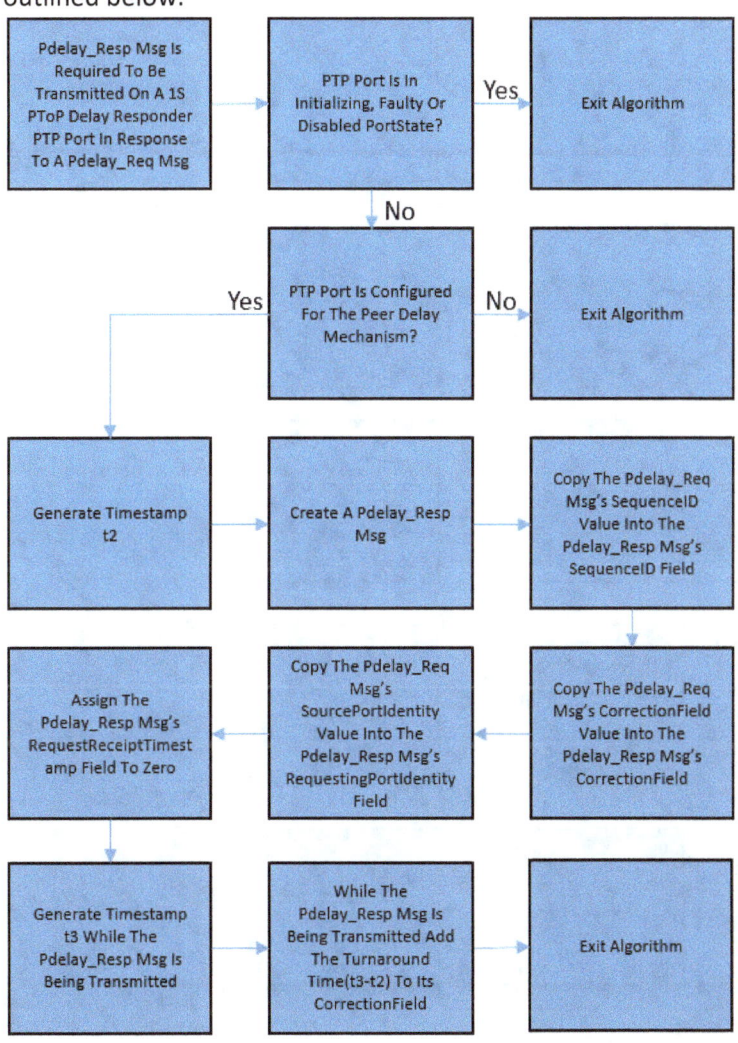

Transmitting Pdelay_Resp And Pdelay_Resp_Follow_Up Messages By A Two-Step Peer-to-Peer Delay Responder PTP Port Algorithm

Pdelay_Resp and Pdelay_Resp_Follow_Up Messages are critical to how the Two-Step Peer Delay Path Mechanism functions and will need to be transmitted reasonably quickly after receiving a Pdelay_Req Message. The logic to how the Pdelay_Resp and Pdelay_Resp_Follow_Up Messages are transmitted by a Two-Step(2S) Peer-to-Peer(PToP) Delay Responder PTP Port is outlined below.

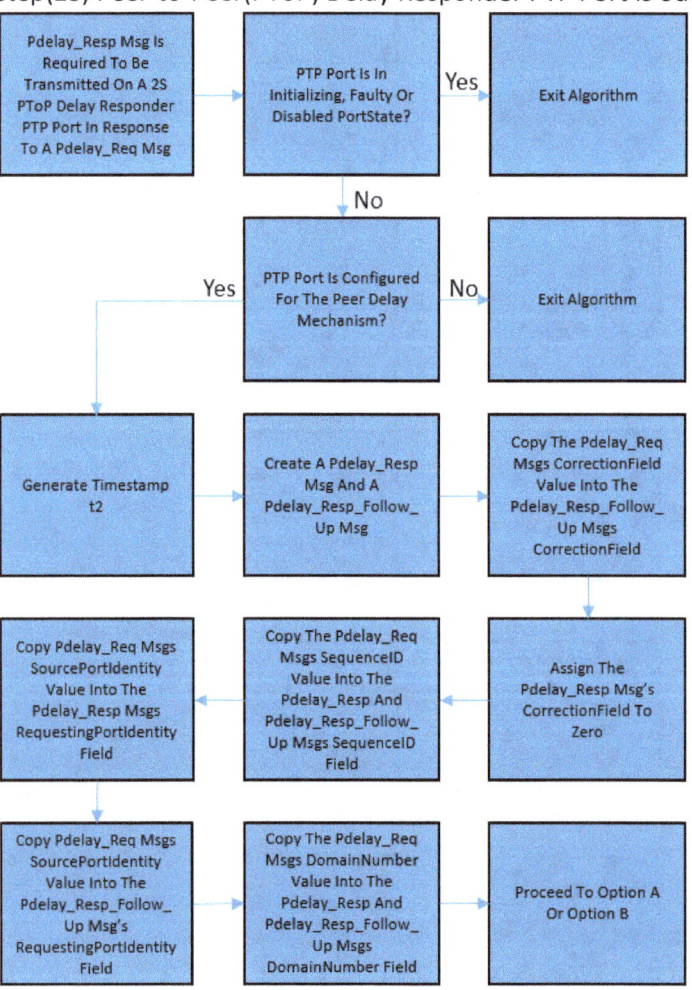

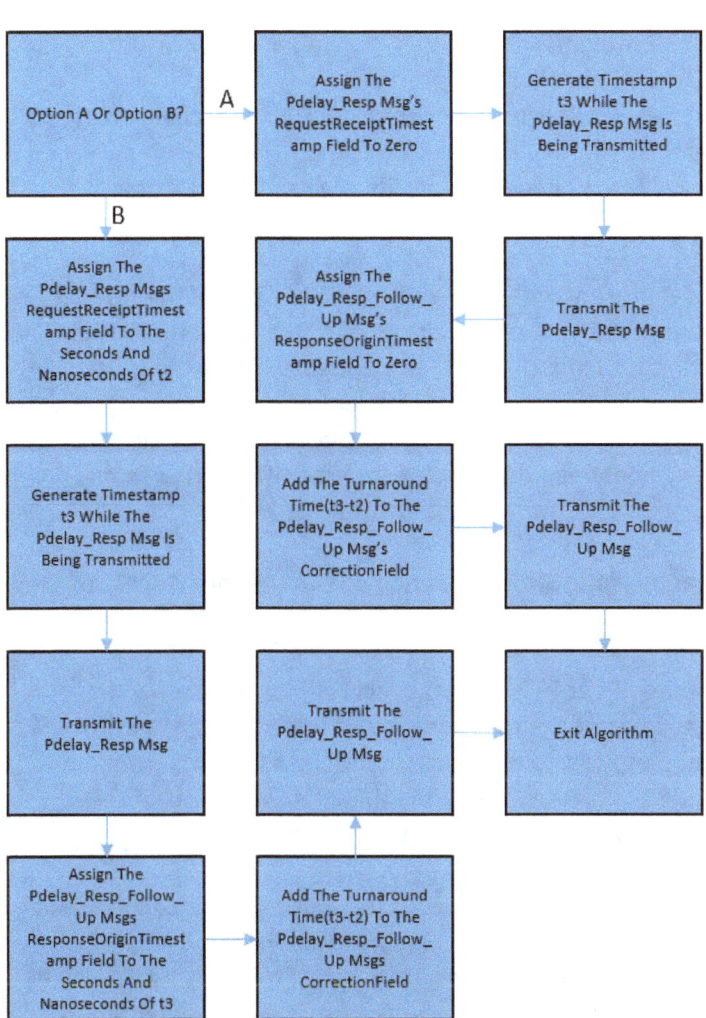

Peer Delay Mechanism Problems

Of course the Synchronization process using the Peer Delay Mechanism has its issues. The first being any difference in the Propagation Times between Pdelay_Req and Pdelay_Resp will result in an Asymmetry Delay Error and an inaccurately calculated MeanLinkDelay Time.

The second issue that is present with Peer-to-Peer PTP Ports is if the frequency is not the same between the two Clocks there will be an error in the turnaround time between Timestamps t3 and t2. If a large frequency difference is occurring a Clocks frequency can be Syntonized to the upstream Timestamping Clock that is closer to the GrandMaster Clock(or is the GrandMaster Clock). Alternatively, the frequency difference between the two Peer-to-Peer PTP Ports can be calculated and fixed.

Syntonized: Syntonization is the Synchronization of two or more Oscillators to the same frequency

The third issue is a Peer-to-Peer PTP Port may receive more than one Pdelay_Resp Messages in response to a transmitted Pdelay_Req Message. These multiple Pdelay_Resp Messages can be identified as coming from more than one Peer-to-Peer PTP Ports by comparing the different values of the SourcePortIdentity field of the received Pdelay_Resp Messages.

Multiple Pdelay_Resp Messages being received is usually a result of the use of a Non-PTP Bridge or Non-PTP Hub. The Peer Delay Mechanism(or even PTP in general!) is not to be used with these types of Multicast Networking Device. PTP can differentiate between Pdelay_Resp Message Responses however there is no way of determining the correct Link Delay. This is due to the fact that there is more than one Peer Delay Transparent Clock attached to the Non-PTP Hub or Non-PTP Bridge and the receiving Peer-to-Peer PTP Port would not know which one to update the Sync Messages CorrectionField with.

In the below example Network, Peer-to-Peer Transparent Clock3 would send a Pdelay_Req Message out to the Non-PTP Hub or Non-PTP Bridge. The Non-PTP Hub or Non-PTP Bridge is not a smart device and would multicast that Pdelay_Req Message out to its other two Ports. Peer-to-Peer Transparent Clock1 and Peer-to-Peer Transparent Clock2 would both respond with their own Pdelay_Resp Messages. Therefore Peer-to-Peer Transparent Clock3 would receive back two different Pdelay_Resp Messages.

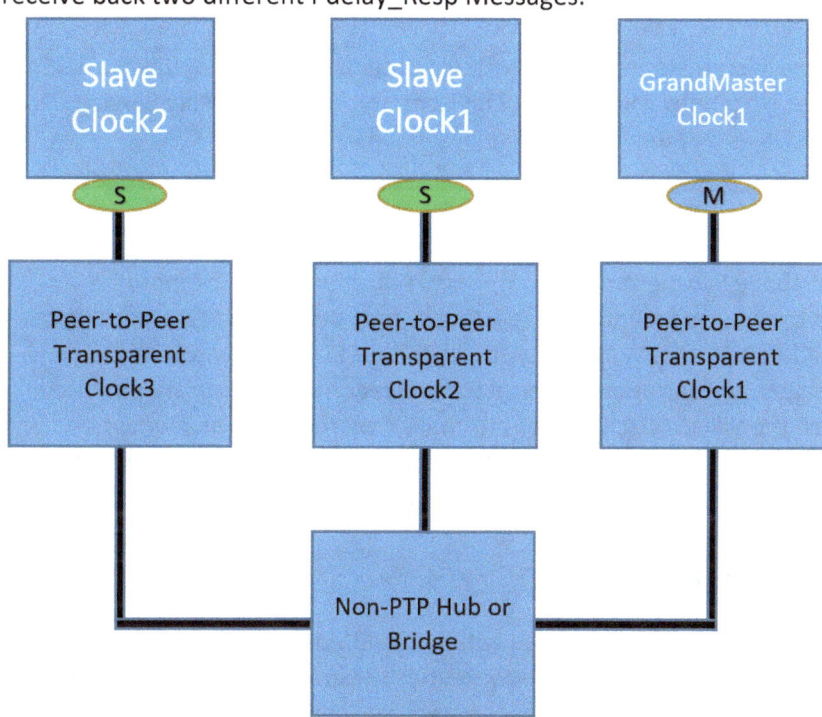

When GrandMaster Clock1 transmits out a Sync Message and Peer-to-Peer Transparent Clock3 receives it. The SourcePortIdentity of the Sync Message indicates it came from GrandMaster Clock1. For Peer-to-Peer Transparent Clock3 this is not useful. Is Peer-to-Peer Transparent Clock3 supposed to update the received Sync Message's CorrectionField with the Pdelay_Resp Message from Peer-to-Peer Transparent Clock2 or the Pdelay_Resp Message from Peer-to-Peer Transparent Clock1? Quite simply it doesn't know which one to use and the PTP Port will enter the Faulty PortState. PTP has no way of knowing which of the Peer-to-Peer Transparent Clocks the Sync Message came from. This is why Non-PTP Hubs or Non-PTP Bridges are never to be used with a Network utilizing the Peer Delay Mechanism.

The fourth issue is a Peer-to-Peer PTP Port may receive no Pdelay_Resp Messages in response to a transmitted Pdelay_Req Message. In this case the Peer-to-Peer PTP Port will at a set interval transmit a Pdelay_Req Message to check if a Peer-to-Peer PTP Port has shown up on the other side of the Network Link.

Common MeanLinkDelay Service

Under normal circumstances a PTP Port will obtain the MeanLinkDelay using the Peer-to-Peer Link Delay Mechanism. The Common MeanLinkDelay Service Service(CMLDS) is an alternative optional service to obtain this value.

Syntonization

As defined above Syntonization is the Synchronization of two or more Oscillators to the same frequency. PTP Clocks may be Syntonized according to the selected PTP Profile. Which may specify either Physical Syntonization or Sync Messages Syntonization. Physical Syntonization uses physical signals to synchronize the Slave's Oscillator or internal clock frequency and would be specified by the selected PTP Profile. Physical Syntonization is not covered by this document.

Adjusting Frequency

Once a Slave Clock has Synchronized with a GrandMaster or Master Clock (using either Peer Delay Mechanism or Delay Request Response Mechanism) and received at least two Sync Messages the frequency difference between the Master and Slave can be found. This frequency difference is called Drift.

Sync Messages Syntonization

A Slave Clock can by Syntonized to a Master Clock by using Sync(and optional Follow_Up) Messages. For this to occur the CorrectedMasterEventTimestamp value will need to be calculated.

When the Slave Clock receives a Sync Message it will generate the values for SyncEventIngressTimestamp and CorrectedSyncCorrectionField detailed in a previous section. For the One-Step Message formula the OriginTimestamp is contained in the Sync Message itself. For the Two-Step Message formula the PreciseOriginTimestamp is contained in the associated Follow_Up Message. The MeanPathDelay is calculated as part of the Request-Response Mechanism as detailed in a previous section.

The MeanLinkDelay is calculated as part of the Peer-to-Peer Mechanism as detailed in a previous section.

One-Step Message Request-Response Mechanism formula for CorrectedMasterEventTimestamp:

CorrectedMasterEventTimestamp = OriginTimestamp + MeanPathDelay + CorrectedSyncCorrectionField

Two-Step Message Request-Response Mechanism formula for CorrectedMasterEventTimestamp:

CorrectedMasterEventTimestamp = PreciseOriginTimestamp + MeanPathDelay + CorrectedSyncCorrectionField + Follow_UpCorrectionField Message

One-Step Message Peer-to-Peer Mechanism formula for CorrectedMasterEventTimestamp:

CorrectedMasterEventTimestamp = OriginTimestamp + MeanLinkDelay + CorrectedSyncCorrectionField

Two-Step Message Peer-to-Peer Mechanism formula for CorrectedMasterEventTimestamp:

CorrectedMasterEventTimestamp = PreciseOriginTimestamp + MeanLinkDelay + CorrectedSyncCorrectionField + Follow_UpCorrectionField Message

The Slave Clock will use the SyncEventIngressTimestamp and CorrectedMasterEventTimestamp to adjust the rate of change of the internal clock or Oscillator to become Syntonized with the associated Master Clock.

Receiving A Sync Message By A Clock PTP Port Algorithm

Sync Messages are critical to how PTP functions and will need to be processed reasonably quickly. The logic to how a received Sync Message is processed by a PTP Port is outlined below.

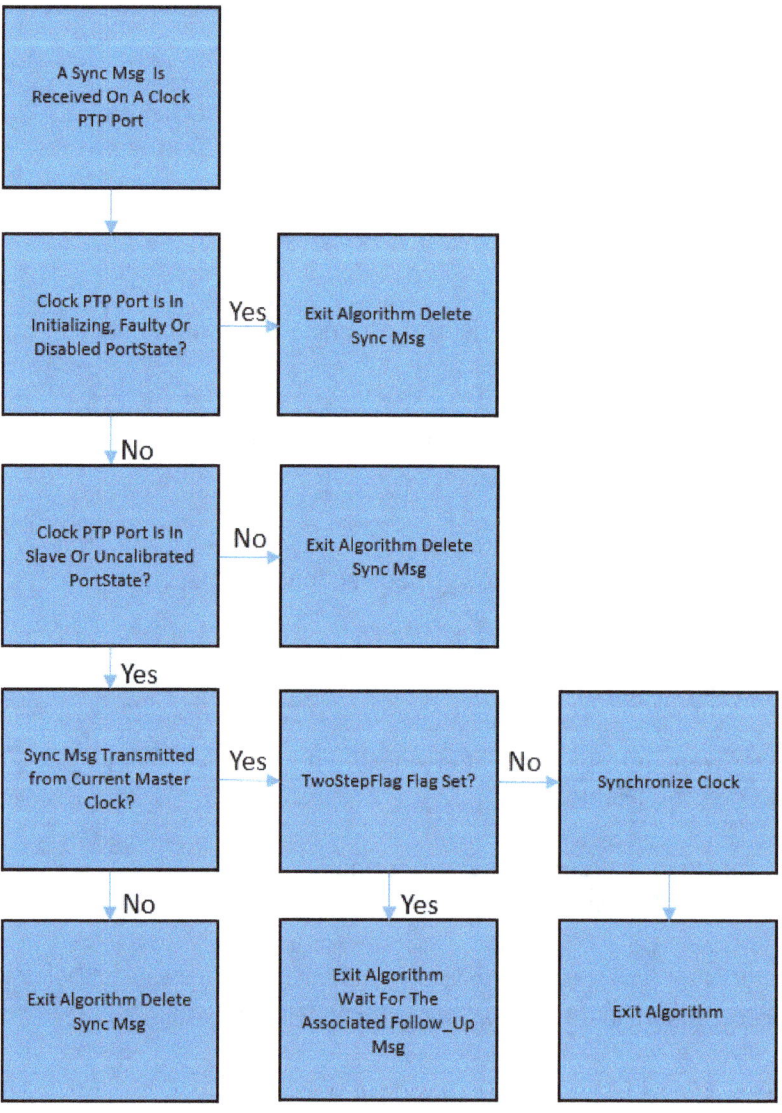

Receiving A Follow_Up Message By A Clock PTP Port Algorithm

Follow_Up Messages are critical to how Two-Step PTP functions and will need to be processed reasonably quickly. The logic to how a received Follow_Up Message is processed by a PTP Port is outlined below.

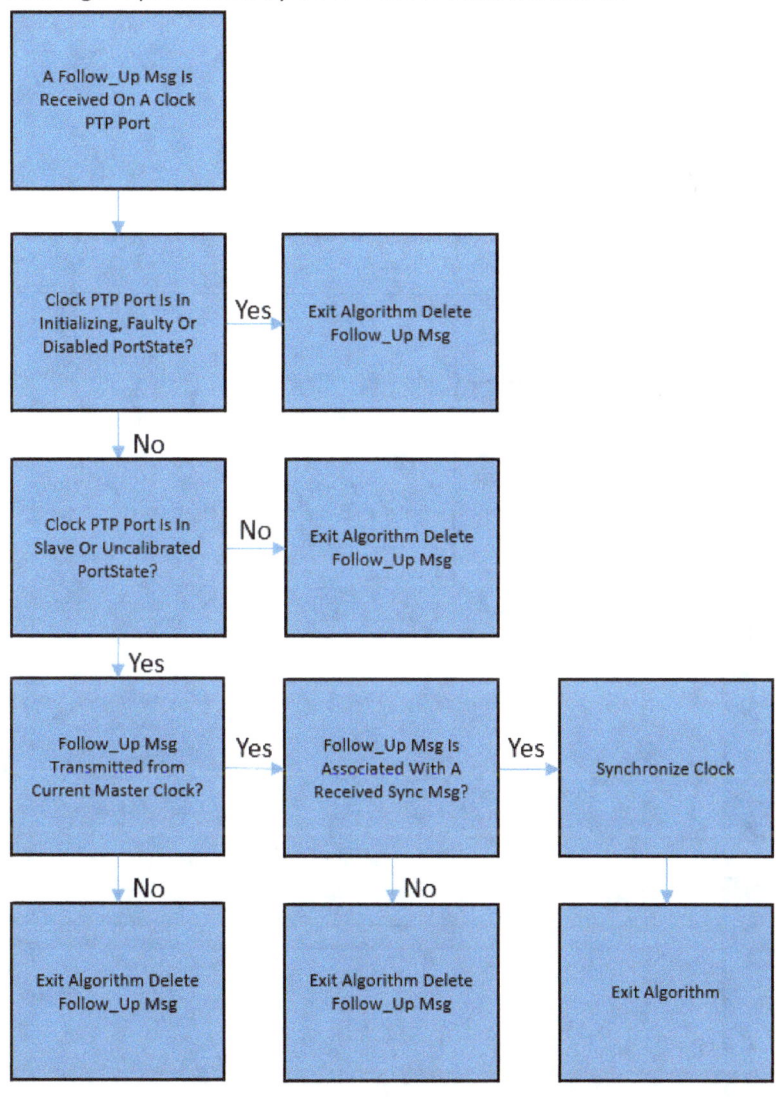

Receiving A Delay_Req Message By A Clock PTP Port Algorithm

Delay_Req Messages are critical to how the Request-Response Mechanism functions and will need to be processed reasonably quickly. The logic to how a received Delay_Req Message is processed by a PTP Port is outlined below.

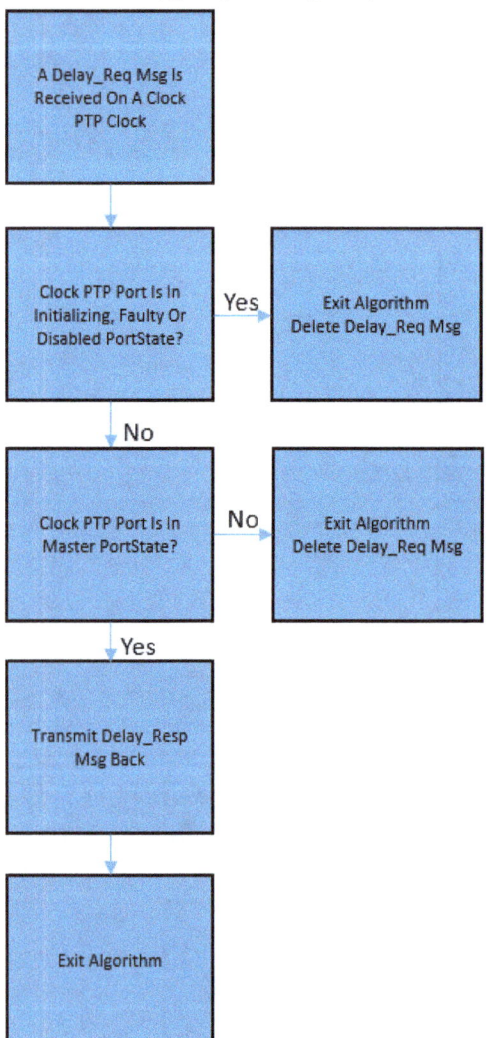

Receiving A Delay_Resp Message By A Clock PTP Port Algorithm

Delay_Resp Messages are critical to how the Request-Response Mechanism functions and will need to be processed reasonably quickly. The logic to how a received Delay_Resp Message is processed by a PTP Port is outlined below.

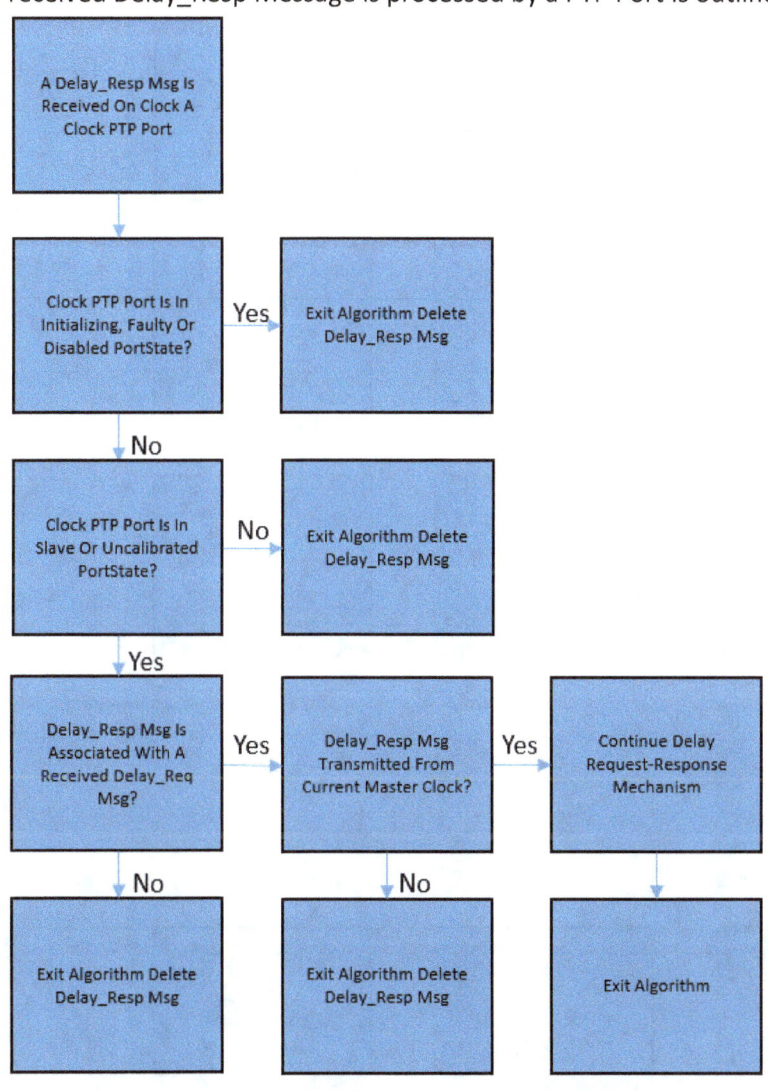

Transmitting A Delay_Req Message By A Clock PTP Port Algorithm

Delay_Req Messages are critical to how the Request-Response Mechanism functions. The logic to how a Delay_Req Message is transmitted by a PTP Port is outlined below.

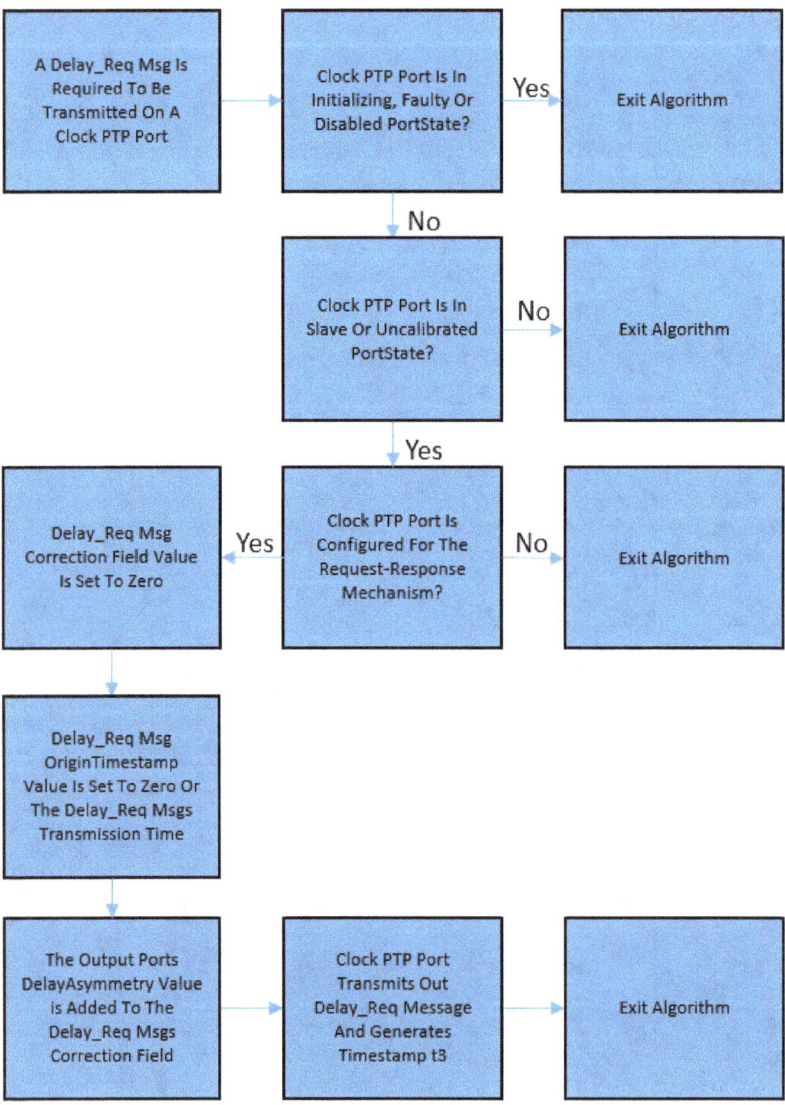

Transmitting A Delay_Resp Message By A Clock PTP Port Algorithm

Delay_Resp Messages are critical to how the Request-Response Mechanism functions and will need to be transmitted reasonably quickly after receiving a Delay_Req Message. The logic to how a Delay_Resp Message is transmitted by a PTP Port is outlined below.

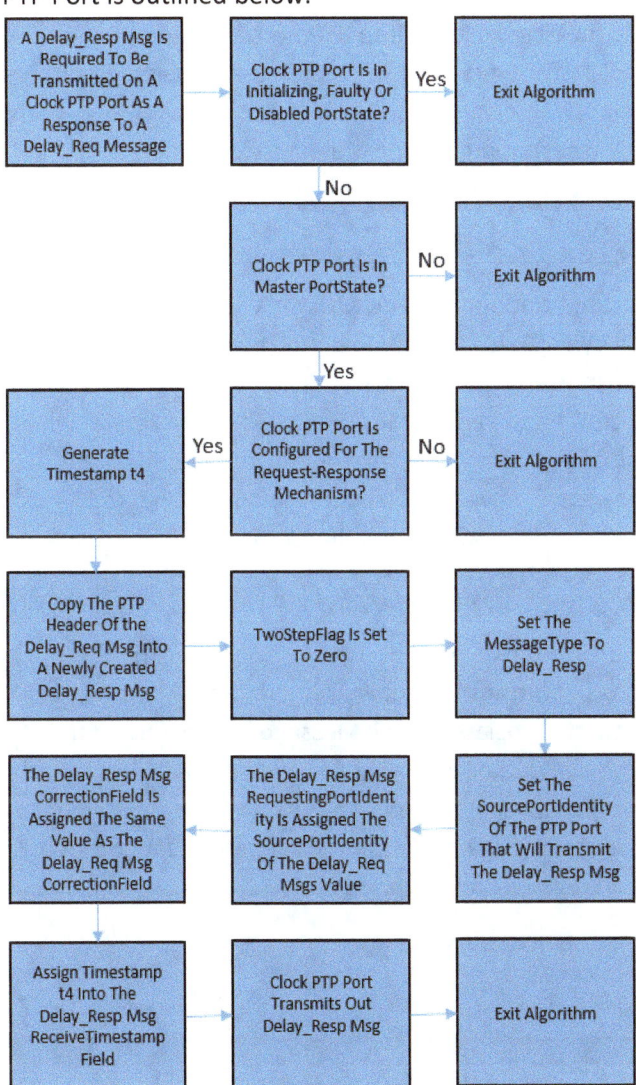

One-Step and Two-Step PTP Ports for Ordinary and Boundary Clocks

As discussed Sync Messages can be One-Step or Two-Step so too can PTP Ports be One-Step or Two-Step. All PTP capable ports must be able to handle both One-Step and Two-Step Sync Messages(and any associated Follow_Up Messages) when receiving. However when transmitting PTP Ports are permitted to only transmit as either a One-Step or Two-Step PTP Port. On some Clocks(especially GPS GrandMaster Clocks) this is a configurable setting.

One-Step PTP Ports will only transmit out a Sync Message with the OriginTimestamp field value intact when the Sync Message was originally transmitted by the Master Port.

Two-Step PTP Ports will transmit out both a Sync with the OriginTimestamp and CorrectionField fields of the Sync Message containing the value zero. After the Sync Message has been transmitted the associated Follow_Up Message will be then transmitted and shall contain the correct PreciseOriginTimestamp of when the Sync Message was originally transmitted from the Master PTP Port. The associated Follow_Up Message will have its CorrectionField field updated by each Transparent Clock it encounters as it is transiting across the PTP capable Network from Master PTP Port to Slave PTP Port.

Follow_Up Messages are transmitted as promptly as possible after the associated Sync Message has been transmitted. Follow_Up Messages must be transmitted before the next(not associated) Sync Message is transmitted from that same PTP Port when they have the same destination address.

If the Sync Message uses the Unicast Transmission Model than the associated Follow_Up Message must as well.

Both One-Step and Two-Step PTP Ports when receiving a Two-Step Sync Message will record the SequenceID value of the Sync Message and use that value to associate the correct Follow_Up Message with the correct Sync Message. The Sync and its associated Follow_Up Message will always have the same SequenceID value. If all requirements are met the operation to process the Follow_Up Message's PreciseOriginTimestamp and CorrectionField is started.

Timestamping PTP Event Messages

As mentioned earlier when PTP Event Messages are received or transmitted Timestamps are made. These Timestamps are created exactly when a PTP Message crosses a particular point between the Physical Layer Preamble and the Physical Layer Header called the Message Timestamp Point.

Message Timestamp Point	
Physical Layer Preamble	Physical Layer Header

Depending on the Transport Mechanism where the Message Timestamp Point is will depend on the Network Transport Protocol. This book focuses exclusively on Ethernet(IEEE802.3).

When a PTP Event Message is received or transmitted it will be passed up or down the Protocol Stack. Timestamps are created when the PTP Event Message passes through a selected point in the Stack. Depending on the Clock it could be at any particular Layer. The closer the Packet is to the actual Physical Layer before the Timestamp is created when received or added to the Packet as it is transmitted out the more accurate the Timestamp will be.

If the Timestamp is added or created at the Physical Layer it will require special Hardware to pass information between the PTP code residing in the Application Layer and the Physical Layer Hardware as depicted below:

Protocol Stack Layer
▸ Application Layer
Transport Layer
Internet Layer
Data Link Layer
Special PTP Hardware
Physical Layer

Special PTP Hardware that operates at or just above the Physical Layer is possible but requires dedicated chips and systems that can function nearly independently of the Clock Operating System.

PTP Ports

PTP Ports are imagined under the standard to separate regular Ethernet Messages(including General PTP Messages) from PTP Event Messages. This is important due to Event Messages requiring action in regards to Timestamping.

Note: In regards to the IEEE 1588 Standard a PTP Port is not necessarily the same as a Physical Ethernet Port. More than one PTP Logical Port can theoretically belong to one Physical Ethernet Port though this is rarely the case

Peer-to-Peer Transparent Clocks Mesh Network Topology

In can be difficult to determine how a Mesh Network Topology would operate when it comes to PTP. We did not explain what would happen between Peer-to-Peer Transparent Clock1 and Peer-to-Peer Transparent Clock2 when it comes to PTP from the above Typical Ethernet Network.

When it comes to Ethernet Networks, Spanning Tree Protocol(or one of its many variants) deactivates duplicate Network Links and thus removes Network Loops. When an active Network Link fails Spanning Tree rapidly modifies the Network to account for the change and will reconnect severed Network Devices.

When it comes to Peer Delay(Peer-to-Peer) Mechanism PTP Messages associated with this Mechanism will still be able to make their way through ports blocked by the Spanning Tree Protocol.

Note: For more information on Spanning Tree Protocol and other Networking topics we recommend The Technicians Guide to Industrial Networking

After a Network Topology change affecting a particular Slave Clock, PTP will automatically change and correct for the new path the PTP Messages must now travel.

We will take our Typical Ethernet Network and modify it to be a Mesh Network:

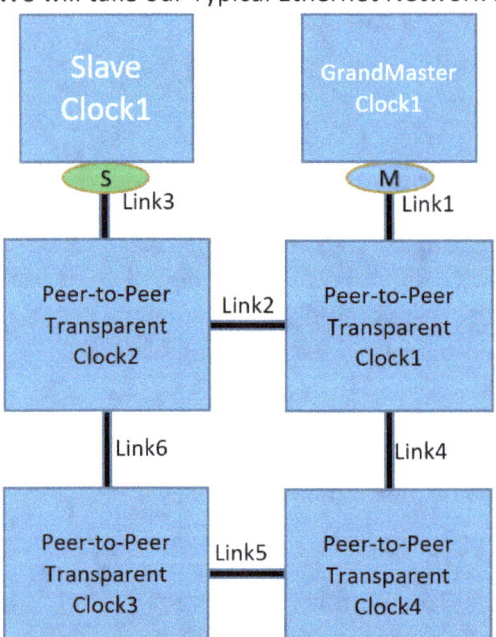

Let us say that the Spanning Tree Protocol has made it so that a One-Step Sync Message transmitted from GrandMaster Clock1 will transit to Slave Clock1 using Link1, Link2 and Link3. It will pass through Peer-to-Peer Transparent Clock1 and Peer-to-Peer Transparent Clock2 on its way to Slave Clock1.

This travel path is illustrated below:

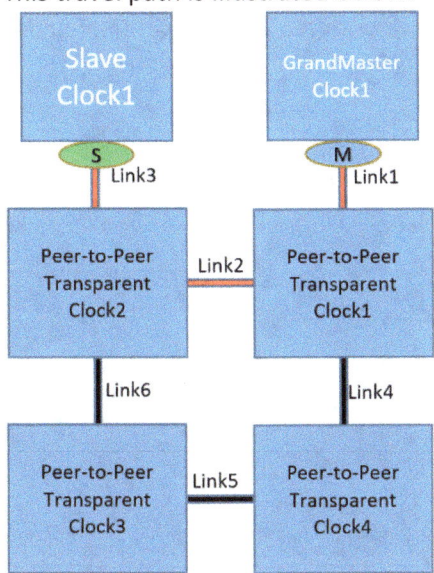

GrandMaster Clock1 will update the OriginTimestamp field of the Sync Message as it is being transmitted out. It will not update the Sync Messages CorrectionField.

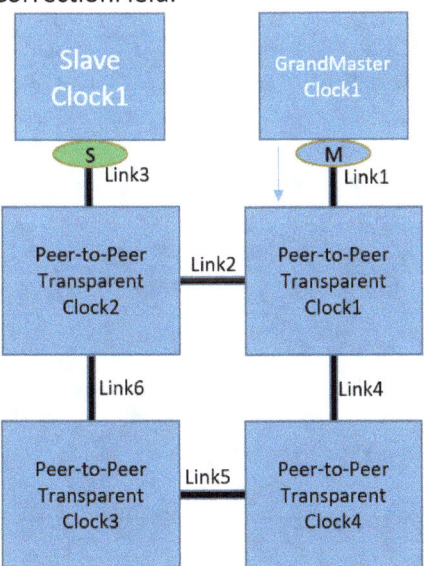

As Peer-to-Peer Transparent Clock1 is transmitting out the Sync Message it will update the Sync Messages CorrectionField with both the Link1 Delay Time and the Peer-to-Peer Transparent Clock1 ResidenceTime.

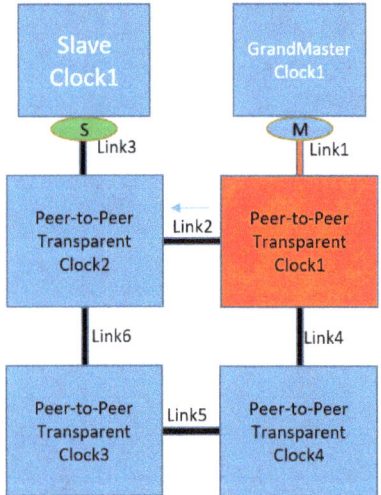

As Peer-to-Peer Transparent Clock2 is transmitting out the Sync Message it will update the Sync Messages CorrectionField with both the Link2 Delay Time and the Peer-to-Peer Transparent Clock2 ResidenceTime.

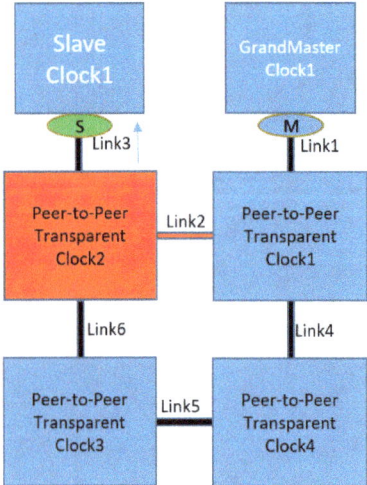

Slave Clock1 will update the Sync Messages CorrectionField with the Link3 Delay Time.

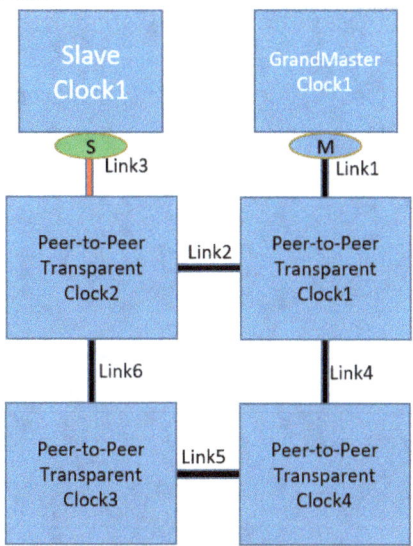

Let us now break the initial path that passes through Link2 as such:

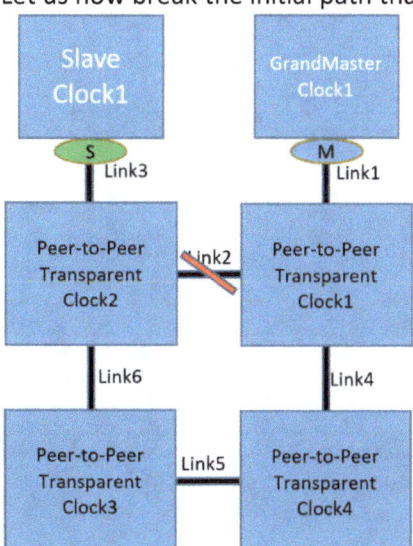

Spanning Tree Protocol would rearrange the Mesh Network to re-establish the connection between GrandMaster Clock1 and Slave Clock1. That One-Step Sync Message transmitted from GrandMaster Clock1 will transit to Slave Clock1 using Link1, Link4, Link5, Link6 and Link3. It will pass through Peer-to-Peer Transparent Clock1, Peer-to-Peer Transparent Clock4, Peer-to-Peer Transparent Clock3 and Peer-to-Peer Transparent Clock2 on its way to Slave Clock1. Each Peer-to-Peer Transparent Clock will update the Sync Messages CorrectionField with its Link Delay Time and its ResidenceTime.

This new travel Path is illustrated below:

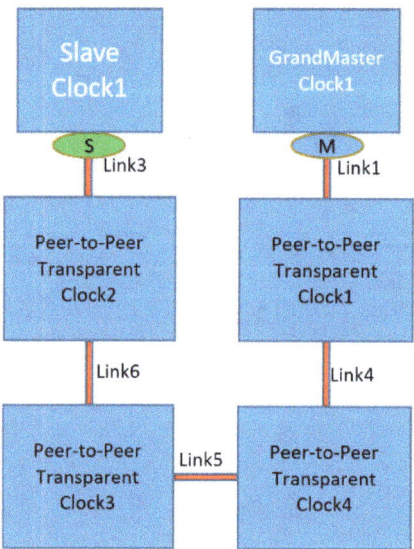

PTP Message Time Intervals and Timeouts

For some PTP Messages a set time interval between consecutive Messages is required. Sync, Delay_Req, Pdelay_Req and Announce Messages are transmitted at regular intervals. Each Message Type has a separate time interval specified.

Announce Message Interval

The Announce Message time interval is specified by the LogAnnounceInterval data set member of the Port Data Set. The AnnounceInterval indicates the amount of time that must pass before another Announce Message will be transmitted. The AnnounceInterval should be the same value throughout the PTP Domain unless otherwise specified by the selected PTP Profile. The Announce Message time interval is a tradeoff between how quickly the Master-Slave Hierarchy updates after a Network change and the additional Network Traffic generated with a shorter time interval.

AnnounceReceiptTimeout

The AnnounceReceiptTimeout data set member of the Port Data Set specifies the amount of AnnounceIntervals that have to elapse without receiving an Announce Message before the PTP Event ANNOUNCERECEIPTTIMEOUTEXPIRES is generated. The selected PTP Profile determines the minimum and maximum values of the AnnounceReceiptTimeout. The AnnounceReceiptTimeout should be the same value throughout the PTP Domain unless otherwise specified by the selected PTP Profile.

Sync Message Interval

The Sync Message time interval is specified by the LogSyncInterval data set member of the Port Data Set. The LogSyncInterval governs the time interval of Sync Messages when Multicast Messaging is used. The PTP standard assumes that Multicast Messaging is always used. The Sync Message time interval is a tradeoff between compensating for the poor quality of Slave Clocks internal clocks and the additional Network Traffic generated with a shorter time interval.

Delay_Req Message Interval

The Delay_Req Message minimum time interval is specified by the LogMinDelayRequestInterval data set member of the Port Data Set. The LogMinDelayRequestInterval indicates the minimum amount of time that must pass before another Delay_Req can be transmitted. The Master Clock publishes this value and it is predicated on the Master Clocks ability to respond to the Delay_Req Messages that it will be sent. The selected PTP Profile determines the minimum and maximum values of the MinDelayRequestInterval. The Delay_Req Message time interval is a tradeoff between responding to Network Path Delay changes and the additional Network Traffic generated with a shorter time interval.

Pdelay_Req Message Interval

The Pdelay_Req Message minimum time interval is specified by the LogMinPdelayReqInterval data set member of the Port Data Set. The LogMinPdelayReqInterval indicates the minimum amount of time that must pass before another Pdelay_Req can be transmitted over a Peer-to-Peer Link. The Pdelay_Req Message time interval is a tradeoff between responding to the Peer-to-Peer Link Delay changes and the additional Network Traffic generated on that one particular Network Link with a shorter time interval.

Parallel Redundancy Protocol and PTP

Note: In order to comprehend how PRP and PTP operate together a basic understanding of Parallell Redundancy Protocol must be we gained, we recommend The Technicians Guide to Parallel Redundancy Protocol

PTP Profiles

PTP Profiles specify a number of options when it comes to how PTP operates. This allows organization or certain industries to use a consistent set of data set member values, configurable attributes and optional features that are tailored for their specific requirements.

This can include:

1. The transport method that are permitted or necessary(Ethernet(IEEE 802.3), UDP IPv4, UDP IPv6, DeviceNET, ControlNET, etc)

2. PTP protocol device settings and configuration options including the default and ranges of PTP Data Set values

3. Defining different BMCA options

4. Specifying the Path Delay Mechanism(Delay Request-Response Mechanism or Peer Delay Mechanism)

5. Closest Clock to the GrandMaster Clock

6. Options that are permitted or necessary

7. The PTP Clock types allowed or not allowed

8. ClockClass values

The purpose of PTP Profiles is to make custom PTP settings for specific industries, environments, or for a specific application by defining PTP Clock settings and other attributes that at the same time meet the needs of that industry.

List of Current IEEE 1588-2019 PTP Profiles

Below is a list of the current PTP Profiles at this time. After this section we go into further detail on the more common PTP Profiles.

PTP Profile Description:	PTP Profile Name:	Industry:	Organization:
Default Delay Request-Response Profile	IEEE Std 1588-2019	NA	IEEE
Default Delay Peer-to-Peer Delay Profile	IEEE Std 1588-2019	NA	IEEE
High Accuracy Delay Request-Response Default PTP Profile	IEEE Std 1588-2019	NA	IEEE
Precision time protocol telecom profile for frequency Synchronization	G.8265.1	Telecommunication	ITU-T
Precision time protocol telecom profile for Phase/Time Synchronization with full timing support from the network	G.8275.1	Telecommunication	ITU-T
Precision time protocol telecom profile for time/phase Synchronization with partial timing support from the network	G.8275.2	Telecommunication	ITU-T
Enterprise Profile for the Precision Time Protocol With Mixed Multicast and Unicast Messages	draft-ietf-tictoc-ptp-enterprise-profile-22	Financial	IETF
SMPTE profile for Synchronization in a professional broadcast environment	SMPTE ST2059-2:2021	Broadcast	SMPTE

AES67 Media Profile	AES67-2018	Audio	AES
IEEE Std 802.1AS	IEEE Std 802.1AS-2020	Industrial Automation	IEEE
C37.238 Power Profile	C37.238-2017	Power Industry	IEEE
Power Utility Automation	IEC/IEEE 61850-9-3	Power Industry	IEC
Automation Networks using PRP & HSR	IEC 62439-3 Annex A.2	Power Industry/ Industrial Automation	IEC
"U" Utility Automation Profile	IEC 62439-3 Annex B	Industrial Automation	IEC
"D" Drives & Process Automation Profile	IEC 62439-3 Annex C	Industrial Automation	IEC
Automotive Ethernet AVB Functional and Interoperability Specification	Auto-Ethernet-AVB-Func-Interop-Spec_v1.6	Automotive	Avnu
LXI IEEE 1588 Profile	LXI IEEE 1588 Profile 1.0, 1 Dec 08	Measurement	LAN eXtensions for Instrumentation (LXI)
GigE Vision	GigE Vision 2.1	Measurement	Automated Imaging Association (AIA)

PTP Profile: Default Delay Request-Response Profile

Data Set Member:	Initial Value(dec):	Range(dec):
Default Data Set DomainNumber	0	0 to 255
Port Data Set LogAnnounceInterval	1	0 to 4
Port Data Set LogSyncInterval	0	-1 to 1
Port Data Set LogMinDelayReqInterval	0	0 to 5
Port Data Set AnnounceReceiptTimeout	3	2 to 10
Default Data Set Priority1	128	0 to 255
Default Data Set Priority2	128	0 to 255
Default Data Set SlaveOnly	False	True/False
Observation Interval(τ)	1s	
Default Data Set SdoID	000(hex)	0 to FFF(hex)

Options:

Optional Features/Services/Mechanism Names:	Inclusions:
Unicast Message Negotiation	Permitted and included but by default are initially disabled
Path Trace	Permitted and included but by default are initially disabled
Alternate Timescale Offsets	Permitted and included but by default are initially disabled
Holdover Upgrade	Permitted and included but by default are initially disabled
Isolation of PTP Instances Running Under Profiles Specified By Different Standards Organizations	Permitted and included but by default are initially disabled
Common MeanLinkDelay Service	Permitted and included but by default are initially disabled
Configurable Correction Of Timestamps	Permitted and included but by default are initially disabled
Calculation Of The <DelayAsymmetry> For Certain Media	Permitted and included but by default are initially disabled
Mixed Multicast/Unicast Operation	Permitted and included but by default are initially disabled

Cumulative Frequency Transfer Method For Synchronizing Clocks	Permitted and included but by default are initially disabled
Slave Event Monitoring	Permitted and included but by default are initially disabled
Enhanced Synchronization Accuracy Metrics	Permitted and included but by default are initially disabled
Message Length Extension	Permitted and included but by default are initially disabled
PTP Integrated Security Mechanism	Permitted and included but by default are initially disabled
Grandmaster Clusters	Permitted and included but by default are initially disabled
Alternate Master	Permitted and included but by default are initially disabled
Unicast Discovery	Permitted and included but by default are initially disabled
Acceptable Master Table	Permitted and included but by default are initially disabled
Mechanism For External Configuration Of A PTP Instance's PTP PortState	Permitted and included but by default are initially disabled
Reduced State Sets And Use Of The <ForeignMasterList> Feature	Permitted and included but by default are initially disabled
Qualification of Announce Messages item e)	Permitted and included but by default are initially disabled

Best Master Clock Algorithm:

BMCA:	Inclusion
Default Best Master Clock Algorithm as described in an above section	Permitted and only BMCA allowed

Path Delay Mechanism:

Path Delay Mechanism:	Inclusion:
Default Delay Request-Response Path Mechanism as described in an above section	Permitted and only Path Delay Mechanism allowed unless Mechanisms are separated by a Boundary Clock

Clock Minimum Specification:

Clock Specification:	Clock Minimum Specification:
GrandMaster Clock Minimum Frequency Divergence	The GrandMaster Clock will not diverge from the selected Timescale by more than 0.01%

PTP Profile: Default Delay Peer-to-Peer Delay Profile

Data Set Member:	Initial Value(dec):	Range(dec):
Default Data Set DomainNumber	0	0 to 255
Port Data Set LogAnnounceInterval	1	0 to 4
Port Data Set LogSyncInterval	0	-1 to 1
Port Data Set LogMinPDelayReqInterval	0	0 to 5
Port Data Set AnnounceReceiptTimeout	3	2 to 10
Default Data Set Priority1	128	0 to 255
Default Data Set Priority2	128	0 to 255
Default Data Set SlaveOnly	False	True/False
Observation Interval(τ)	1s	
Default Data Set SdoID	000(hex)	0 to FFF(hex)
Transport Clock Default Data Set PrimaryDomain	0	

Options:

Optional Features/Services/Mechanism Names:	Inclusions:
Unicast Message Negotiation	Permitted and included but by default are initially disabled
Path Trace	Permitted and included but by default are initially disabled
Alternate Timescale Offsets	Permitted and included but by default are initially disabled
Holdover Upgrade	Permitted and included but by default are initially disabled
Isolation of PTP Instances Running Under Profiles Specified By Different Standards Organizations	Permitted and included but by default are initially disabled
Common MeanLinkDelay Service	Permitted and included but by default are initially disabled
Configurable Correction Of Timestamps	Permitted and included but by default are initially disabled
Calculation Of The <DelayAsymmetry> For Certain Media	Permitted and included but by default are initially disabled
Mixed Multicast/Unicast Operation	Permitted and included but by default are initially disabled

Cumulative Frequency Transfer Method For Synchronizing Clocks	Permitted and included but by default are initially disabled
Slave Event Monitoring	Permitted and included but by default are initially disabled
Enhanced Synchronization Accuracy Metrics	Permitted and included but by default are initially disabled
Message Length Extension	Permitted and included but by default are initially disabled
PTP Integrated Security Mechanism	Permitted and included but by default are initially disabled
Grandmaster Clusters	Permitted and included but by default are initially disabled
Alternate Master	Permitted and included but by default are initially disabled
Unicast Discovery	Permitted and included but by default are initially disabled
Acceptable Master Table	Permitted and included but by default are initially disabled
Mechanism For External Configuration Of A PTP Instance's PTP PortState	Permitted and included but by default are initially disabled
Reduced State Sets And Use Of The <ForeignMasterList> Feature	Permitted and included but by default are initially disabled
Qualification of Announce Messages item e)	Permitted and included but by default are initially disabled

Best Master Clock Algorithm:

BMCA:	Inclusion:
Default Best Master Clock Algorithm as described in an above section	Permitted and only BMCA allowed

Path Delay Mechanism:

Path Delay Mechanism:	Inclusion:
Default Peer Delay Path Mechanism as described in an above section	Permitted and only Path Delay Mechanism allowed unless Mechanisms are separated by a Boundary Clock

Clock Minimum Specification:

Clock Specification:	Clock Minimum Specification:
GrandMaster Clock Minimum Frequency Divergence	The GrandMaster Clock will not diverge from the selected Timescale by more than 0.01%

Optional Features

The IEEE 1588-2019 standard has optional features that may be included in your selected implementation of PTP:
1. Unicast Message Negotiation
2. Path Trace
3. Alternate Timescale Offsets
4. Holdover Upgrade
5. Isolation Of PTP Instances Running Under Profiles Specified By Different Standards Organizations
6. Common MeanLinkDelay Service
7. Configurable Correction Of Timestamps
8. Calculation Of The <DelayAsymmetry> For Certain Media
9. Mixed Multicast/Unicast Operation
10. Cumulative Frequency Transfer Method For Synchronizing Clocks
11. Slave Event Monitoring
12. Enhanced Synchronization Accuracy Metrics
13. Message Length Extension
14. PTP Integrated Security Mechanism

In this document we will only cover optional features that are most relevant to an Ethernet Network PTP Implementation.

Unicast Message Negotiation Mechanism

Unicast Messages and Unicast Negotiation is allowed in PTP however it is an optional feature that must follow the below conventions.

Signaling Messages with attached TLV's are what allow for the operation of Unicast Negotiation. If a TLV is transmitted, sent or responded with a TLV it usually is enclosed in a Signaling Message. Signaling Messages are very simplistic and were covered in a previous section. They are removed from the explanation going forward.

The Requesting PTP Port will transmit a REQUEST_UNICAST_TRANSMISSION TLV enclosed in a Signaling Message to the Grantor PTP Port to transmit Unicast Sync, Delay_Resp, Pdelay_Resp or Announce Messages. If the Grantor or Requestor PTP Ports are in Initializing, Faulty or Disabled PortState then the Request for Unicast Messages cannot be completed. If an involved Transparent Clock PTP Port is in Fault PortState then the Request for Unicast Messages cannot be completed.

PTP Ports already with the Unicast Message Negotiation option turned on that receive a Signaling Message with a REQUEST_UNICAST_TRANSMISSION TLV attached will reply with a Signaling Message with a GRANT_UNICAST_TRANSMISSION TLV attached. The responding GRANT_UNICAST_TRANSMISSION TLV is what grants or denies the request for Unicast Messages. If the DurationField of the GRANT_UNICAST_TRANSMISSION TLV was set to a value of zero the request for Unicast Messages was denied.

Note: A PTP Port which has been approved to transmit Unicast Messages to another PTP Port is called a Grantee

Note: A PTP Port which has approved another PTP Port to transmit Unicast Messages to it is called the Grantor

A Grantee PTP Port can advise the Grantor PTP port that it no longer requires the Unicast Messages granted service. This is done by transmitting a CANCEL_UNICAST_TRANSMISSION TLV with the MaintainRequest Flag value set to zero. The Grantee PTP Port once it receives the CANCEL_UNICAST_TRANSMISSION TLV with the MaintainRequest Flag value at zero will reply with an ACKNOWLEDGE_CANCEL_UNICAST_TRANSMISSION TLV. After that the Grantee PTP Port will stop the Unicast Messages granted service.

If a Grantor PTP Port that can no longer maintain the Unicast Messages granted service it will transmit a CANCEL_UNICAST_TRANSMISSION TLV with the MaintainGrant Flag value at zero to the Grantee PTP Port. The Grantee PTP Port once it receives the CANCEL_UNICAST_TRANSMISSION TLV with the MaintainGrant Flag value at zero will reply with an ACKNOWLEDGE_CANCEL_UNICAST_TRANSMISSION TLV and then will stop the Unicast Messages granted service. If the Grantor PTP Port does not receive an ACKNOWLEDGE_CANCEL_UNICAST_TRANSMISSION TLV from the Grantee PTP Port it will continue transmitting CANCEL_UNICAST_TRANSMISSION TLVs until a specific number of them have been sent.
If a Grantor PTP Port receives a receipt of a MaintainGrant Flag or MaintainRequest Flag set to True it will continue maintaining the current contract and not abandon it.

Between a Grantor PTP Port and a Grantee PTP Port there can only be one Grant for each MessageType going in one direction. When a Grant Message is received granting transmission of a MessageType between the Grantor and Grantee it will abort the previous contract.

Once a Unicast Contract has been decided upon between the Grantor PTP Port and the Grantee PTP Port if any Multicast Messages are received they will not be processed and will be promptly dropped.

Allowing Unicast Message Negotiation Mechanism

To allow for Unicast Message Negotiation turn on the UnicastNegotiationPort data set member Enable. Usually when the Network Professional selects a specific PTP Profile this will turn on or off automatically. By default it is turned off.

When Unicast Messaging Is Turned Off

If a PTP Clock is configured to turn off its Unicast Messaging it will revoke all Unicast Message Negotiated Grants by issuing CANCEL_UNICAST_TRANSMISSION TLV Messages as detailed above.

When Unicast Message Negotiation is turned off the PTP Clock will not:
1. Transmit a REQUEST_UNICAST_TRANSMISSION TLV Message
2. Respond to a REQUEST_UNICAST_TRANSMISSION TLV Message
3. Transmit a GRANT_UNICAST_TRANSMISSION TLV Message

Renewing An Unicast Message Grant

Before an existing agreement concludes the Requesting PTP Port may transmit a new Unicast Message Negotiation Request. The Granting PTP Port is obligated(but not required) to respond with a Grant that is equal to or greater than the unexpired time of the prior Unicast Message Grant.

Bidirectional Unicast Messaging

A PTP Clock may Request Unicast Messaging and Grant Unicast Messaging simultaneously. There may be two Unicast Message Contracts between two PTP Clocks at a time. The two Unicast Message Contracts would cover all receiving and transmitting Messages and all Messages would be Unicast between them. When a PTP Clock holds two Unicast Contracts with a single PTP Clock it is said to hold a Bidirectional Contract with the other PTP Clock.

REQUEST_UNICAST_TRANSMISSION TLV

The IEEE 1588-2019 REQUEST_UNICAST_TRANSMISSION TLV is 10bytes in length and contains the following:

Byte1		Byte2
TLVType		
LengthField		
MessageType	Reserved	LogInterMessagePeriod
DurationField		
DurationField(cont)		

TLVType: The TLVType Field will be a value of 4(hex) to indicate a REQUEST_UNICAST_TRANSMISSION TLV. The TLVType Field is 2bytes in length

LengthField: The LengthField value is the number of bytes in the ValueField of the TLV which is 6(dec). The ValueField value for the REQUEST_UNICAST_TRANSMISSION TLVs includes the number of bytes for the MessageType Field, Reserved, LogInterMessagePeriod Field and the DurationField. The LengthField contains an unsigned integer 16bits in length

MessageType: The MessageType Field specifies the PTP Message type this REQUEST_UNICAST_TRANSMISSION TLV is requesting for. This field specifies whether the PTP Message is a Sync, Follow_Up, Delay_Req, Delay_Resp, Pdelay_Req, Pdelay_Resp, Pdelay_Resp_Follow_Up, Announce, Management or a Signaling Message. This is the exact same MessageType from the PTP Message Header detailed earlier. Sync, Delay_Resp, Pdelay_Resp and Announce Messages are the only MessageTypes that will be accepted by the Unicast Message Negotiation process. The MessageType Field is 4bits in length

Note: If the PTP Port is a Two-Step Port and it grants a Unicast Transmission Contract for Sync Message it will also be granted for Follow_Up Messages as well. This is true for Pdelay_Resp and their associated Pdelay_Resp_Follow_Up Messages as well

Reserved: This Reserved Field is 4bits in length

LogInterMessagePeriod: The LogInterMessagePeriod Field value will be the time period between the requested Unicast PTP Messages. The value will be in logarithm to base2 in seconds. The LogInterMessagePeriod Field contains a signed integer 1byte in length

DurationField: The DurationField is the desired period of time that the requested Unicast PTP Messages will be transmitted. The period of time will be in seconds. The DurationField contains an unsigned integer 4bytes in length

GRANT_UNICAST_TRANSMISSION TLV

The IEEE 1588-2019 GRANT_UNICAST_TRANSMISSION TLV is 12bytes in length and contains the following:

Byte1		Byte2							
TLVType									
LengthField									
MessageType	Reserved	LogInterMessagePeriod							
DurationField									
DurationField(cont)									
Reserved		0	0	0	0	0	0	0	R

TLVType: The TLVType Field will be a value of 5(hex) to indicate a GRANT_UNICAST_TRANSMISSION TLV. The TLVType Field is 2bytes in length

LengthField: The LengthField value is the number of bytes in the ValueField of the TLV which is 8(dec). The ValueField value for the GRANT_UNICAST_TRANSMISSION TLVs includes the number of bytes for the MessageType Field, Reserved Field, LogInterMessagePeriod Field, DurationField, Reserved Field and the 8bit Flag Field. The LengthField contains an unsigned integer 16bits in length

MessageType: The MessageType Field specifies the PTP Message Type this GRANT_UNICAST_TRANSMISSION TLV is granting permission for. This is the exact same MessageType from the PTP Message Header detailed in an earlier section. The MessageType value will be the same as the associated REQUEST_UNICAST_TRANSMISSION TLV request. The MessageType Field is 4bits in length

Reserved: This Reserved Field is 4bits in length

LogInterMessagePeriod: The LogInterMessagePeriod Field value will be the time period between the requested Unicast PTP Messages. The value will be in logarithm to base2 in seconds. The LogInterMessagePeriod Field contains a signed integer 1byte in length

DurationField: The DurationField is the desired period of time that the requested Unicast PTP Messages will be transmitted. The period of time will be in seconds. If this value is zero the request has been rejected. The DurationField contains an unsigned integer 4bytes in length

Reserved: This Reserved Field is 1byte in length

R: The R(or Renewal Invited) Flag is a value of one when the Granting PTP Port will probably resume the Grant when the Requesting PTP Port asks to renew the request. The R Flag is 1bit in length

CANCEL_UNICAST_TRANSMISSION TLV

The IEEE 1588-2019 CANCEL_UNICAST_TRANSMISSION TLV is 6bytes in length and contains the following:

Byte1					Byte2
TLVType					
LengthField					
MessageType	0	0	G	R	Reserved

TLVType: The TLVType Field will be a value of 6(hex) to indicate a CANCEL_UNICAST_TRANSMISSION TLV. The TLVType Field is 2bytes in length

LengthField: The LengthField value is the number of bytes in the ValueField of the TLV which is 2(dec). The ValueField value for the CANCEL_UNICAST_TRANSMISSION TLVs includes the number of bytes for the MessageType Field, the 4bit Flag Field, and the Reserved Field. The LengthField contains an unsigned integer 16bits in length

MessageType: The MessageType Field specifies the PTP Message Type this CANCEL_UNICAST_TRANSMISSION TLV is canceling permission for. This is the exact same MessageType from the PTP Message Header detailed earlier. The MessageType Field is 4bits in length

G: The G(or MaintainGrant) Flag is a value of one when the Granting PTP Port wants to advise the Grantee PTP Port that it intends to continue to provide the currently Unicast Transmission Service for that particular MessageType. When the value is zero the Granting PTP Port wants to advise the Grantee PTP Port that it intends to stop the currently Unicast Transmission Service for that particular MessageType. The G Flag is 1bit in length

R: The R(or MaintainRequest) Flag is a value of one when the Grantee PTP Port wants to advise the Grantor PTP Port that it still needs the Unicast Transmission Service for that MessageType. When the value is zero when a Grantee PTP Port wants to advise the Grantor PTP Port that it does not need the Unicast Transmission Service for that MessageType any longer. The R Flag is 1bit in length

Reserved: This Reserved Field is 1byte in length

ACKNOWLEDGE_CANCEL_UNICAST_TRANSMISSION TLV

The IEEE 1588-2019 ACKNOWLEDGE_CANCEL_UNICAST_TRANSMISSION TLV is 6bytes in length and contains the following:

Byte1					Byte2
TLVType					
LengthField					
MessageType	0	0	G	R	Reserved

TLVType: The TLVType Field will be a value of 7(hex) to indicate a ACKNOWLEDGE_CANCEL_UNICAST_TRANSMISSION TLV. The TLVType Field is 2bytes in length

LengthField: The LengthField value is the number of bytes in the ValueField of the TLV which is 2(dec). The ValueField value for the ACKNOWLEDGE_CANCEL_UNICAST_TRANSMISSION TLVs includes the number of bytes for the MessageType Field, the 4bit Flag Field, and the Reserved Field. The LengthField contains an unsigned integer 16bits in length

MessageType: The MessageType Field specifies the PTP Message Type this ACKNOWLEDGE_CANCEL_UNICAST_TRANSMISSION TLV is confirming the canceling of permission for. This is the exact same MessageType from the PTP Message Header detailed earlier. The MessageType value will be the same as the associated CANCEL_UNICAST_TRANSMISSION TLV request. The MessageType Field is 4bits in length

G: The G(or MaintainGrant) Flag value of the ACKNOWLEDGE_CANCEL_UNICAST_TRANSMISSION TLV will be the same as the associated CANCEL_UNICAST_TRANSMISSION TLV G Flag value request it is acknowledging. The G Flag is 1bit in length

R: The R(or MaintainRequest) Flag value of the ACKNOWLEDGE_CANCEL_UNICAST_TRANSMISSION TLV will be the same as the associated CANCEL_UNICAST_TRANSMISSION TLV R Flag value request it is acknowledging. The R Flag is 1bit in length

Reserved: This Reserved Field is 1byte in length

Mixed Multicast And Unicast PTP Messages

Mixing Unicast Messages and Multicast Messages is allowed in PTP but should only be done when Delay_Req and Delay_Resp Messages are being utilized. The purpose of using mixed Multicast and Unicast PTP Messages is to not allow purposeful handling of Delay_Req and Delay_Resp Messages at PTP Ports which are always listening at PTP Multicast Logical Ports but are not the intended Receiving Clock of the Message.

Mixed Multicast and Unicast PTP Messages is an optional feature that is typically enabled by the selected PTP Profile. If this feature is enabled all Ordinary and Boundary Clocks in the same Network will have it turned on.

If this option is turned on Sync and optional Follow_Up Messages can be transmitted Unicast or Multicast. Follow_Up Messages will be transmitted whatever the associated Sync Message was transmitted as. Delay_Req and Delay_Resp Messages will be transmitted Unicast. Announce Messages are to be transmitted Multicast.

Unicast Discovery

Unicast Discovery is an optional mechanism turned on by the selected PTP Profile or is enabled by default by the Clock manufacturer. This mechanism allows for PTP to be used over Ethernet Networks that do not allow for Multicast Messaging.

The Unicast Discovery mechanism is turned off by setting the UnicastDiscoveryPort data set member MaxTableSize to a value of zero. A PTP Clock with Unicast Discovery turned on will also have the Unicast Negotiation feature turned on. A PTP Clock with Unicast Discovery enabled will need the Addresses of possible Master PTP Clock Ports that it will need to initiate Unicast Communications with. The Clock can ask that the Master PTP Clock transmit Unicast Announce, Sync, and Delay_Resp Messages to itself.

A Unicast Discovery enabled PTP Clock will construct a list of possible Master Clocks and their PTP Ports. This list is detailed in the UnicastDiscoveryPort Data Set. A Unicast Discovery enabled PTP Clock may try to initiate communications with possible Master Clocks from its constructed list. From the constructed list the PTP Ports are listed by PortAddress and each entry details the logical/protocol address.

If the constructed list has no entries the Unicast Discovery Mechanism will not operate apart from overseeing the Unicast Discovery Port Data Set.

The PTP Clock with Unicast Discovery turned will regularly ask the PTP Ports from its list to transmit a Unicast Announce Message to its self. This is done using Unicast Message Negotiation. If one of the requested PTP Ports does not grant the request the requesting PTP Clock will ask again after an interval determined by the LogQueryInterval data set member.

Alternate GrandMaster Clock/Alternate Master Clock

The topic of Alternate GrandMaster Clock or Alternate Master Clock was briefly discussed in a beginning section but is covered in greater detail here.

When the Alternate Master Clock optional feature is enabled by the selected PTP Profile(or manually or by the manufacturer) this kind of PTP Master Clock may exist on a PTP capable Network. More commonly this option describes how a PTP Port will operate as an Alternate Master Port not the actual Clock. An Alternate Master PTP Port will communicate PTP timing info with other PTP Ports on the same Network. The other PTP Ports will also gather the transmission path characteristics of every Alternate Master PTP Ports.

The Alternate Master feature is turned off by setting the AlternateMasterPort Data Set NumberOfAlternateMasters data set member to a value of zero. Slave Clocks that will not be using the Messages or information from Alternate Master Clocks will disregard PTP Messages with the AlternateMasterFlag turned on.

An Alternate Master PTP Port will transmit Announce Messages with the AlternateMasterFlag turned on. As with all Announce Messages they are transmitted at the interval described by the Ports LogAnnounceInterval data set member.

The Alternate Master PTP Port will transmit Sync Messages and if it is a Two-Step Clock the optional Follow_Up Messages as well. As with the Announce Messages the Sync and optional Follow_Up Messages will also have their AlternateMasterFlag turned on with a one as well. These Sync and Follow_Up Messages are transmitted out at the interval determined by the AlternateMasterPort data set member LogAlternateMulticastSyncInterval.

Delay_Resp Messages will also have their AlternateMasterFlag turned on with a one as well.

The AlternateMasterPort data set member NumberOfAlternateMasters sets a maximum amount of PTP Ports that can transmit PTP Messages with the AlternateMasterFlag turned on. This data set member is what determines the maximum number of Alternate Master PTP Ports on a Network.

Acceptable Master Table

Acceptable Master Table is an optional mechanism turned on by the selected PTP Profile or is enabled by default by the Clock manufacturer. This mechanism allows for PTP Slave Clocks to only Synchronize to PTP Master Clocks that are on the Acceptable Master Table. This is often done to stop Slave Clocks from Synchronizing to inadequate or unsuitable Master Clocks. When the AcceptableMasterTable Data Set MaxTableSize data set member is set to a value of zero this mechanism is turned off.

PTP Network Physical Layout

For this book we are only focused on using PTP on Ethernet based Networks. PTP is inherently limited and becomes more inaccurate when it comes to large distances and each separate site using PTP should be its own "island of time". Sites that are kilometers away from each other should have their own source of time. Having a GPS GrandMaster Clock distribute the Time Signal at each local site is a common solution.

Communication within the site between Clocks should be done exclusively by Transparent Clocks and if absolutely required Boundary Clocks as well. Selecting Peer Delay Path Delay Mechanism or Request Response Path Delay Mechanism Transparent Clocks is an important consideration when building a PTP capable Network. As well the selected PTP Clocks should be consistently One-Step or Two-Step as well.

Reducing the amount of time delay between Clocks is an important topic. The less Transparent Clocks and Boundary Clocks between the Master PTP Port and the Slave PTP Port the better the Synchronization accuracy.

NonTransparent Clocks can create timing inconsistencies and Path Asymmetry and are best not used at all when using PTP.

PTP Network Logical Layout

When implementing PTP at a site most often a single PTP Domain using a single Network is more than sufficient. However if the operation requires groups of Clocks with separate timescales at a single site than there are two available options.

One option is to use separate physical Ethernet Networks that cannot communicate with each other(except through a Router-if absolutely required). Both PTP Domains could use the default PTP Domain settings.

The second option is for the different groups of Clocks to all use the same physical Ethernet Network but each separate group would be assigned to different PTP Domains. This can be a useful solution however caution is advised as having more than one PTP Domain on an Ethernet Network can negatively affect individual Transparent Clocks performances.

PTP Clock Hardware

To get the absolute best Synchronization accuracy the following PTP Clock practices by the Network Professional are advised:
1. Select PTP Clocks that are able to handle the required accuracies
2. Select PTP Clocks that support the optional features and mechanisms that will allow for the required accuracies
3. If a timescale based on TAI or UTS is important than consideration of the GrandMaster Clock is a necessary concern. If a PTP Network with the GrandMaster Clock loses its power it may lose its epoch and therefore its date and time.
4. A GrandMaster Clock may also stop working correctly so its frequency or Time Signal may stop being accurate. To combat this failure a well-designed Slave Clock may be able to detect for it by comparing its own internal clock time to the Time Signal received from the now dysfunctional GrandMaster Clock. If the Slave Clock also has access to Alternate GrandMaster Clocks it may also be able to compare and detect for the GrandMaster Clocks inaccurate Time Signals.

PTP Designed Clocks

Applications and Services constructed to use PTP may reduce the PTP Clocks ability to accurately Synchronize using PTP. PTP has set time limits on Messages being processed and other timing requisites on their transmission and receiving times. All PTP Clock manufacturers need to assure their designs are able to provide the processing capabilities and memory required to meet these PTP Message timing requirements. PTP related operations will need to be allotted greater preference over other applications in a PTP Clock. At every opportunity PTP related operations must take precedent over other Non-PTP Applications and Services as their use can affect PTP Synchronization accuracies.

Getting the best PTP Clock Synchronization accuracy in a PTP capable Network is determined by:
1. DelayAsymmetry
2. Precise Timestamping
3. Stability
4. Inconsistent Delays in the PTP Clocks Protocol Stack
5. Inconsistent Delays in Network Hardware

DelayAsymmetry

DelayAsymmetry is when the Transit Time for a Packet is not the same transmitting to Device2 from Device1 as transmitting to Device1 from Device2. DelayAsymmetry was discussed at length in previous sections.

Precise Timestamping

The internal clock of all participating PTP Clocks need to be of high enough precision to allow for the required accuracy of PTP Event Message Timestamps. The GrandMaster Clock, Transparent Clocks and Slave Clocks each need to be equipped with a precise enough internal clock in order for PTP to create reliably precise Timestamps for PTP Event Messages in order to allow for the accurate Synchronization of all participating PTP Clocks.

Stability

The accuracy required of the PTP Clocks internal clock can be very high. Often this high accuracy and therefore the consistent stability overtime goes hand in hand with higher costs. Often times the internal clocks are made using quartz crystals that will as time goes on experience thermal expansion and regression, mechanical fatigue and other types of degradation contributing to a reduction in their accuracy.

Inconsistent Delays in the PTP Clocks Protocol Stack

Inconsistent Delays in the Clocks Protocol Stack are usually created when applying Application Layer Timestamps. The cheapest PTP Clocks will only run a PTP Application at the Application Layer with no aspect of it interfacing at the Hardware/Physical Layer. PTP Clocks that have no special PTP based Hardware at the Physical Layer will have errors in their Timestamps. These Timestamp Errors can be up to milliseconds in time. Application Based Timestamping Delay Errors can be reduced by using interrupts when a Timestamp is required thus reducing the error to tens of microseconds.

Inconsistent Delay in Network Hardware

Transparent Clocks and NonTransparent Clocks Physical Layer Hardware can cause Inconsistent Delays in the receiving, processing and transmission of PTP Messages. All Ethernet Switches(whether PTP capable or not) employ a Store and Forward model to the receiving and transmission of Ethernet Messages. When an Ethernet Message is received it is placed in an Input Buffer as part of its processing and then passed to an Output Buffer to be queued up in preparation for retransmission. If Network Traffic is inconsistent or heavy the Output Buffering Delay will be inconsistent. This causes inconsistency in the delay between receiving and retransmission of a PTP Event Message. Networks designed with PTP in mind need to take the Inconsistent Output Buffering Delay into account. Transparent Clocks do sort regular Network Traffic from PTP Event Messages moving the PTP Event Messages to the front of the Output Buffer allowing for a faster turnaround time and thus less Inconsistent Delays in the Network Hardware.

PTP Capable Ethernet Network Best Practices

Enabling an Ethernet Network to work effectively with PTP especially being able to realize 100ns(dec) Synchronization or better on a local PTP capable Network can be difficult when first beginning. For the most basic of PTP capable Networks the following devices are required: Transparent Clocks, at least one GPS PTP capable GrandMaster Clock, and PTP capable Slave Clocks.

As time goes on with the implementation of a PTP capable Ethernet Network PTP compatible devices are selected for(and tested), internal organizational standards are developed, subject matter experts emerge and inter device operability is discovered. The following sections touch on a variety of subjects and best practices to help contribute towards this goal.

GPS GrandMaster Clocks

PTP GrandMasters are usually Synchronized using a GPS or GLONASS signal collected from a GNSS Receiver transmitted from orbiting satellites. When the GPS GrandMaster is locked to a GPS Satellite the Synchronization accuracy can be better than 30ns(dec). The GPS GrandMaster Clock will have an internal Oscillator that acts as the reference clock that is updated using this GPS signal. Outgoing Sync Messages or replied Delay_Req Messages will have accurate Timestamps due to this inbuilt hardware. This is known as Hardware Timestamping and is not negatively influenced by Network Traffic or an Operating System and will have a better internal Oscillator.

GrandMaster Clock Oscillators are not to deviate in their period more than 0.01% from what a perfect Oscillator would at an identical frequency.

GPS GrandMaster Clocks

When purchasing a GPS GrandMaster Clock for use with PTP you will also be required to select the Antenna, Co-Ax Cable and any other accessories.

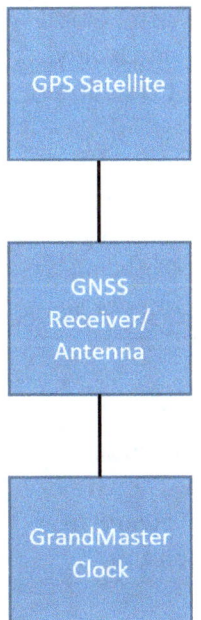

When signal interference(current or future) is a concern the GrandMaster Clock will simply use an internal crystal or Oscillator. Holdover is the term used to describe how long a GrandMaster Clock's internal Oscillator can retain its accuracy following the loss of the reference source(GPS Signal). GrandMaster Clocks that have lost their reference source will need to stay inside the operational tolerances to remain functioning. In this context Holdover becomes an essential metric.

There are usually at least a few options when selecting the model of your chosen GrandMaster Clocks internal Oscillator. Good Quartz Oscillators can uphold a +/-600µs Holdover for more than 24hours. Top Performing Quartz Oscillators can uphold a +/-10µs Holdover for more than 24hours. Lastly Rubidium Oscillators can uphold a +/-10µs Holdover for more than a week.

Having two GrandMaster Clocks is common. The BMCA will compare both GrandMaster Clocks and choose the preferred Clock. The comparison is done using the information contained in the Announce Messages. With default PTP the GrandMaster Clock selected will become the Preferred GrandMaster and it will serve out Sync Messages. With default PTP the other GrandMaster Clock will become the Backup GrandMaster Clock. The Backup GrandMaster Clock would wait for the Preferred GrandMaster Clock to degrade in ClockQuality, have a lower Priority1 or Priority2 or just stop serving time then it would start serving time.

Keep the option Alternate GrandMaster Clock/Alternate Master Clock that was mentioned in an earlier section in mind. If this option is enabled the Backup GrandMaster Clock would instead be an Alternate GrandMaster Clock and it would serve time out on the same Network. However no Slave Clocks or Slave Ports would synchronize to it unless the Preferred GrandMaster Clock was degraded or stopped serving time for some reason.

In some cases Network Professionals may want to configure Slave Clocks manually to switch to a specific Backup GrandMaster Clock. If the Preferred GrandMaster Clock fails it is better for each Slave Clock on that Network to select the same new GrandMaster Clock instead of them Synchronizing to different GrandMaster Clocks based on the BMCA.

Another GrandMaster Clock consideration is the adjustment of the frequency of transmitting Sync Messages. To reduce Network Traffic or just make use of a minimum bandwidth Sync Messages can be transmitted less frequently.

Hardware Versus Software Timestamping Slave Clocks

Slave Clocks equipped with Hardware Timestamping though more expensive has the advantage of providing separate hardware that results in better Synchronization accuracy than Software Timestamping. Hardware Timestamping will as with the GrandMaster Clock Hardware Timestamping have the following benefits: the Slave Clock will not be negatively influenced by Network Traffic or an Operating System and will have a better internal Oscillator. Synchronization of better than 100ns is possible only with Hardware Timestamping Slave Clocks.

Software Timestamping Clocks use the inferior Timestamping method but are cheaper in price. They will use the existing Device's Hardware with no separate PTP Hardware to handle PTP mechanisms and PTP Messages. The Oscillator on the Devices motherboard is usually not great. Software Timestamping must be used and will be negatively affected by the Operating System latency and inconsistency. Synchronization of between 10μs and 100μs is possible with Software Timestamping Clocks.

Problems With NonTransparent Clocks

As mentioned in an earlier section a Non PTP capable Ethernet Switch is called a NonTransparent Clock and a PTP capable Ethernet Switch is called a Transparent Clock. A NonTransparent Clock will in the short-term store and process Packets before transmitting them out the correct Port. This short term storage and processing is not consistent and varies considerably depending on Network Traffic. Packet Delay Variation is considerable and without the separate PTP hardware that supports Timestamping Synchronization accuracy will be very poor. Using Transparent Clocks either Delay Request Response or Peer Delay is essential when Synchronizing Slave Clocks with PTP. Boundary Clocks are also an acceptable solution but do not perform as well as their Transparent Clock cousins.

Limitations And Rules For PTP

1. A PTP capable Network that uses Two-Step Sync Messages must be planned for in such a way as to allow the Sync and Follow_Up Message to take the same Network Path. The Path Delay will not be calculated correctly if the Sync and Follow_Up Messages take different paths. PTP will likely still run but it will not be working correctly

2. PTP is usually not supported on Stacked Network Devices

3. Use only PTP Clocks that use the same PTP Version throughout the PTP capable Network or the same PTP Domain. If the same PTP Domain is to have Clocks using different PTP Versions with those PTP Versions not able to operate together the Domain will need to be broken down into different Regions separated by Boundary Clocks capable of negotiating different PTP Versions

4. A GrandMaster Clock should only serve PTP Messages on one VLAN

5. Only use one Best Master Clock Algorithm throughout the PTP capable Network or at the very least the same PTP Domain

6. A Unicast Frame Model or Mixed Unicast/Multicast Model is accepted only if the conduct of PTP is maintained similar to the originally planned Multicast Frame Model. For a Transparent Clock Announce Messages are presumed by PTP to be received by a single PTP enabled Port and then retransmitted through all other Ports that have PTP enabled on them

7. Use only the same PTP Profile throughout the PTP capable Network or at least the same PTP Domain. If the same PTP Domain is to have Clocks using different PTP Profiles with those PTP Profiles not able to operate together the Domain will need to be broken down into different Regions separated by Boundary Clocks capable of negotiating different PTP Profiles. Even including Boundary Clocks may not solve this problem and is generally never advised

8. One-Step and Two-Step Transparent Clocks usually do work together but cannot be guaranteed to do so

9. It is assumed that the Network will not allow for Network Loops due to some variation of Spanning Tree Protocol. Regardless built right into the PTP protocol is a method of not allowing for the Network Looping of PTP Messages

10. Only use the same optional features, Path Mechanisms and configuration options throughout the PTP capable Network or at the very least the same PTP Domain. When a Boundary Clock is employed to communicate between two PTP Domains there can be no guarantee that the two Domains will operate together if they use different optional features, mechanisms or configurations

11. If an optional feature, mechanism or configuration option is enabled on one or only a few PTP Clocks in a PTP capable Network there maybe issues between those with and those without them. Conversely, depending on the option there be no issues at all between those with and those without. If considering this approach you will need to studying the option in question to see if this is a possibility. This of course isn't an issue if only one PTP Profile is in use on the PTP capable Network

12. It is recommended to not have Non-PTP End Devices on the same Network as PTP capable End Devices as it will decrease Synchronization accuracy

13. It is recommended to not use NonTransparent Clocks when employing PTP

14. No more than 255(dec) Boundary Clocks are to be used as part of a Master-Slave Hierarchy. No Boundary Clocks should be employed if possible

15. IPv6 is usually not supported by PTP capable devices

16. MACsec(IEEE 802.1AE) is not compatible with PTP

17. Do not use Transparent Clocks or NonTransparent Clocks as a Master or GrandMaster Clock as they usually have a reduced internal clock accuracy. Although using a Transparent Clock as a Backup GrandMaster Clock to reduce costs is an interesting consideration

18. Non-PTP capable Network Devices especially Ethernet Switches, Hubs or Bridges should not be used in a PTP capable Network

19. Unsuccessful, double or out of sequence PTP Messages are permitted if they occur infrequently

20. For Peer Delay Transparent Clocks the better the local Clocks internal Oscillator the less error will occur when calculating the Link Delay and ResidenceTime

21. Use only data set member values that function together throughout the PTP capable Network or the same PTP Domain. If the same PTP Domain is to use different data set member values that do not operate together they will need to be broken down into different Regions separated by Boundary Clocks.

22. Only use one Transport Mechanism. In this case Ethernet

23. When using a Management Mechanism only use one for the whole PTP capable Network. With the default method of PTP Management Messages be preferable or if the selected PTP Profile specifies it use its chosen Management Mechanism

24. Only use the same Path Delay Mechanism throughout the PTP capable Network. If the same PTP capable Network is to use different Path Delay Mechanisms it will need to be broken down into different Path Delay Mechanism Regions separated by Boundary Clocks.

25. Data set members that have a minimum and maximum value limits should have the same values for each PTP Clock in the PTP capable Network

www.ingramcontent.com/pod-product-compliance
Lightning Source LLC
Chambersburg PA
CBHW052146220526
45471CB00004B/1551